I0822075

ROSE GUIDE TO THE FEASTS, FESTIVALS AND FASTS OF THE BIBLE

Paul H. Wright,
Editor

Rose Guide to the Feasts, Festivals and Fasts of the Bible

Published by Rose Publishing
An imprint of Tyndale House Ministries
Carol Stream, Illinois
www.hendricksonrose.com

ISBN 978-1-64938-021-0

Photos by Paul H. Wright, Brian Negin, Becca McDonald, Diane Wright, Ophir Yarden, and Heidi Kinner; used by permission

Other photos used under license from Shutterstock.com; cover photo by Seth Aronstam/Shutterstock

"From Agricultural Plenty to Failure" diagram courtesy of Biblical Backgrounds, biblicalbackgrounds.com

Relief maps by Michael Schmeling, www.aridocean.com

Art by Matthew Berkowitz, used by permission; Balage Balogh, ArchaeologyIllustrated.com

Cover by Sergio Urquiza; book design by Sergio Urquiza and Cristalle Kishi

---

Library of Congress Cataloging-in-Publication Data
Names: Wright, Paul H., Dr., author.
Title: Rose guide to the feasts, festivals and fasts of the Bible / Paul H. Wright.
Description: Carol Stream, Illinois: Rose Publishing, [2022] | Includes bibliographical references and index. | Summary: "Description of the meanings and history of Jewish feasts in the Bible, divided by time period. Includes information about which feasts are celebrated today and their significance to various religious groups"-- Provided by publisher.
Identifiers: LCCN 2021046429 | ISBN 9781649380210 (hardcover)
Subjects: LCSH: Fasts and feasts--Judaism.
Classification: LCC BM690 .W75 2022 | DDC 296.4/3--dc23
LC record available at https://lccn.loc.gov/2021046429

Printed in the United States of America
021122VP

Contents

Celebrations. Festivals. Observances. Feasts. Times to celebrate—and to remember—are an important part of our lives. Often they're joyous, with lots of bustle and noise. Now and then they're solemn and full of awe. Some focus on the power of individual reflection; others don't seem right unless they are empowered by a crowd. *How* we celebrate differs widely with who we are, what the occasion is, and where we live. *That* we celebrate seems to be a universal human trait. And the wider our circle of connections, the greater the number of occasions we have to celebrate.

I lived in Jerusalem for a quarter century, a city blessed with people hailing from every corner of the world and representing a wide spectrum of what it means to be human: Jews, Muslims, Christians, Druze; people secular and people religiously observant; those of means and those needing means; people with a large circle of family and friends and people on their own; people native to the Middle East and those from elsewhere. Here, irrespective of ethnic, national, or religious allegiance, there is always something to celebrate. Usually, it seems, food is involved, often something prepared specially for the occasion. I imagine it's the same where you live as well.

This book is about the feasts, festivals, and fasts of the Bible. We will explore the celebrations and observances kept by ancient Israel in the time of the Old Testament and those kept by the Jews in and after the time of the Gospels. (The lists overlap but are not exactly the same.) Together, these provide context for how Jews, Christians, and messianic believers celebrate today. Some of ancient Israel's celebrations were holidays; others were holy days. Some were at first holidays that over time became holy

days; others were holy days right from the start. Several had their roots in agricultural activities, especially those of harvest times. Others are embedded in events specific to Israel's founding, the mighty acts of God that have continued to shape Jewish identity ever since. Some, such as the great pilgrimage festivals of Pesach, Shavuot, and Sukkot (Passover, Weeks, and Booths, respectively), combine Israel's agricultural calendar with portions of Israel's founding epic to mark passages of time—a year, a single lifetime, the lifetime of a people—in powerful ways. In doing so, these feasts bind the Jews to each other and to their ancestral homeland, even when celebrated in parts of the world where the agricultural seasons and national origin stories are quite different. For example, in October, the Sukkot order of service includes prayers for rain, fully in tune with the climate of Israel but wildly out of place in New England or northern Europe. And we must note that the fast on the most significant of all the holy days—the Day of Atonement (Yom Kippur)—is such a solemn observance that nothing is eaten at all. Perhaps we can better understand the power of the great fasts when we view them alongside the many holy days that are feasts. We will explore them all.

Christians are drawn in particular to the Jewish festivals that appear in the Gospels. Jesus, we read, celebrated Passover and the Feast of Booths. The holy drama of Passion Week occurred at the same time as the feasts of Passover and Unleavened Bread, and the Holy Spirit came with "tongues as of fire" at Pentecost (Shavuot). Today, many messianic followers of Jesus—of *Yeshua*—also keep other holy days that he would have known as an observant Jew in the first century, including Yom Kippur, Rosh HaShanah, and the Sabbath on the seventh day of the week.

Celebrations and remembrances take on an extra dimension when they happen at times or in places of danger and risk. Over a lifetime, we may encounter many situations prone to famine, pestilence, or war, where life is never quite as secure as we would like it to be. On nearly every account of what makes life uncertain or insecure, ancient Israel was such a place. Over thousands of years, Jews have celebrated the biblical festivals in spite of their many wounds or, perhaps, in part because of them. The topic of feasts, festivals, and fasts of the Bible is a topic of victories anticipated and victories gained.

We should expect to find a wide variety of ways that the biblical feasts have been celebrated through the ages, but there is a core that makes Passover *Passover,* just as there is a core that makes Christmas *Christmas.* Attached to the core, we find an endless variety of creative traditions—differences that may be due to the locations, the circumstances, or the accumulation of cultural trappings over time. To people who are used to one way of celebrating Christmas, for instance, Yuletide festivities in other parts of the globe can be barely recognizable, as would holiday traditions be to someone who time traveled even two centuries into the past. We should expect no less with the biblical observances. Part of our difficulty, as we explore the richness of the biblical festivals, will be to determine what is "core" and what is "creative tradition," both for the times of the Bible and for today.

Chapter 1, written by myself, is a survey of the feasts, festivals, celebrations, and observances that were part of the life of ancient Israel during the time of the Old Testament. These, we will see, were many, varied, and tied closely to the land and experiences of the people. A few became the primary feasts and fasts best known to Jews and Christians today, although details about how that began to happen during the time of the Old Testament are not as clear as we might assume or want them to be.

Chapter 2 presents observances that were a dynamic part of Jewish life in the centuries leading up to and following the time of the New Testament. Many Christians are curious about the ways that Jesus observed the festivals and what it would have been like for him to journey to Jerusalem to celebrate. We have some information about the festivals during this time, but we have much more from the centuries immediately following the New Testament, when the rabbis wrote profusely about all aspects of Jewish life. The author of chapter 2 is Moshe Silberschein, a conservative Jewish rabbi living in Jerusalem with a sensitive passion for understanding the shared heritage of Judaism and early Christianity, and the place of Jesus within early Judaism.

Chapter 3 describes ways that Jews keep the biblical holidays today. Around a common core of what it means to "keep" the feasts, we can see a wide variety of creative activities that bind Jews together and root them into a rich heritage of faithfulness before God. Ophir Yarden, an educator in Jewish and Israel studies who lives in Jerusalem, will guide us on a journey into the celebratory and commemorative world of modern Judaism.

Chapter 4, written by Pastor Steven Lancaster, examines ways that messianic congregations—be they Jewish, gentile, or of mixed membership—observe the biblical feasts and holidays today. Steve, who is a teacher with a pastor's heart and a pastor with a teacher's heart, guides a congregation that seeks to follow the lifestyle and teachings of Yeshua as believers would have done in the first century. Although he now lives in north central Ohio, he lived in Jerusalem for several years, so he also has a comprehensive understanding of the larger historical, geographical, and cultural context in which Yeshua lived.

Chapter 5 closes the circle by considering ways that churches and congregations that do not label themselves as messianic have adopted elements of the biblical feasts into their liturgies, theologies, and expressions of Christian life. Our expert here is The Very Reverend Heidi Kinner, a former company commander in the Marine Corps, who has since served as dean of several Anglican congregations in the United States. Heidi writes from a conviction that active participation in the gospel message includes expressions of worship and response that are rooted in the faith and practices of the early church.

Come along with us on a journey through time and across the lands of the Bible, a trek that will lead you home, as we explore the feasts, festivals, and fasts of the Bible. Together, we bring a variety of perspectives on a subject that is far more complex than it may first appear.

It is likely that you picked up this book because you are already observing some of the biblical feasts, festivals, and fasts. Or perhaps the festivities are new to you and you wonder how knowing about them, or keeping them, would help you understand the Bible, or even Jesus, better. It's also okay to just read out of curiosity. You will quickly see that each of the authors has a very different perspective on the biblical celebrations and observances. There is much we agree on and much that we see differently; the topic has many facets to explore and in which to find meaning for our lives. No matter the case, we hope that by reading through these chapters, you will better appreciate the ways that these celebrations and observances shape our understanding of God's care for our world, for our places in it, and for us.

Reverend Paul H. Wright, PhD

Mt. Zion, Jerusalem and Evanston, Illinois

with

Rabbi Moshe Silberschein, MHL

Talpiyot Mizrah, Jerusalem

Ophir Yarden, MA, MA

Abu Tor, Jerusalem

Pastor Steven P. Lancaster, ThM

Marion, Ohio

The Very Reverend Heidi Kinner, MDiv

Clancy, Montana and Hobe Sound, Florida

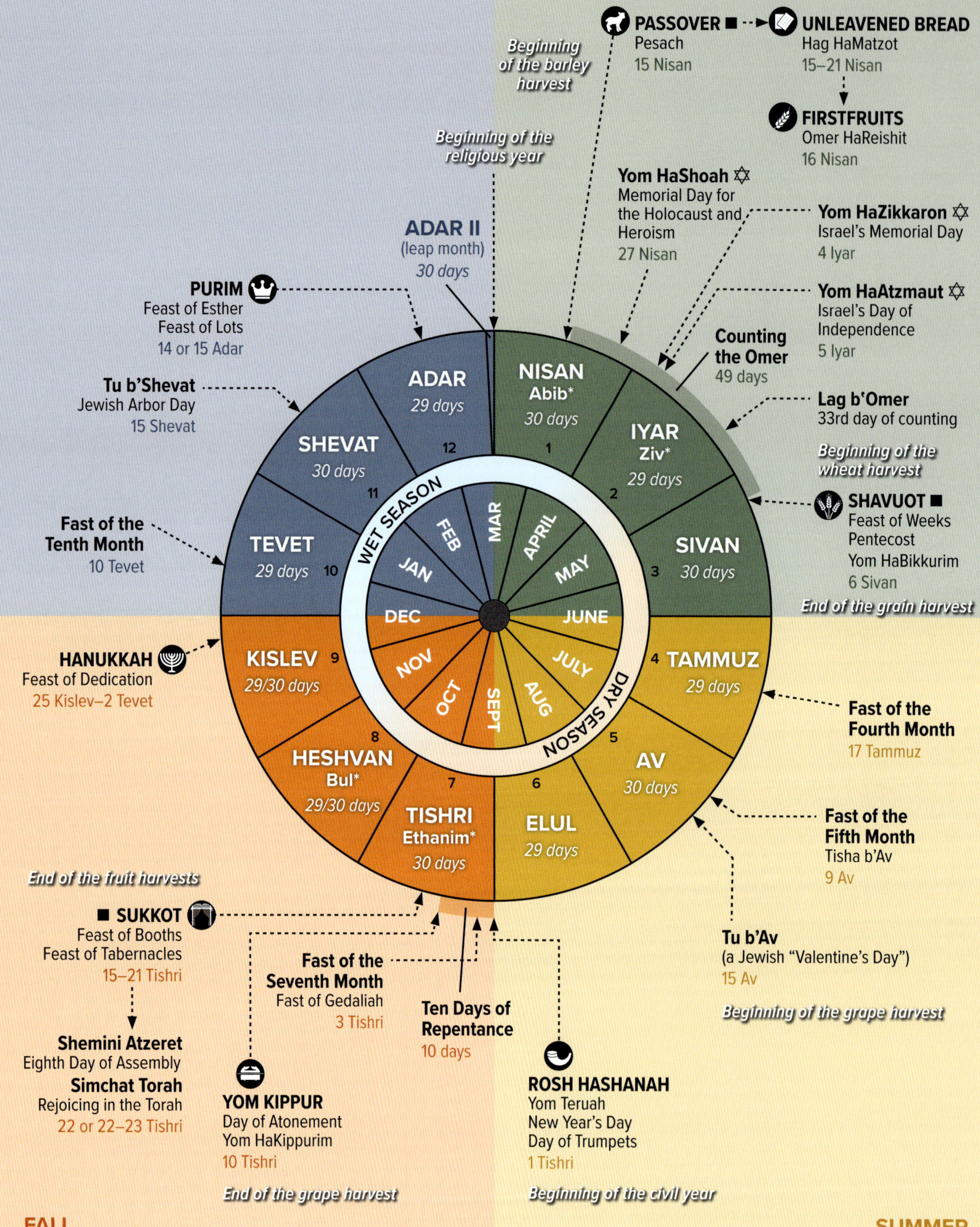
WINTER
SPRING
FALL
SUMMER
PASSOVER ■
Pesach
15 Nisan
UNLEAVENED BREAD
Hag HaMatzot
15–21 Nisan
FIRSTFRUITS
Omer HaReishit
16 Nisan
Beginning of the barley harvest
Beginning of the religious year
Yom HaShoah ✡
Memorial Day for the Holocaust and Heroism
27 Nisan
Yom HaZikkaron ✡
Israel's Memorial Day
4 Iyar
Yom HaAtzmaut ✡
Israel's Day of Independence
5 Iyar
Counting the Omer
49 days
Lag b'Omer
33rd day of counting
Beginning of the wheat harvest
SHAVUOT ■
Feast of Weeks
Pentecost
Yom HaBikkurim
6 Sivan
End of the grain harvest
ADAR II
(leap month)
30 days
PURIM
Feast of Esther
Feast of Lots
14 or 15 Adar
Tu b'Shevat
Jewish Arbor Day
15 Shevat
Fast of the Tenth Month
10 Tevet
HANUKKAH
Feast of Dedication
25 Kislev–2 Tevet
NISAN
Abib*
30 days
1
IYAR
Ziv*
29 days
2
SIVAN
30 days
3
TAMMUZ
29 days
4
AV
30 days
5
ELUL
29 days
6
TISHRI
Ethanim*
30 days
7
HESHVAN
Bul*
29/30 days
8
KISLEV
29/30 days
9
TEVET
29 days
10
SHEVAT
30 days
11
ADAR
29 days
12
WET SEASON
DRY SEASON
MAR
APRIL
MAY
JUNE
JULY
AUG
SEPT
OCT
NOV
DEC
JAN
FEB
Fast of the Fourth Month
17 Tammuz
Fast of the Fifth Month
Tisha b'Av
9 Av
Tu b'Av
(a Jewish "Valentine's Day")
15 Av
Beginning of the grape harvest
End of the fruit harvests
■ SUKKOT
Feast of Booths
Feast of Tabernacles
15–21 Tishri
Shemini Atzeret
Eighth Day of Assembly
Simchat Torah
Rejoicing in the Torah
22 or 22–23 Tishri
Fast of the Seventh Month
Fast of Gedaliah
3 Tishri
Ten Days of Repentance
10 days
YOM KIPPUR
Day of Atonement
Yom HaKippurim
10 Tishri
End of the grape harvest
ROSH HASHANAH
Yom Teruah
New Year's Day
Day of Trumpets
1 Tishri
Beginning of the civil year
✡ Modern Israeli Holidays
■ Pilgrimage Feasts
* Name of the month in the Old Testament

COUNTING THE OMER – The 49 days (7 weeks) from Firstfruits (Omer HaReishit) to the Feast of Weeks.

FAST OF THE FIFTH MONTH – Tisha b'Av (TIH-sha b'AV). Marks the destruction of the First and Second Temples.

FAST OF THE FOURTH MONTH – Marks the date Jerusalem's walls were breached in the Babylonian siege.

FAST OF THE SEVENTH MONTH – Fast of Gedaliah. Marks the assassination of the Jewish governor Gedaliah under the Babylonians.

FAST OF THE TENTH MONTH – Marks the date the Babylonian siege of Jerusalem began.

FIRSTFRUITS – This word identifies two festivals: Omer HaReishit (OH-mer ha-ray-SHEET), "sheaf of the firstfruit," which is part of Passover week and marks the start of the barley harvest and Counting the Omer; and Yom HaBikkurim (YOHM ha-bi-kur-REEM), "day of the firstfruits," another name for Shavuot.

HANUKKAH (KHA-nu-kah) – Feast of Dedication. Celebrates the rededication of the temple after the Maccabean victory. Celebrated for eight days with lighting candles on a menorah each day.

LAG B'OMER (Lahg b'OH-mer) – Minor holiday on the 33rd day of Counting the Omer. A happy day that serves as break from the solemnness of the Omer period.

LUNISOLAR CALENDAR – The Jewish lunisolar (moon and sun) calendar with 12 months numbering 29 or 30 days each. Nisan marks the beginning of the religious year and Tishri the civil year. A leap month, Adar II, is added about every three years.

PASSOVER – Pesach (PAY-sakh). Commemorates Israel's exodus from Egypt. Observed after sundown of 14 Nisan, hence the start of 15 Nisan. Today, it is a weeklong festival beginning with a Seder (SAY-der) meal.

PILGRIMAGE FEASTS – Three major feasts of ancient Israel: Passover (Pesach), Weeks (Shavuot), and Booths (Sukkot). Usually designated in the Bible as "feasts" using the Hebrew word *haggim* (kha-GEEM, plural), *hag* (KHAG, singular).

PURIM (PUR-im) – Feast of Esther, Lots. Celebrates the Jews' deliverance as told in the book of Esther. Today, it is a joyous holiday with reading the Scroll of Esther, costumes, and pastries.

ROSH HASHANAH (ROHSH ha-SHA-nah) – New Year's Day, Yom Teruah, Day of Trumpets. First of the High Holy Days and begins the civil year with sounding the shofar (ram's horn).

ROSH HODESH (ROHSH KHOH-desh) – New Moon. In biblical times, it announced the monthly sighting of the crescent moon, the start of each month. A minor holiday today.

SABBATH – Shabbat (Sha-BAHT). Observed weekly (Saturday), beginning at sunset on Friday with lighting candles and sharing a Sabbath meal. A day to rest and cease from work.

SHAVUOT (Sha-vu-OHT) – Feast of Weeks, Pentecost (in Greek), Yom HaBikkurim ("day of the firstfruits"). Observed the 50th day at the end of Counting the Omer. Marks the start of the wheat harvest. Believed to be the day God gave Torah to Israel on Mount Sinai and the Holy Spirit to believers in Jesus in Acts 2.

SHEMINI ATZERET (Sheh-ME-ne ah-TZER-et, Eighth Day of Assembly) and **SIMCHAT TORAH** (Sim-KHAT to-RAH, "Rejoicing in/of the Torah") – Observed at the end of the week of Sukkot. Today, marks the conclusion of the annual Torah reading cycle. Celebrated as two days outside Israel and one day in Israel.

SUKKOT (Su-KOHT) – Feast of Booths, Tabernacles. Weeklong commemoration of Israel's wilderness sojourn after the exodus. Today, Jews construct booths and share meals in them.

TEN DAYS OF REPENTANCE – Ten days from Rosh HaShanah through Yom Kippur, a period of penitence, prayer, and Torah reading.

TU B'AV (TOO b'AV) – A "Valentine's Day" of sorts, a day for matchmaking and romance. Marks the beginning of the grape harvest.

TU B'SHEVAT (TOO b'sheh-VAHT) – Jewish Arbor Day marking the start of the year for orchards.

UNLEAVENED BREAD – Hag HaMatzot (KHAG ha-ma-TZOHT), Feast of Matzah. For seven days unleavened bread (matzah) is eaten to recall Israel's hasty exodus from Egypt.

YOM HAATZMAUT (YOHM ha-atz-ma-OOT) – Independence Day celebrating the establishment of the modern State of Israel in 1948.

YOM HASHOAH (YOHM ha-SHO-ah) – A day to honor those who died in the Holocaust and the heroism of those who resisted.

YOM HAZIKKARON (YOHM ha-zik-ka-ROHN) – Israel's Memorial Day remembering fallen soldiers and victims of hostile acts, observed the day before Independence Day.

YOM KIPPUR (YOHM kih-PUR) – Day of Atonement, Yom HaKippurim (YOHM ha-kih-pu-REEM "day of atonements"). Final High Holy Day, a most solemn day of fasting. In biblical times, it was the day the high priest entered the tabernacle/temple and made atonement for sins. Also marks the end of the grape harvest.

"This day shall be for you a memorial day,

and you shall keep it as a feast to the LORD.*"*

—Exodus 12:14

Feasts of the Bible During the Time of the Old Testament

Paul H. Wright

We start our journey exploring the feasts of the Bible at the beginning, the time of the Old Testament. Perhaps we are better off saying up front the *times* of the Old Testament, since the events of Genesis through Malachi covered more than a millennium, and we might rightly expect that the ways the Israelites feasted changed over time. As we journey, we will see that there were many reasons to feast in ancient Israel, as there are everywhere. Eating together in family groups or communities is an important part of living together, even more so when it marks special occasions and when special foods are part of the meal. Feasts provide food not only for the body but also for the soul, a connection that was intentional in ancient Israel (and I think it still should be).

The biblical feasts that are most prominent today—Passover, Weeks, and Booths—started to take shape during the time of the Old Testament, as Israel forged and then strengthened its identity as a people called out of the nations by God. It is not something that happened all at once. It took a long time for Israel to work out what it meant to keep Moses's commands. For this reason, our journey through the Old Testament will be a winding course as we follow the Israelites, tracking their interactions not only with each other but also with the larger world around them, a world that itself found ample occasion to feast. In the process, not only will the Bible become more alive, but we will also become more alive to it. Let's start our journey with some examples of feasting in the Bible that are perhaps not as clear-cut as they might at first seem yet are crucial for understanding how and why Israel's feasts came to be.

PICTURING THE FEASTS OF THE BIBLE

It was sometime shortly after the year 715 BC, the first year of the reign of Hezekiah, king of Judah.[1] The king sent word to all Judah and the remnant of Israel, decreeing that everyone come to Jerusalem to celebrate the Passover.[2] Judah was on the cusp of a renewed Golden Age, led by a charismatic young monarch who was about to embark on a comprehensive program of national renewal in the face of the greatest threat to the kingdom to date—the invasion of the ruthlessly efficient war machine that was Assyria. The description of Hezekiah's Passover celebration, recorded in 2 Chronicles 30, is magnificent in its detail, telling us how the feast was prepared, who came, and how they celebrated.

> And many people came together in Jerusalem to keep the Feast of Unleavened Bread [Passover] . . . a very great assembly. . . . The people of Israel who were present at Jerusalem kept the Feast of Unleavened Bread seven days with great gladness, and the Levites and the priests praised the LORD day by day, singing with all their might to the LORD. . . . So they ate the food of the festival for seven days. . . . So there was great joy in Jerusalem. (2 Chron. 30:13–26)

We can read a similar account of a Passover celebrated in Jerusalem nearly a century later, in 622 BC, the eighteenth year of the reign of King Josiah (2 Kings 23:21–23; 2 Chron. 35:1–19). Some of its details about how the festival was celebrated and what was eaten differ from the description of the Passover of Hezekiah. We will come back to both celebrations toward the end of this chapter. For now, it is important to recognize that the Passovers of Hezekiah and Josiah have become a kind of template in the minds of many Bible readers for what Passover and the rest of the biblical feasts must have been like throughout the time of the Old Testament.

But this is to move too fast. A careful reading of the accounts of these two Passovers suggests a different picture. For instance, Hezekiah celebrated the Passover in the second month of the year rather than the first month as stipulated in the Law of Moses[3] (Ex. 12:2–6; 23:15; 34:18; Lev. 23:5;

Deut. 16:1). This was "because the priests had not consecrated themselves in sufficient number, nor had the people assembled in Jerusalem" (2 Chron. 30:2–3). *Interesting.* A short command in Numbers 9:9–13 allows people who were not able to celebrate Passover because they either had been away on a journey or had become ritually unclean by touching a dead body, to do so on the fourteenth day of the second month instead. But this surely was exceptional, never meant to be the rule, and cannot explain what seems to be a wholesale lack of preparation, even by the priests in the days of Hezekiah. The most likely explanation of Hezekiah's late date for Passover seems to be that it had not been celebrated as an all-Israel event in Jerusalem before that time, at least not regularly. Dare we even think that maybe it had not been celebrated on a regular, widespread basis anywhere? For Christians, this would be like celebrating Christmas on January 25 because not enough people had remembered to put up the tree, buy the presents, and schedule the church service for December!

But there is more. Many who ate the Passover in Hezekiah's day did so in a way that was "otherwise than as prescribed.... [that is,] not according to the sanctuary's [the Jerusalem temple's] rules of cleanness," having first been properly excused by the king (not by the priests!) for either not knowing what to do or simply not doing it (2 Chron. 30:18–19). Whatever Passover might have meant to the masses or even to the priests up to the time of Hezekiah, it wasn't this template.

Nonetheless, in the end, everyone had such a wonderful time celebrating together that Hezekiah himself stretched the instruction of Moses and doubled the length of the feast from seven to fourteen days (2 Chron. 30:22–23). Clearly, there was room for flexibility in celebrating the holy day. The writer of Chronicles then admits, "For since the time of Solomon the son of David king of Israel there had been nothing like this in Jerusalem" (2 Chron. 30:26), be it the Passover or any other celebration. And putting an exclamation point on the end of the narrative about the Passover of Josiah a century later, the chronicler also writes, "No Passover like it had been kept in Israel since the days of Samuel the prophet. None of the kings of Israel

Fresco of King Hezekiah in the church Neuottakringer Pfarrkirche, Vienna, by Felix Jenewien (Renata Sedmakova/ Shutterstock)

had kept such a Passover as was kept by Josiah" (2 Chron. 35:18, emphasis added). The Bible does not record a single Passover in Samuel's day, nor does it mention that any were celebrated by the kings between Samuel and Josiah, save a brief note about Solomon (2 Chron. 8:12–13) and the detailed Passover of Hezekiah, making our search for the necessary details elusive. Our hunt is further complicated by the fact that the chronicler's statement is a bit ambiguous. Does saying that none of the kings "had kept such a Passover" mean that earlier kings (and others) had kept the Passover throughout the history of ancient Israel but just in very different ways? Or does it mean that no one was really keeping it at all?

We have a similar account about the Feast of Booths (Sukkot) in the book of Nehemiah. In the mid-fifth century BC, after Nehemiah had rebuilt the walls of Jerusalem, following the return of Jews from their Babylonian exile, the priests, Levites, and heads of all the households studied "the words of the Law" with the priest Ezra and "found it written in the Law that the LORD had commanded by Moses that the people of Israel should dwell in booths during the feast of the seventh month" (Neh. 8:13–14). Apparently, it was either a new thing for them or something they had totally forgotten—not that there was a feast of the seventh month, but that the celebrations should include dwelling in booths (the Hebrew word for booths is *sukkot*). And we note that Nehemiah did not call

Ezra and Nehemiah read the scroll of the Law to the Israelites assembled in the temple court (Neh. 8:1–12). (Art by Balage Balogh)

it the Feast of Booths but simply "the feast of the seventh month," a name that is generic enough to tell us that making booths and all that went with doing that apparently had not been a significant part of the feast before. The key sentence again comes as a conclusion: "For from the days of Jeshua [Joshua] the son of Nun to that day the people of Israel had not done so" (Neh. 8:17). Then we read, "They kept the feast seven days, and on the eighth day there was a solemn assembly, *according to the rule*" (Neh. 8:18, emphasis added). This last phrase implies that however the feast of the seventh month may have been celebrated throughout the history of ancient Israel prior to Nehemiah, it hadn't typically—if at all—been done in a way that was kosher to the commands of Moses.

All of this raises some interesting and relevant questions:

- If Passover, the premier springtime festival in the Jewish calendar today, wasn't celebrated as often or in the manner that we usually think it was during the time of the Old Testament, what *might* it have looked like?
- And if the Israelites hadn't been making booths during their seventh month festival, a practice that is integral to how the Feast of Booths, the major Jewish autumn festival, is celebrated today, what *were* they doing?
- Or, to expand our inquiry, if ancient Israel wasn't celebrating these feasts as we—who peer backward from a position that has inherited thousands of years of accrued traditions—would like them to have done, what, or what else, *were* they celebrating? And how? And why?

These questions are important, not only because they help us flesh out the development and significance of the biblical feasts, but also because they prompt us to take the context of ancient Israel seriously, at face value. The great American geographer of the early twentieth century, Carl Ortwin Sauer, urged his students to ponder human and geographical landscapes slowly, in order to "see the land with the eyes of its former occupants, from the standpoint of their needs and capacities" rather than our own.[4] Sauer went on to say that this is "about the most difficult task in all human geography," and he is right, except that we must add that it is about the most difficult task in all biblical studies as well. C. S. Lewis said a similar thing when he spoke of "chronological snobbery," the tendency to read the past through the familiar categories of our own present.[5]

What all this points us toward is the need for a deep dive into the ancient world of the feasts, festivals, and fasts of Israel, as earthy, divine, or different from today as they may prove to be.

Hezekiah, king of Judah in the late seventh century BC, set his kingdom on a path of revival in the face of a ruthless Assyrian threat. His Passover, celebrated nationally in Jerusalem, is preserved in the biblical record. One of the more visible examples of his success preserved in the archeological record is the broad wall that he built to protect Jerusalem's vulnerable northern side. (Photo by Paul H. Wright)

THE BIBLICAL WORLD

Before we begin our deep dive into the world of ancient Israel, our first task is to recognize that there are foundational differences between the cultural world in which we live today and the world of the Bible.[6]

Ancient Biblical World	Modern Western World
Largely rural and agricultural	Essentially urban and industrial
Communal relationships grounded in a person's extended family	Highly individualistic
Fulfillment found in what was good for the group	Fulfillment often defined by what is good for an individual
Time is cyclical, always coming around to something familiar, welcomed, and safe.	Time is a linear march into the future, to be experienced and explored by each individual as they see fit, typically with the goal of discovering something new.
Recognizes an essential connection between what is earthly and what is spiritual	Tends to separate what is divine from what is material—or deny the reality of the spiritual world altogether

By "biblical world," I don't mean just the world of Israel and Judah, but everyone living in the same region at the time of the Bible. This includes the Canaanites, Ammonites, Moabites, Edomites, Syrians, Phoenicians, and Philistines, as well as, to a large extent, the Egyptians, Assyrians, Babylonians, and Persians, and later the Greeks and Romans. The people of Israel and Judah were immersed in this larger world (whether or not they were aware of it on a daily basis) and shared many aspects of the cultures of their neighbors. They also differed from them in some significant ways. We will unpack all of this as we go along, but for now we can anticipate that ancient Israel celebrated events in their lives that were grounded in the yearly agricultural cycle, in family or village settings, and in ways that recognized God's connection to the natural world in which they lived.

Our next task is to appreciate the limits of what we know and what we can reasonably conclude about the biblical feasts. As we study the celebrations of ancient Israel, it's important to note the following key points.

The Bible provides a treasure trove of information about the world of the people we meet on its pages, but it is neither a complete encyclopedia, nor did its authors intend it to be. Some things are left unsaid, either because they are not particularly important to the point that the biblical author was making or because they are things that he assumed his readers already knew. For instance, the authors of the Bible often do not give us the reasons for Israel's actions. "This month [the month of the first Passover celebration in Egypt] ... shall be the first month of the year for you" (Ex. 12:2). God told this to Moses and Aaron without reminding them (or us) what their first month was otherwise or exactly why he was changing the calendar.

The available archaeological data, for all its richness, is also incomplete and subject to the interpretation of the observer. Complete bowls, for instance, found in the antechambers of tombs in which the mortal remains of Judeans were placed tell us something about what the dinnerware used for special occasions was like. But why were they placed in a tomb in the first place? And exactly *what* was being eaten, or celebrated, *there?*

The world of the Bible was very diverse, just as our world is today. Even if we look at only ancient Israel and ignore its neighbors, we see a host of cultural details that differ over time and at various places in the land. Was what was celebrated in northern Israel the same as what was celebrated in Judah in the south? How might people whose lives were wholly immersed in farming have celebrated compared to steppe-land shepherds or city dwellers? Did the common people celebrate differently than the priests or government officials who were more likely to have been literate and hence had better access to the written instructions of Moses (see 2 Chron. 17:3–9)? And as Israel grew as a distinct people group over time—from "the house of Jacob" (Ex. 19:3) to "the people of Israel" (1 Kings 8:63) to "Jews" (Neh. 5:8, 17)—how did their celebrations develop to reflect that transition from tribe to kingdom to peoplehood?

We must be on guard not to overgeneralize bits of evidence by stretching them to times and places within the context of ancient Israel itself where they don't properly belong. This is especially important when we realize that the values and priorities of the biblical authors were often different from the values and priorities of the biblical people whose exploits they recorded, and these differences only increase the longer the period of time between when the event happened and when it was written down.

Stone houses of the Al-Jaya village huddle against a cave-pocked cliff in the area of ancient Edom, now southern Jordan. Village wheat fields lie above. Both are in the shadow of Montreal, the Crusader castle at Shawbak. Residents of the village preserve patterns of social life that have roots in ancient times—and in the biblical record. (Photo by Paul H. Wright)

We need to ask the question, what was Israelite and what was pagan? More specifically, during the time of the Old Testament, what was *distinctively* Israelite about their celebrations that was different from how Israel's neighboring nations celebrated? Given that Israel shared essentially the same physical and economic world as its near neighbors (the same climate, growing season, agricultural and shepherding practices, etc.), might we not expect that their festivals would have been more, rather than less, similar? This question is particularly relevant when we consider the *reasons* why ancient Israel celebrated, and whether those reasons were personal or shared with a community.

One question that Bible readers often miss asking is, what might be the realistic differences between what the Bible *prescribes* as proper behavior for celebrating and how the people of Israel on the ground *actually* celebrated? We read in Deuteronomy, "Three times a year all your males shall appear before the Lord your God at the place that he will choose" (Deut. 16:16). But did they? Or as another example, Deuteronomy 31:10–11 relates Moses's command: "At the end of every seven years, at the year of release, at the Feast of Booths when all Israel comes to appear before the Lord at the place that he will choose, you shall read this law before all Israel in their hearing." It's a wonderful command, but one for which there is no explicit evidence in the rest of the Bible that it actually happened, certainly on a regular basis.

Is what we might call "biblical culture" the things that *should* have happened or what actually *did* happen—with as many variations over time and place as we can possibly imagine? To sharpen this question further, when the authors of the Old Testament describe how people actually did celebrate, are they describing what was normal behavior of the majority of people or an instance of something unusual or a once-and-only event? Were Hezekiah's Passover and Ezra's Feast of Booths representative of Judean culture or something that, given the reality of their life and times, was countercultural?

All of these are big considerations that take work to address. Nevertheless, they are critical for understanding not only what ancient Israel celebrated during the time of the Old Testament but also how some of the feasts we read about in the Bible came to be the Jewish High Holidays that we know today. We are faced with limited evidence and big questions that stare into our faces as we peer into the ancient past, so the search for answers can turn out to be a surprising adventure. It's an exercise in seeing how God works with real human beings, culturally embedded people like you and me, exactly where we are, in order to meld us together into a people who are able to shape our lives more closely to the image that he put in all of us (Gen. 1:27; Rom. 12:2).

FOUR CONTEXTS

We will start by peering into four contexts that help us open for our viewing the celebratory world of ancient Israel:

1. The context of climate and land
2. The context of mealtime and eating
3. The context of time
4. The context of worldview

Each provides important background information that will help bring the feasts of Israel into sharper focus.

1. The Context of Climate and Land

One of the first things we notice when we look at the geographical setting of the biblical story is that the lands bordering the southeastern Mediterranean Sea, including ancient Israel, have two distinct growing seasons. These are at opposite times of the year in what we call winter into spring

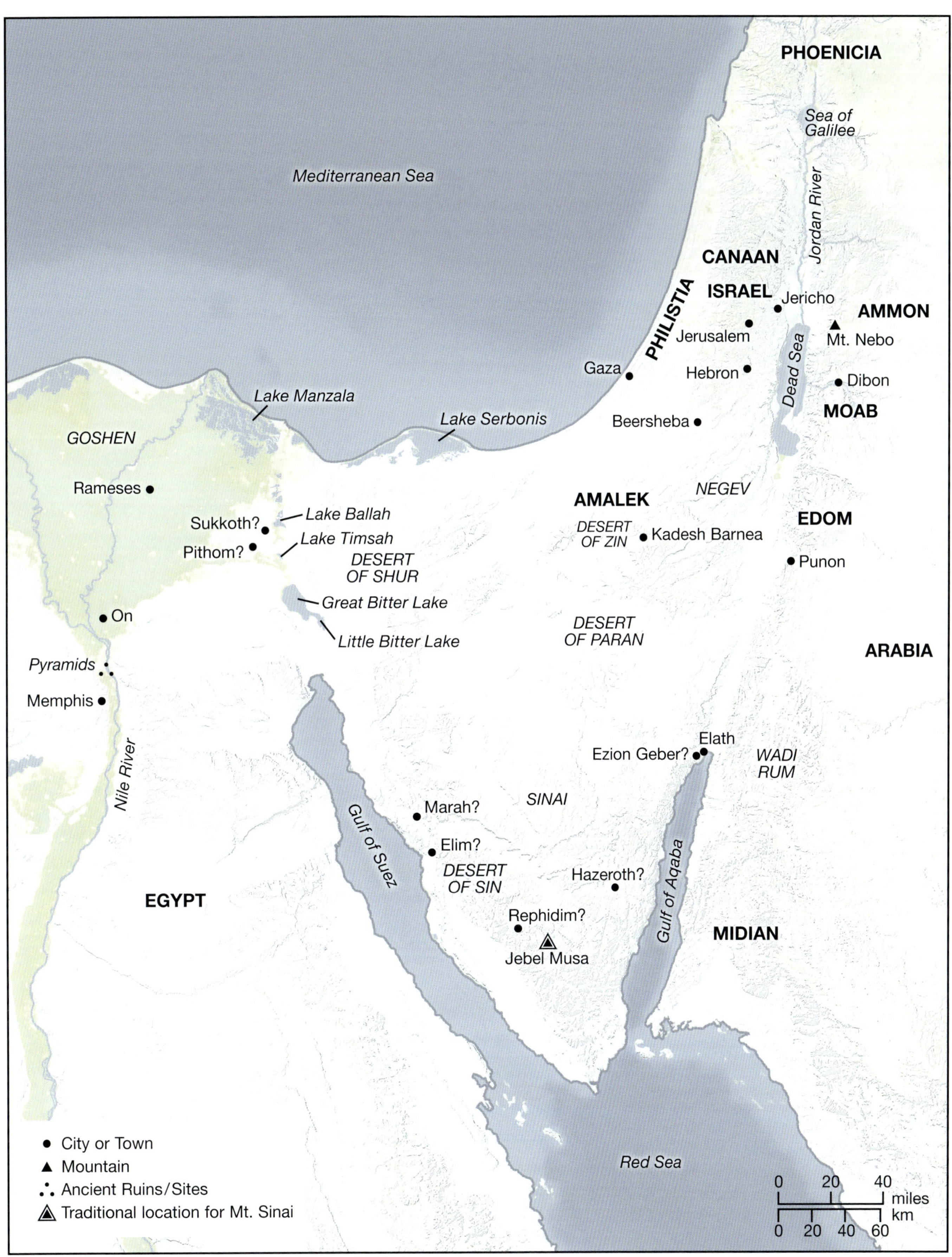
PHOENICIA
Sea of Galilee
Jordan River
Mediterranean Sea
CANAAN
PHILISTIA
ISRAEL
Jericho
AMMON
Jerusalem
Mt. Nebo
Dead Sea
Gaza
Hebron
Dibon
Lake Manzala
Lake Serbonis
Beersheba
MOAB
GOSHEN
Rameses
AMALEK
NEGEV
Sukkoth?
Lake Ballah
EDOM
DESERT OF ZIN
Kadesh Barnea
Pithom?
Lake Timsah
DESERT OF SHUR
Punon
Great Bitter Lake
On
DESERT OF PARAN
Little Bitter Lake
ARABIA
Pyramids
Memphis
Elath
Ezion Geber?
WADI RUM
Nile River
Gulf of Suez
Marah?
SINAI
Elim?
DESERT OF SIN
Hazeroth?
Gulf of Aqaba
EGYPT
Rephidim?
MIDIAN
Jebel Musa
City or Town
Mountain
Ancient Ruins/Sites
Traditional location for Mt. Sinai
Red Sea
0 20 40 miles
0 20 40 60 km

At left is what ripening wheat ought to look like (Galilee) and at right is what in the land of ancient Israel it too often was (desert areas south and east). The former says "feast," the latter, "famine." (Photos by Paul H. Wright)

and summer into autumn. These are terms for our convenience, not those of an ancient Israelite who would have divided the year into a wet season and a dry season, differentiating parts of the wet season by the amount of rain that fell. Each season produces its own crops with distinct harvest times.[7]

Due to seasonal patterns of rainfall, the land experiences cool wet winters (November through April) followed by hot dry summers (May through October). The usual rainfall comes from the west-northwest, carried by storm clouds that blow off the Mediterranean Sea and bring life to what is otherwise a mostly rocky landscape. The agricultural year begins in the autumn with the onset of the early rains (*yoreh;* Deut. 11:14; Ps. 84:6). These soften the rock-hard ground for the blade of the plow. The cooler winter months are blessed with the winter rains (*geshem* or *matar;* Ezra 10:9, 13), pushed ashore through a stationary trough of low pressure over the eastern Mediterranean Sea. These dump their abundance into the wadis, hollows, and aquifers of the land. The winter rains taper off as temperatures rise throughout the spring, giving way to the softer latter rains (*malqosh;* Deut. 11:14) that ripen the barley and wheat, bringing splashes of color to hillsides and meadows that become filled with wildflowers and grass (Ps. 65:12–13). Then follows five to six months of no rain whatsoever. The vineyards and orchard crops suck moisture from beneath the summer-parched ground through roots that run deep, doubly blessed by summer dew from above. In the biblical landscape, dew was God's gentle blessing—quiet, refreshing, and always welcome in a land scorched by the summer sun (Gen. 27:28; Deut. 32:2; Hos. 14:5).

> Let us fear the Lord our God,
> who gives the rain in its season,
> the autumn [early] rain and
> the spring [latter] rain,
> and keeps for us
> the weeks appointed for the harvest.
> (Jer. 5:24)

This annual pattern, as timeless as the land itself, proved to be an effective way for its residents—Canaanites, Israelites, Philistines, Phoenicians, Arameans, Ammonites, Moabites, and Edomites—to coax food to grow based on the seasonal rainfall throughout the year. The winter wet-season crops are annuals, mostly barley needing a minimum of eight inches of rainfall to mature and wheat requiring twelve inches or more. Orchard crops are sustainable throughout the heat of the dry summer: grapes, figs, pomegranates, olives, dates, and almonds, to name a few. Grain is harvested mid-March through early June—first barley and then wheat. The orchard crops are picked from August (grapes) through November (figs and olives). When the rains are plentiful, these harvests are the two best times of the year: storehouses overflow, debts can be settled, and tithes and offerings are brought to the temple (see Deut. 31:10). Harvest time is a time to plan for the future and peer with favor into the next new year:

> Be glad, O children of Zion,
> and rejoice in the Lord your God,
>
> for he has given the early rain for
> your vindication;
> he has poured down for you abundant rain,
> the early and the latter rain, as before.
>
> The threshing floors shall be full of grain;
> the vats shall overflow with wine and oil.
> (Joel 2:23–24)

> For the Lord your God is bringing you into a good land, a land of brooks of water, of fountains and springs, flowing out in the valleys and hills, a land of wheat and barley, of vines and fig trees and pomegranates, a land of olive trees and honey. (Deut. 8:7–8)

But all is not always well. Yes, Israel was "a land flowing with milk and honey" (Ex. 3:8) and "a land in which you will eat bread without scarcity, in which you will lack nothing" (Deut. 8:9). However, these statements perhaps should be read in the context of Israel's forty years of wandering in the Sinai wasteland where they had witnessed firsthand the meaning of want.[8] Israel's homeland was blessed but still subject to unpredictable disasters and strife, and one of the first that we notice is famine.[9]

The weather patterns that carry the blessing of rain were not always as predictable, or timely, as the Israelites hoped they would be (Jer. 14:2–6; Amos 4:7–8). Squeezed by the Mediterranean Sea that only sometimes provided sufficient rainfall and the vast expanse of the north Arabian Desert from which the "fierce breath … of the east wind" blows (Isa. 27:8), ancient Israel was always susceptible to the subtle shifts in international weather patterns that wreaked havoc on their land between.[10] More than that, its north-south mountain ranges blocked the prevailing rains from adequately penetrating the entire land, creating local deserts on the leeward side. "The earth under you shall be [as hard as] iron," we read in the curses of Deuteronomy 28:23–24, and "the rain of your land [will be] powder;" unfortunately, that was all too often the case. Other factors such as locust plagues or marauding armies could lengthen the biannual hungry gap between harvests to weeks or even months, plunging people

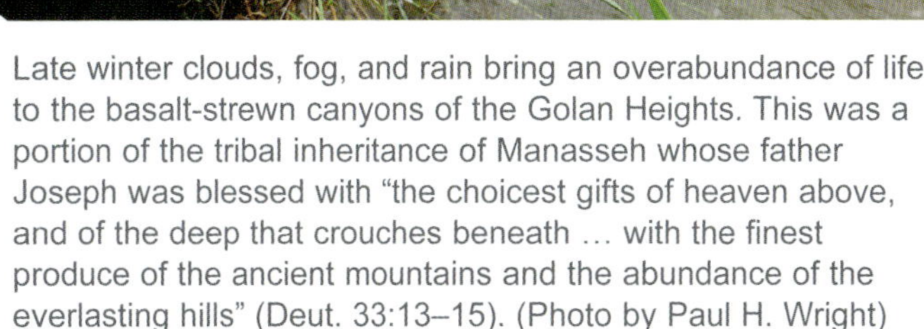

Late winter clouds, fog, and rain bring an overabundance of life to the basalt-strewn canyons of the Golan Heights. This was a portion of the tribal inheritance of Manasseh whose father Joseph was blessed with "the choicest gifts of heaven above, and of the deep that crouches beneath … with the finest produce of the ancient mountains and the abundance of the everlasting hills" (Deut. 33:13–15). (Photo by Paul H. Wright)

and animals alike into desperation.[11] Wracked by disease, wholly consumed by the daunting task of sheer survival, and left even to cannibalism or eating their own bodily waste, these, too, were part of the experience of ancient Israel (2 Kings 6:28–29; 18:27; Lam. 4:9–10).

But the Bible remains clear. In spite of the forces for good or bad that lay beyond ancient Israel's control, theirs was "a land that the Lord your God cares for. The eyes of the Lord your God are always upon it, from the beginning to the end of the year" (Deut. 11:12). Israel's land and their situation in life—as difficult as it may have been at any given time—was something that God knew and cared about. As best we can tell from available sources, Israel's neighbors held to worldviews in which their gods cared primarily only for themselves and not so much—if at all—for people.[12] This, we will see, provides the foundational difference between *how* and *why* the feasts of ancient Israel differed from those of their neighbors, even though they shared the same arc of untamable land.

2. The Context of Mealtime and Eating

From the produce of the land, we move quite naturally to the context of mealtime and eating. Given the uncertainty of rainfall and an adequate harvest, plus the ever-present threat of famine, it is natural that mealtime—and especially feasting—was something not to be taken for granted. The idea of three square meals a day with a balanced, tasty, and diverse diet was something quite unfamiliar to most of the ancient world—and still is to large parts of our own. An Israelite life "lived in safety ... every man under his vine and under

The Beth Netopha Valley from atop Khirbet Qanah, ancient Cana of Galilee. Rich soil and ample water secure lives tied to the land and its cycle of seasons. (Photo by Paul H. Wright)

his fig tree" (1 Kings 4:25) was the ideal, though perhaps generous in terms of everyday reality.

From the Bible, other ancient texts, and archaeology we have a good idea of the kinds of foods actually available to the Israelites.[13] We also know what was and wasn't (or at least should or shouldn't have been) eaten by looking at the food laws in the books of Leviticus (11:1–47; 17:10–16) and Deuteronomy (14:3–21). Often mentioned in passing, the Bible records many instances of people eating and drinking in normal circumstances; these are a valuable window into life on the ground. For instance, Boaz offered Ruth bread dipped in wine and roasted grain, a workaday meal for reapers (Ruth 2:14), and Jael gave milk and curds to Sisera, a man on the run (Judg. 4:19; 5:25).

The main meal of the day, taken late afternoon or early evening, was typically the equivalent of a bowl the size of cupped hands containing soup, gruel, or stew made of lentils, vegetables, or foraged plants, almost never with meat (Gen. 25:29–34; 2 Kings 4:38–41). Summer fruits, such as olives and grapes, together with winter grain, were staples, able to be made into oil, wine, and bread (Deut. 7:13). For most families, meat was reserved for special festive occasions (Passover, for example), for serious hospitality (Gen. 18:1–8; Judg. 6:19–20), or to enable hard workers (1 Sam. 25:11). Killing the proverbial fatted calf (or sheep or goat) depleted a family's store of capital, while drinking milk was more like consuming only the interest earned. For protein, sheep and goat milk and their derivatives had to suffice, as well as things that scampered or hopped along the ground; at least the book of Leviticus declared locusts, crickets, and grasshoppers to be ritually clean to eat (Lev. 11:22).

The Bible includes a number of menus for meals eaten on specific occasions, usually in the context of courting good will.

- King Solomon's daily diet included large quantities of meat, much of it not native to his Jerusalem home. Such foods were meant to feed (and also appease) the king's royal court and retainers, but "fine dining" like this was surely the exception for Israel as a whole (1 Kings 4:22–23).
- The shepherd boy David hurried parched grain and loaves of bread to his encamped brothers, making sure to bring protein-rich cheeses—something even better—to their field commander (1 Sam. 17:17–18). With an all-volunteer army, care packages from home were a survival necessity.
- Abigail pacified David and his men with significant quantities of loaves of bread, skins of wine, parched grain, clusters of raisins,

Mansaf is a traditional Middle Eastern dish of lamb, or sometimes chicken, cooked in a sauce of fermented yogurt poured over rice. It is served on special occasions. As has been the custom for thousands of years, everyone uses flatbread and their fingers as the only utensils to eat off a common plate. In this way, the very act of eating lowers guards and builds community. Pictured here is such a meal shared by students of biblical life and culture. (Photo by Paul H. Wright)

fig cakes, and even sheep, after her husband Nabal (his name means "fool") had refused to share with David's men the food that he had already prepared for his feast (1 Sam. 25:2–25).

- Following the weary march through the Judean wilderness to intercept the royal interloper Absalom, King David and his men were relieved by local supporters with a generous spread of "wheat, barley, flour, parched grain, beans and lentils, honey and curds and sheep and cheese" (2 Sam. 17:28–29).
- Ezekiel gives us a recipe for bread: mix together wheat, barley, beans, lentils, millet, and emmer. What we take as health food today was to him probably cleaning out the cupboard so that he could survive a lengthy siege on his city (Ezek. 4:9).

From menus such as these, we see something of the variety of foods that could be eaten. What we don't know is how typical they were to one's daily diet. Most likely, the best determiner of what was actually consumed on a daily basis was hunger pangs plus whatever might have been available on any given day, grubs and all.

So the Israelites ate to stave off hunger. But mealtime was also a social event. At least once a day, everyone in the same social unit—for ancient Israel, it was the extended family—focused on the same activity at the same time. The act of eating together is a powerful binding agent, especially when people outside one's normal in-group are invited.[14] For ancient Israel, this was particularly so when the meal was eaten off a single shared platter or out of a single large bowl (a krater), with fingers or dipped bread as the only utensils.[15] (The same habit is practiced by Bedouin in traditional settings yet today.) Eating from a common dish breaks down boundaries, recognizes those who might otherwise be "the other," and places high value on building acceptance and trust. Meals shared in this way are the great leveler, with an emphasis on "done with" rather than "done to," cooperation rather than hostility.[16] By implication, choosing not to invite someone to a meal or choosing to refuse an invitation arouses suspicion, enmity, and resentment (1 Sam. 25:9–13).

We can see the values of table fellowship most clearly in the context of hospitality.[17] The practical need to care for travelers, people journeying outside the reach of their own in-groups, became a sacred duty for the Israelites, as it still is in cultures across the globe: "You know the heart of a sojourner, for you were sojourners in the land of Egypt" (Ex. 23:9; see also Isa. 58:6–7).

Home was not so much a place of possessions as it was a place of shelter, and it came with the obligation to provide shelter and provision to others.

> "An Egyptian delivered us out of the hand of the shepherds and even drew water for us and watered the flock," [said Reuel's daughters]. . . . "Then where is he?" [asked Reuel, dumbfounded that his daughters failed to bring the "Egyptian," Moses, home after he had defended their water rights at the local well]. "Why have you left the man? Call him, that he may eat bread." (Ex. 2:19–20)

Given as a gift to strangers at mealtime, food is a kind of sacrifice for the sake of the other. While an act of hospitality in the biblical world carried an expectation that hospitality would flow the other way too, the interchange was not "you did it because you expect something back." Rather, hospitality was the first step in initiating an ongoing relationship of mutual responsibility and aid.[18] In this light, "you prepare a table before me in the presence of my enemies" (Ps. 23:5) is not a gloat by the psalmist at a banquet but a call for reconciliation, even with those intent on doing the psalmist harm.

Since the act of eating a meal together meant far more than just filling one's belly, sharing a meal in sacred, religious contexts carried even more significance. In these settings, the participants recognized that God himself was present at the meal. Whether meals took place around a family table, within the larger village community, on the national level, or as part of a peoplehood that transcended boundaries, table fellowship with God implied an orderly and ideal world, one that was full, satisfied, and wholly accepting of all its participants.[19]

From Meals to Feasts

Some meals in ancient Israel became feasts, with the attendees drawn from communities larger than the family unit itself. The most common Hebrew word for feast, or banquet, is *mishteh,* from the root *shatah*, which means "to drink" or "to imbibe." The occasions could be:

- Celebratory, such as weddings (Judg. 14:10);
- Satisfying, as at sheep-shearing time (1 Sam. 25:2, 36);
- Momentous, as when a covenant was ratified (Gen. 26:26–31; 2 Sam. 3:20–21);
- Showy, such as the banquet of King Ahasuerus (Est. 1:1–9); or
- Judicious, like the banquet of Esther (Est. 5:1–8).

Cooking flatbread, a timeless staple in the Middle East, on a griddle. (Art by Balage Balogh)

As for the meal itself, there was always plenty of food and drink. Indeed, eating and drinking to excess was often the goal so as to honor the generosity of the host, although having a good time came in a close second. Feasts were appropriate times to eat and drink something not normally part of daily fare, such as meat or fine spiced wine (see Song 8:2). We should add, of course, that there were other elements: music from the lyre, harp, tambourine, and flute (Isa. 5:12), giving and receiving gifts (Est. 2:18), plenty of boasting and talk, and all those other things that do not need to be mentioned when guests become merry of heart (Job 1:4–5). All this exuberance is quite understandable, given ancient Israel's otherwise toilsome search for survival, as is the Bible's condemnation of the celebrants' natural tendency toward excess.

From Feasts to Festivals

Some feasts also became festivals. The Hebrew word *hag* is a term that identifies in particular the three great festivals of ancient Israel:

- Passover (Pesach)
- Feast of Weeks (Shavuot)
- Feast of Booths (Sukkot)

We should think of a *hag* as a feast held in a sacred place and at a sacred time, on holy ground where people met or sensed the special presence of God. This implies a pilgrimage or sacred journey, which is itself a sacrifice of personal hardship for the honor of being present with others who also made the same journey to celebrate the festival.[20]

The food and drink for these festivals typically was similar to what was served for other feasts—though perhaps the revelry in eating and drinking was done with all due sacred restraint. Some festivals included foods specific to the occasion, such as unleavened bread at Passover (Ex. 12:17–20).

Pomegranates, figs, grapes, and olives are four summer fruit staples in the hilly heartland of Israel. Their harvest rounds out the agricultural year. "You crown the year with your bounty ... the hills gird themselves with joy" (Ps. 65:11–12). (Photos by Paul H. Wright)

It is with the festivals in particular that we can sense how awesome the otherwise essential act of eating—something never to be taken for granted—actually was when done on holy ground in communal fellowship with God. It's no wonder that mealtime, anytime, was a time of blessing.

3. The Context of Time

We move now to the context of time and why certain points of the week, month, or year in the ancient world became significant enough to be marked by celebration. Let's start by looking at how Israel and their neighbors measured time.

Agricultural Time

With the rise of the monarchy in the tenth century BC, Israel developed a civil calendar that marked the passage of years by the length of a king's reign.[21] Reckoning a sequence of years this way was necessary for official administrative purposes, but it rarely reached down to the priorities of people in the villages, except at tax time. What was more relevant for the daily life of villagers was to note the passage of time *within* each year. On the most practical level, this was done simply by noting that certain events happened within the natural annual agricultural cycle, rather than by labeling them according to segments of a calendar *per se*. The Bible provides many examples, each earthy and quite sufficient for the practicalities of life dominated by the field.[22]

- When the rains come "in their season … your threshing shall last to the time of the grape harvest, and the grape harvest shall last to the time for sowing" (Lev. 26:4–5).
- Moses sent his twelve spies up the hilly backbone of Canaan when "the time was the season of the first ripe grapes" (Num. 13:20).
- Samson, a newlywed not particularly mindful of his bride, paid a visit to his wife "after some days, at the time of wheat harvest" (Judg. 15:1).
- Ruth and Naomi returned from the land of Moab to the fields of Bethlehem "at the beginning of the barley harvest" (Ruth 1:22), and Ruth gained the right to glean in the fields "until the end of the barley and wheat harvests" (Ruth 2:23).
- Rizpah, widow of Saul, wronged when King David executed her two sons, brought attention to her plight through a silent outdoor vigil "from the beginning of [the barley] harvest until rain fell upon them from the heavens" (2 Sam. 21:9–10).
- Amos witnessed a locust plague "when the latter growth was just beginning to sprout … the latter growth after the king's mowings" (Amos 7:1).
- The earliest mention of two of Israel's great festivals are set according to harvest times: "You shall keep the Feast of Harvest [Hag HaQatzir], of the firstfruits of your labor, of what you sow in the field. You shall keep the Feast of Ingathering [Hag Ha'Asif] at the end of the year, when you gather in from the field the fruit of your labor" (Ex. 23:16).

We can think of this as reckoning time at the local level, with "time zones" based on local growing conditions. The exact time of year "when the latter growth was just beginning to sprout," for instance, would differ from place to place or from year to year depending on local topography, climate, and rainfall. And as long as life was lived in small social circles, from village to village, we might expect that the specific dates of their harvest-related celebrations would vary as well.

Lunar Time

Even though the cycle of growing seasons corresponds to the solar year ("seedtime and harvest, cold and heat, summer and winter;" Gen. 8:22), the most visible and consistent way to mark time over the course of the year is by the phases of the moon. From earliest times, ancient Israel, like most of its neighbors, did exactly this. For each of twenty-nine consecutive nights, the shape of the moon and its location when first visible in the arc of the sky is different from the night before and the night following. This lunar cycle of waxing and waning, from new moon to full moon to no moon, happens twelve times in a bit less than the length of a solar year, giving a predictable and evocative order to the passage of time.

Largely because of its nightly phases, the moon begs to be paid attention to, so this "lesser light to rule the night" (Gen. 1:16) became a powerful force in the ancient world. This was especially so among desert dwellers, who favored its gentle light—fully adequate in the cool of the night—over the intensity of the sun and whose shepherding lifestyle was much less dependent on the growing seasons.[23] In fact, it was the first visibility of the moon in the evening sky that prompted the idea—common but not universal in the ancient world—that a day started in the evening. For this reason, a new month also began in the evening, when the first sliver of the crescent moon hung low in the western sky, shortly after the sun dipped below the horizon.

It is important at this point to notice that of the six days of creation described in Genesis 1, only once, on the fourth day, is there a reason given for the thing that was created:

> And God said, "Let the lights in the expanse of the heavens be for separating the day from the night. And let them be for signs and for seasons, and for days and years." (Gen. 1:14)[24]

This mosaic floor from the sixth-century AD Bet Alpha synagogue in the Jezreel Valley, Israel, depicts a zodiac wheel labeled with the Hebrew months. The sun is represented in the center and one of the four seasons in each corner. (Photo by Paul H. Wright)

The Gezer and Ugarit Calendars

An example of a Canaanite calendar comes from a short inscription etched on a small slab of limestone found at Gezer, a large city overlooking the coastal plain about twenty miles (32 km) west of Jerusalem.[25] The tablet, popularly known as the Gezer calendar, dates to the late tenth century BC, the time of the reign of Solomon when control of Gezer was passing from the Canaanites (with Egypt's help) to Israel (Judg. 1:29; 1 Kings 9:15–17). Its language is most likely Canaanite (Phoenician), although it could be Hebrew; in either case, the content of the text fits both peoples. The text organizes agricultural activity throughout the year by units of one or two months, starting in the autumn but without giving any actual month names:

His two months: ingathering

His two months: seed [or sowing]

His two months: late sowing

His month: flax cutting

His month: barley harvest

His month: [wheat] harvest and measuring

His two months: vine harvest

His month: summer [fruit] harvest[26]

Because the list starts in our autumn, we can assume that the Canaanites saw each new year as starting then. It probably also reflects the growing season at Gezer itself, where the warm weather would allow the grape harvest to take place in June/July, about a month earlier than in the Judean highlands. We would expect, on this account, the barley harvest to be at least in March/April, but we find instead a month of cutting flax, bumping the Gezer barley month to April/May. This is evidence that the ways to reckon time varied in different locations, since flax is a crop that does well in the warmer, wetter coastal flatlands stretching westward from Gezer but cannot be grown in most other parts of the country, including the hill country of Judah. We also see that the terms *harvest* (*qatzir*) and *ingathering* (*asif*) match the original names of two of Israel's pilgrimage festivals (Ex. 23:16).

The Gezer calendar divides the year into months according to agricultural activities. The text mirrors the Israelite agricultural year. (Photo by Osama Shukir Muhammed Amin/Wikimedia)

As another example, scholars have been able to re-create the calendar that the people of Ugarit used in the fifteenth to thirteenth centuries BC.[27] Ugarit was a large port city on the north Syrian coast that lay within the broad cultural realm of the Canaanites. Even though some of the month names are difficult to translate, we see that the people of Ugarit also began their year in the early autumn and thought of the annual passage of time not just in terms of seasonal agricultural activity but of their own life passages as well. And there is harmony between the rhythms of individual life and the seasons: the month of *pgrm*, "the dead" or "funeral offerings," takes place in the darkest time of the year (December/January) when the fate of the crops sown is still in doubt; the month of *hlt*, probably "phoenix," corresponds to renewed life that is possible with the start of the spring harvest; and the hot summer months, post-grain harvest, are labeled with devotion to the gods. This suggests that the people of Ugarit combined agricultural activities with ritual acts, a tendency common throughout the ancient (and modern) world.

Immersed in a world where all other people made gods of the sun, moon, and stars, the writer of Genesis is clear that the celestial lights are things that were created, and that was done by *one* God. More than that, they were made for a specific purpose—and that was to serve people, rather than function as gods for people to serve. Genesis 1:14 is a clear statement of Israel's belief in one God (monotheism), but it also recognizes that Israel, by noticing the patterns of movement made by the sun and the moon, participated with their neighbors in the most natural way of measuring the passage of time.

Hebrew has two words for month. One is *yerah*, which comes from the word for "moon," *yareah*; and the other is *hodesh*, "new," a term frequently used to refer to the new moon marking the start of each month. That there are two terms in Hebrew for month suggests that it was the phases of the moon, not the agricultural season, that provided the underlying basis for a calendar that not only the Israelites but also their neighbors could follow.

The Months

The Bible preserves only four month names used by Israel during the time of the Old Testament before the exile. It is likely that these were also the actual month names of the Canaanite calendar adopted by Israel, given their shared natural environment. Again, we see a clear connection between the time of year and activity on the ground.

- The month of **Ethanim**, "perennial," was the last month of the annual summer drought, when the only reliable water sources were perennial springs.
- Ethanim was followed by the month of **Bul**, "rain" or "produce," and the onset of the early rains (see Deut. 11:14).
- The month of **Abib** (or Aviv) has a technical name. *Abib* is a term for the head of barley grain when it first has nutritional value (it is the consistency of soft wax), the last developmental stage before harvest.[28]
- Then follows the month of **Ziv**, "beauty," the time of year when the land is most lush with later rain (see Deut. 11:14).

The names of the Jewish months today come directly from the names of the months in the Babylonian calendar. The Jews most likely adopted these names during their time in exile in the sixth and fifth centuries BC, leaving behind the Canaanite names they had previously used. The Babylonian names also are tied directly to the seasons, which in Babylon were not too different from those in Canaan.

There was of course a problem. As natural as it is to follow the phases of the moon when calculating the passage of time, it is difficult for agricultural societies to keep to a strict lunar calendar. This is because the annual solar cycle consists of 365¼ days, while twelve lunar cycles of 29½ days each make a year of only 354 days. This puts the system out of sync by about one month every three years. It becomes a problem only if particular months are tied to specific agricultural activities such as the harvest festivals, as they are for Israel. Left alone, people in villages would probably tend to celebrate whenever their particular crops were in the barn. But to have any sort of larger tribal or national unity, the people needed to pick a date, as it were, and stick with it. To solve the problem, the Babylonians, and then Israel, adopted a lunisolar (moon and sun) calendar, adding an additional month every two or three years to synchronize the calendar with the seasons. For Israel, this was the month of Adar, the month prior to the barley harvest, repeated when needed as Adar II so that Passover, which by Torah command must be celebrated on the fourteenth day of Nisan, would correspond to the barley actually being ripe in the field (Lev. 23:5).

Months in the Ancient Near East

This comparison chart starts in the autumn, when in the land of ancient Israel the harvest of summer fruit overlapped the beginning of the early rains.

Modern Equivalent	Gezer Calendar	Ugarit Calendar	Old Hebrew (Canaanite) Calendar	Babylonian Calendar	Jewish Calendar
Sept/Oct	"ingathering"	*rish yn* "first wine"	*Ethanim* "perennial [springs]" 1 Kings 8:2	*Tashritu*	*Tishri*
Oct/Nov	"ingathering"	*nql* "cultivation"* or "sickle"*	*Bul* "rain"* or "produce"* 1 Kings 6:38	*Arahshamnu*	*Heshvan*
Nov/Dec	"seed" or "sowing"	*mgmr* translation unknown	unknown	*Kislimu*	*Kislev*
Dec/Jan	"seed" or "sowing"	*pgrm* "the dead" or "funeral offerings"	unknown	*Tebetu*	*Tevet*
Jan/Feb	"late sowing"	*iblt* "ritual acts"*	unknown	*Shabatu* described in texts as "a favorable month; a month of frost"	*Shevat*
Feb/Mar	"late sowing"	*hyr* "the dead"* or "donkey"*	unknown	*Addaru* described in texts as "a favorable month"	*Adar* (and *Adar II*)
Mar/Apr	"flax cutting"	*hlt* "phoenix"*	*Abib* (*Aviv*) "young grain of barley" Ex. 13:4; 23:15; 34:18; Deut. 16:1; see also Ezek. 3:15	*Nisannu*, "first produce of the season" The *akitu* (New Year's) festival celebrated on days 10–11.	*Nisan*
Apr/May	"barley harvest"	*gn* "garden"	*Ziv* "beauty" 1 Kings 6:1, 37	*Ayaru*	*Iyar*

Modern Equivalent	Gezer Calendar	Ugarit Calendar	Old Hebrew (Canaanite) Calendar	Babylonian Calendar	Jewish Calendar
May/Jun	"wheat harvest and measuring"	*itb* "Ashtabi" (a deity)	unknown	*Simanu* a month of settling debts and obligations	*Sivan*
Jun/Jul	"vine harvest"	*dbhn* "sacrifice"	unknown	*Dumuzi* the name of the dying grain-god	*Tammuz*
Jul/Aug	"vine harvest"	unknown	unknown	*Abu* described in texts as when "the fire-god comes down from the sky and vies with the sun-god"	*Av*
Aug/Sep	"summer (fruit) harvest"	*ittbnm* "Ashtabi" (a deity*)	unknown	*Ullulu*	*Elul*

*translation uncertain

Appointed Times

One of the Hebrew words that is particularly descriptive of the great pilgrimage feasts of Israel is *mo'ed*, which means "appointed or fixed time." There were times fixed in the calendar for these special feasts to take place:

> Let the people of Israel keep the Passover at its appointed time [*mo'ed*]. On the fourteenth day of this month [Nisan], at twilight, you shall keep it at its appointed time [*mo'ed*]; according to all its statues and all its rules you shall keep it. (Num. 9:2–3)

We note that Genesis 1:14 uses the word quite intentionally: the sun and moon were created with the expressed purpose of being "for signs and for seasons" (*mo'edim,* plural), literally "for appointed times." This wording points directly to their role in determining the specific dates of Israel's great feasts. We recall that, unlike the beliefs of Israel's neighbors, the heavenly lights are not objects of worship, but things created to help point us toward the Creator. But the word *mo'ed* also means an "appointed or fixed *place.*" By combining the concepts of time and place, we might say "a rendezvous" is indicated.[29] One of the names for the tabernacle is "tent of meeting" (*ohel mo'ed*; Ex. 27:21), making it early Israel's point of spiritual and social rendezvous. Thus the term *mo'ed* eventually came to identify both the Jerusalem temple and the feasts held there (Lam. 2:6)—one term for both the place and time of Israel's sacred rendezvous with God.

The Weeks

The Israelites divided the month into weeks of seven days each; in fact, the Hebrew word for "week," *shavu'a*, comes from *sheva*, "seven." But having a week of seven days is not so obvious a choice. Unlike the day, month, and year, a seven-day week cannot be precisely calculated based on the movement of the sun, the moon, or the stars. While the elements of the fourth day of creation were intended to mark the seasons, days, and years, the word *week* is not mentioned in Genesis 1:14. The most obvious division of the month is by halves—new moon and full moon—which the early Israelites, along with just about everyone else, also recognized. For their part, the Egyptians, among whom the Israelites lived from the time of Joseph to Moses, divided the month into three ten-day weeks, realizing that 30 (3 x 10) was the best whole number to represent each lunar month of 29½ days, while four weeks of seven days (4 x 7 = 28) is not.[30] The moon's phases between quarters last approximately 7.4 days each, but that extra 0.4 days of time was never reconciled in the Israelite calendar to keep the weeks in sync with each lunar month the way that the lunar months were reconciled on an ongoing basis to the solar year. So it seems that because the seven-day week cannot be explained naturally and because it corresponds to the most foundational event of all—creation (Gen. 1)—it became the most distinctive passage of time for ancient Israel, marked of course by the holy seventh day, the Sabbath. Let's call it a "God thing" rather than just another cycle of nature.

4. The Context of Worldview

Our fourth context is that of worldview. This is the most difficult context to enter, but it's also the most important for getting to the heart of Israel's feasts. Knowing what the people we see on a daily basis are thinking is hard enough; to know the mind of an ancient Israelite—someone separated from us by three millennia and the wide span of the globe—is probably the most challenging task for any Bible

Sunrise from Jebel Musa, the traditional site of Mount Sinai. "God came from Teman [on the eastern horizon], and the Holy One from Mount Paran. His splendor covered the heavens, and the earth was full of his praise. His brightness was like the light; rays flashed from his hand; and there he veiled his power" (Hab. 3:3–4). (Photo by Paul H. Wright)

reader. So we gaze through two windows, flexing our mental muscles and trusting the Holy Spirit to sharpen our view. Through one window, we observe the actions and words of people whose lives are recorded on the pages of the Bible. Through the second window, we examine the life and times of the biblical authors who recorded these words and deeds. And peering into both, we see that even though the Israelites participated in the world of the ancient Near East, they also stood apart from it. As previously mentioned, Israelite celebrations did not develop in isolation, and we should expect to find similarities between the ways they feasted and the ways of their neighbors. These similarities are important to take into account in spite of the fact that Israel's neighbors were pagan. We should also expect to find some differences when we compare any two people groups. But most important is to recognize differences *of essence*—of the ways of thinking and understanding and believing that made ancient Israel unique.[31]

- The first significant difference is monotheism: "Hear, O Israel: The Lord our God, the Lord is one" (Deut. 6:4). One God, creator not created, who acts in history and whose interests and control are not limited by the borders of ancient Israel but rather inclusive of the entire universe (Isa. 42:5–10).
- The second difference is that God knows about and cares for people (Deut. 11:12; Isa. 40:28–31; 43:1–7). By clear contrast, all of the written texts that we have from ancient Israel's neighbors indicate that their gods

It was at Mount Sinai where Moses experienced the fullness of monotheism: "Hear, O Israel: The Lord our God, the Lord is one" (Deut. 6:4). This is the view northward from the summit of the traditional location of Mount Sinai. (Photo by Paul H. Wright)

> (or, to be more accurate, their *conception* of what were gods) were many, that these gods were subject to the same concerns, foibles, and tendencies to self-centeredness that characterize humanity, and that they did not care very much for people.

These differences are differences *of essence.* The peoples round about Israel, living in an uncertain world and conceiving that the actions and attitudes of their gods were also uncertain, sought stability for their own lives by trying to nudge the gods in their direction. Through a series of activities that included celebrating religious festivals, they sought to appease their gods so that the gods would, at the very least, not bring harm and, they hoped, also act favorably toward them and their loved ones. Festivals that celebrated primal events (such as creation or the annual re-creation of plant growth through rain) or that honored passages of life (such as birth and death) included reciting founding myths or ceremonies where people ate with the gods. It was personal: *If I reenact the great cosmic myths, the gods may be compelled to instill order in my corner of the universe, favorably altering my uncertain destiny in the month or year to come.* And, as we can see from the invectives against paganism spoken by Elijah, Isaiah, Jeremiah, and the other biblical prophets, many Israelites tended to believe the same thing, either in connection with the Canaanite god Baal or even in thinking about the Lord God. The seduction of syncretism—the fusion of different belief systems—has always been strong.

All of this stands in stark contrast to the reasons why the biblical authors said Israel should celebrate. Primary among those reasons was the need to establish a memorial to God's great saving acts in the past and his ongoing provision, in spite of the harsh daily circumstances of life. Passover, for instance, was celebrated to "remember the day when you came out of the land of Egypt" (Deut. 16:3) and the Feast of Booths so that "your generations may know that I made the people of Israel dwell in booths when I brought them out of the land of Egypt" (Lev. 23:43). This is rooted in the idea of covenant, a special relationship that God chose to forge with Israel that bound the two in a mutual relationship of loyalty, provision, and trust (Ex. 34:10–27). Israel's great feasts (the *haggim*) were not occasions to try to control God but to learn to understand him and how to follow him better. We note the language of Deuteronomy:

> For seven days you shall keep the feast [of booths] to the LORD your God at the place that the LORD will choose, because the LORD your God will bless you in all your produce and in all the work of your hands, so that you will be altogether joyful. (Deut. 16:15)

In other words, keep the feast because of what God does, not *so that* he will act in such and such a way. There is no hint in the Bible that the turn of the year was a time when evil spirits were particularly active and on the prowl, as many ancients believed; that through careful rituals and ceremonies the malevolent forces could be checked lest they bring harm to one's home and family; and that harvest time celebrations were intended to entice the spirits to act kindly. No, the great biblical feasts—Passover, Weeks, and Booths—were about expressing the true character of God and acknowledging who is in control.

Israel was also to celebrate the feasts so that others less fortunate—the sojourner, the fatherless, and the widow—could share in their abundance (Deut. 16:11–12, 16–17). By doing so, they (and we!) learn to care for others the same way that God cared for Israel in Egypt or sustained them (and sustains us!) during long, trying years of wilderness wandering.

And of course, one of most practical reasons to celebrate the feasts was to have an opportunity to rejoice together in community and be grateful for the things God has done (Deut. 16:11, 14–15). Celebrations were one way to say, *Yes we are part of humanity, but we are also unique.*

FEASTS OF HEARTH AND HOME

It's time to take a look at specific feasts that are mentioned in the Old Testament. Our approach will be to take a comparative view. This means we'll look at which feasts ancient Israel celebrated, how they differed from the feasts of their neighbors, and how they differed from what we know as the "biblical feasts."

The first thing we notice is that the Israelites celebrated a great many feasts, more than the well-known pilgrimage festivals of Passover, Weeks, and Booths. So we'll start our discussion with feasts that the Bible typically calls *mishteh*, the common term for a feast or banquet. We will also include some other feasts that Israel celebrated early on, as well as other instances where feasting is implied, such as on the Sabbath or at the new moon. Some of these feasts marked family events or life passages. Others were tied to seasonal activities. Many observed cyclical passages of time, either weekly, monthly, or annually. Typically, they were celebrated locally, in the village or out in the countryside, in a home (tent, house, or palace) or at a shrine, for a select group of people such as a family or clan, members of a work gang, or even the royal court. Some required a short pilgrimage to a shared high place or the site where the tabernacle was set up, before all the elaborate trappings of the Jerusalem temple and priesthood had developed. Overall, we can characterize these more common and local observances as "feasts of hearth and home."

At every level, these celebrations were communal and nearly always involved eating something that was above and beyond one's normal daily diet. In addition, in one way or another, all served to recognize, embrace, and reinforce the participants' identity, whether it was with their family, their clan or tribe, their people, or their God.

The biblical prophets help us see that all too often the identity that many Israelites reinforced had more in common with that of the pagan Canaanites than it did with the commands of the Lord God. But, we recall, we can assume that *some* of the ways and *some* of the reasons that the Israelite celebrations were similar to those of their neighbors were due to a shared climate, agricultural cycle, and moon-based calendar. (As today, Christmas trees are put up by believers and non-believers alike.)

Even though Israel participated in the world of the ancient Near East, they also stood apart from it. In the end, all of the biblical feasts, including those of hearth and home, helped define Israel's cultural and personal identity just as much as they were occasions to celebrate normal passages of life.

Feasts that Marked Stages of Life

Our list of biblical feasts of hearth and home starts with celebrations that marked stages of life, each quite normal in the human lifespan. Each was a feast (*mishteh*) that usually involved drinking—sometimes to excess.

- Pharaoh celebrated his birthday by holding a feast for all his royal officials (Gen. 40:20). Much later, Herod Antipas did the same (Matt. 14:6–10). On both occasions, subjects were elevated to, or removed from, power. Ordinary people also celebrated birthdays, such as the sons of Job, who held "a feast in the house of each one on his day," inviting their sisters to join in (Job 1:4).
- Abraham held a great feast to mark the day that Isaac was weaned, formally confirming that his son had survived infancy (a not-so-easy thing in the ancient world) and acknowledging that Isaac, not Ishmael, was to be his rightful heir (Gen. 21:8).
- A wedding feast was given by Laban to celebrate the marriage of his eldest daughter Leah to Jacob (Gen. 29:21–23). There is no mention of a second feast for Rachel a week

later (v. 28); either that one is implied, or Laban felt that the marriage of his unloved older daughter was more deserving of the event.

- In the time of the judges, Samson hosted his own wedding feast, "for so the young men used to do" (Judg. 14:10); his was a boastful guy-thing that lasted seven days (vv. 11–19).
- To complete the cycle of life, Jeremiah tells us that at a person's death, mourners typically ate and drank with members of the surviving family in a "house of feasting" (*beit mishteh;* Jer. 16:8).

There is every reason to think that such celebrations were part of the social fabric of all ancient Israel, as they are in most cultures today.

Though birthday and wedding feasts were common in the ancient Near East, perhaps as widespread was the *marzeah*.[32] This was a ceremony centered around a drinking banquet. At times it seems to have been associated with funerals and events to honor or commune with the dead. In these instances, the marzeah was typically hosted by the oldest living son on behalf of his dead ancestors, especially for his father. When possible, the banquet took place in the large antechamber of the rock-hewn tomb in which the bodies of the dearly departed lay, its living participants calling on the dead to join the meal. This was a recurring feast held on the anniversary of the death or on astronomically significant days such as the new moon, moments of time when, in pagan belief, life and death hung together in the balance. Because the marzeah was associated with the passage from life to death, the celebrations often included a sexual element so as to cause, or at least symbolize, the beginning of a new cycle of life. The marzeah was as common as it was widespread in the ancient world, mentioned in texts dating from the fourteenth century BC to the Byzantine period in the fourth through sixth centuries AD,

An Iron Age tomb located just north of Jerusalem on the grounds of the Saint Etienne Monastery. Bodies were laid on the stone-hewn ledges on either side. Once the flesh decayed, the bones were placed in a common repository into which the photographer is peering. (Photo by Paul H. Wright)

Ceramic vessels for food storage and consumption fill this reconstructed model of a tomb from the Iron Age (time of the Judean monarchy) excavated at Ketef Hinnom opposite the southwestern corner of ancient Jerusalem. This reconstruction is in the Israel Museum, Jerusalem. (Photo by Paul H. Wright)

and stretching from Egypt to Mesopotamia, a wide geographical run of two thousand years.

This feast is mentioned by name twice in the Bible:

> Woe to those who lie on beds of ivory
> and stretch themselves out on their couches,
> and eat lambs from the flock
> and calves from the midst of the stall,
> who sing idle songs to the sound of the harp
> and like David invent for themselves instruments of music,
> who drink wine in bowls
> and anoint themselves with the finest oils,
> but are not grieved over the ruin of Joseph!
> Therefore they shall now be the first of those who go into exile,
> and the revelry [marzeah] of those who stretch themselves out shall pass away.
> (Amos 6:4–7)

> For thus says the LORD: Do not enter the house of mourning [marzeah], or go to lament or grieve for them, for I have taken away my peace from this people, my steadfast love and mercy, declares the LORD. (Jer. 16:5)

Amos mentions some of the elements of the marzeah, and we can see why most English Bibles translate the word not as "banquet" but "revelry." Amos doesn't specifically mention the marzeah's association with the dead (it sometimes was just a raucous banquet), but Jeremiah clearly does. Because according to ancient Near Eastern texts the marzeah was most often associated with ceremonies in which people banqueted with the dead, it seems that it also could have been part of other scenes mentioned in the Old Testament that either described what people did or what the biblical writers urged them *not* to do.

> When you have finished paying all the tithe of your produce in the third year ... then you shall say before the LORD your God ... "I have not eaten of the tithe while I was mourning ... or offered any of it to the dead." (Deut. 26:12–14)

> Then they yoked themselves to the Baal of Peor [the rapacious lord of the wide-open mouth], and ate sacrifices offered to the dead.
> (Ps. 106:28; see also Num. 25:1–9)

> Should they inquire of the dead on behalf of the living? (Isa. 8:19).

As uncomfortable as the answer might be, these references surely prompt the question, why would the biblical prophets condemn practices associated with the marzeah, if their people weren't participating in it or something like it and doing so to such an extent that its pagan values shaped

Abraham and the Three Angels by Avanzino Nucci (1629)

Israel's behavior in a way that needed correcting? Indeed, rock-hewn family tombs from the time of the Judean monarchy found in Jerusalem include bowls for food, jugs for liquids, lamps for light, jars and juglets for scented oils, talismans, and fertility figurines.[33] Such finds suggest similar questions: Why were things meant for the living placed in tombs of the dead? And who was using them in there? While it is difficult to know what any given ancient Israelite was *thinking*, there is enough evidence to allow us to see what they were *doing*. At least in part, they tended to mark passages of life with feasts that were common to the world around them.

Feasts for Hospitality

Another occasion for feasting that the Bible mentions is hospitality, and here we are on more familiar, comfortable ground. Examples are numerous, since acts of hospitality that centered on a meal were an essential part of ancient Near Eastern culture. Offering food and drink was expected nearly every time people met, whether it is mentioned in the texts or not. This makes hospitality an underlying value for all our categories of feasting.

The template for hospitality is the detailed account of Abraham and Sarah entertaining strangers—angels unaware—in their tent (Gen. 18:1–8). They spared no effort, giving the best that they had of food, drink (milk rather than wine due to their status as herders, not farmers), and attention to their visitors' needs, without rushing the moment in any way.

> Abraham went quickly into the tent to Sarah and said, "Quick! Three seahs of fine flour! Knead it, and make cakes." And Abraham ran to the herd and took a calf, tender and good, and gave it to a young man, who prepared it quickly. Then he took curds and milk and the calf that he had prepared, and set it before them. And he stood by them under the tree while they ate. (Gen. 18:6–8)

Later, when the angelic visitors arrived at Sodom, Lot hosted them in his house, preparing a feast (*mishteh*) that included unleavened bread (Gen. 19:3). That the people of Sodom were decidedly *in*hospitable that night only heightens our picture of what proper table fellowship should be (Gen. 19:4–22).

Feasts for Special Occasions

Many of the feasts and celebrations (*mishteh*) recorded in the Bible mark special occasions that were above and beyond the norms of common hospitality. Some were held to seal a covenant, celebrate a victory, confirm kingship, or mark a grand accomplishment. Others came with ulterior motives: to curry favor or entice and entrap an enemy. Many were "political" on one level or another. Here are just five of the many examples found in the Bible:

- Isaac reestablished the covenant that Abimelech, the king of Gerar, had made with his father Abraham by hosting a feast: "they ate and drank" together (Gen. 26:26–31; compare with Gen. 21:22–34). The mutual oaths that Isaac and Abimelech made the next morning sealed their relationship, allowing each their own grazing land and, by implication, the obligation of mutual aid.
- After Saul's death, David, newly anointed as king of Judah, hosted Saul's close relative and general, Abner, at a feast. It was at this feast where Abner pledged his loyalty and that of all Israel to David, even though Abner had been a natural candidate for the throne (2 Sam. 3:17–21). Shortly afterward David's general Joab killed Abner under the pretext that his pledge was a trap (vv. 22–30).

- The newly crowned Solomon offered sacrifices to the Lord and gave a celebratory feast for his servants after God, in a vision at the high place of Gibeon, had granted his request for wisdom (1 Kings 3:4–15).
- The prophet Isaiah described a great feast that God will make for all people following his victory over death, the greatest of enemies, where death itself is an item to be consumed: "He will swallow up death forever" (Isa. 25:8). "On this mountain the LORD of hosts will make for all peoples a feast of rich food, a feast of well-aged wine, of rich food full of marrow, of aged wine well refined" (v. 6).
- Perhaps the most garish feast described in the Bible was the one hosted by Ahasuerus, king of the Medes and Persians, who threw a seven-day drinking party with his royal court in his opulent palace garden (Est. 1:1–10). During the feast, "the heart of the king was [a bit too] merry with wine" (v. 10)—and thereby unfolds the story of Esther.

Feasts Connected with Sacrifice

Sacrifices of animals, grain, or baked goods offered to God were also, quite naturally, occasions for feasting.[34] The Israelites made most of their sacrifices at local shrines, even during time periods when the temple stood in Jerusalem.[35] Before mentioning examples of sacrifices, we might first reflect a bit on the act of sacrifice itself.

Full of intention and awe, sacrifice is denying oneself in favor of the absolute weightiness of the Other.[36] This weightiness is felt most strongly when the sacrifice is a living being, an act that involves shedding blood—an animal alive, then dead, bringing life (Lev. 17:11, 14). Hostile and impure before the sacrifice, the offerer leaves the high place or altar purified and at peace. God accepted the sacrifices of the people of Israel under the framework of his covenant, whereby the sacrifice demonstrated the unbreakable link between God and his people; a community seared together; bound in obedience and will; manifest by righteousness, forgiveness, and grace.

The Israelites sacrificed animals, foods, and drinks common to feasts, with the best portions designated as the offering. This is most clearly seen in Leviticus, parts of which are a kind of priests' manual. With the exception of the burnt offering (*olah;* Lev. 1:1–17; 6:8–13; 7:8) and drink offering (*nesek;* Num. 15:7, 10; 28:7), the act of sacrifice included the act of either the priest or the offerer (or both) eating the largest portion of what was given. The priests were to eat their portions of meat and grain within the confines of the tabernacle or temple, a sacred duty that also met their daily practical needs.

Sacrifices on the altar at the dedication of the First Temple built by King Solomon. The Levitical priests are depicted in the foreground with musical instruments, as other priests line the ramp of the altar. (William Brassey Hole, 1846–1917)

Offering	Hebrew	Description	Biblical Reference
Grain offering	*minhah*	Grain, either raw, cooked, or baked into bread and sometimes spread or mixed with olive oil; a small portion was burned on the altar while the priests ate the rest.	Lev. 2:1–16; 6:14–23; 7:10
Sin offering	*hattat*	Bull, lamb, birds (turtledoves or pigeons), or fine flour; the fat portions and a small amount of the flour were burned on the altar while the priests ate the rest.	Lev. 4:1–5:13; 6:24–30
Peace offering	*shelamim*	Bull, lamb, or goat; the fat, kidneys, and liver were burned as a sacrifice to God while the meat was divided between the priests and the offerer. If the offering was given as a thanksgiving to God, it included unleavened bread or wafers and loaves of fine flour, all spread or mixed with oil; the largest portion of these was eaten by the priests.	Lev. 3:1–17; 7:11–34

The peace offering is particularly interesting. In this sacrifice, the offerer ate his meat portion of the offering as a feast, together with his family and anyone else in need of the sacrifice. For this reason, we can think of the peace offering as a fellowship or communion offering, signaling not only the well-being of God with his people but the communal well-being of the people themselves.[37] When a person offered multiple sacrifices, the peace offering came last to conclude with the wholeness represented by the shared feast. The sequence of offering sacrifices was to sacrifice first for atonement, then for holiness, and then for fellowship.[38]

We must note that though the sacrifices mentioned in the Bible were eaten with God in his divine presence, he was not consuming (or eating) the sacrifice as the offerers were. This is important to note because Israel's neighbors believed that their gods had to be fed in order to be content and in turn bless the one making the sacrifice. For them, the sacrifice was a meal eaten together with their gods.[39] Contrary to this popular belief, the Bible is clear that God neither needs nor consumes the sacrificial item (Ps. 50:12–13). He is, however, present with the offerer and pleased by the aroma when the food is burned, the smell being the tangible sign that the sacrifice was complete (Gen. 8:20–21; Lev. 1:9). It is significant that the very act of sacrificing to God—replete with menus and recipes describing how the food should be prepared (Lev. 3:9–17; 6:19–23; 7:12; Num. 15:1–10; 28:1–8)—strengthened the same values that accompanied feasting: reconciliation between two parties, forging a shared identity, building community, and establishing trust.

Thus far, this is a summary of the Torah instructions for sacrifice, as they relate to feasting. What might have actually happened throughout the time of the Old Testament, especially before the Jerusalem temple was built, is a different matter altogether—and we have little archaeological or textual evidence to see anything other than basic shapes. But the sweeping condemnations by the psalmists and prophets do clue

Remains of a small sanctuary dedicated to the Egyptian goddess Hathor, at Timna in southern Israel, enclose an offering bench and incense altars. During its latest architectural phase (the late twelfth century BC), this sanctuary was enclosed by a tent of heavy red and yellow cloth typical of Midianite shrines. (Photo by Paul H. Wright)

A horned altar for live animal sacrifice found at Beersheba, ancient Israel's southernmost city. The altar was in use during the early Judean monarchy in the tenth and ninth centuries BC. It is now in the Israel Museum, Jerusalem. (Photo by Paul H. Wright)

us in to the fact that all too often the sacrifices that Israelites made—and the accompanying meals eaten, whether by priests or people—were not offered with the convictions that either God or his spokespersons approved (Ps. 50:8–13; 51:16–17; Isa. 1:11; 43:23–24; Hos. 8:13; 9:4). The Bible includes specific examples: extorting the fatty cuts of meat for oneself (1 Sam. 2:12–17), burning incense to Baal (2 Kings 23:5), and making cakes for the queen of heaven (Jer. 7:18)!

Yet we also read of peace offerings and other, non-specific sacrifices that were not condemned by the biblical writers. Rather, these they recorded matter-of-factly at a variety of high places, shrines, or altars throughout the Land of Israel:

- Elkanah and Hannah in Shiloh (1 Sam. 1:1–3, 9)
- Samuel and Saul at the high place of an unnamed city, perhaps Ramah, where the future king, not the priest, received the best cuts of meat (1 Sam. 9:12–14, 19)
- Saul at Gilgal (1 Sam. 11:15)
- The clan of David in Bethlehem for their yearly sacrifice (1 Sam. 20:5–6)
- David and his men eating the "bread of the Presence" offered daily at the high place in Nob (1 Sam. 21:1–6)
- David at the threshing floor of Araunah the Jebusite, the place that later was designated the location of the Jerusalem temple (2 Sam. 24:18, 25)

It is likely (maybe certain) that these sacrifices included meals, all within the context of family and clan, which characterizes them as being of hearth and home. There is just enough evidence to indicate variety, especially in the early years of ancient Israel, and we must be content to be left to wonder about the actual nature of sacrifice and feasting on the ground in the time of the Old Testament.

SABBATH: THE WEEKLY FEAST

Another biblical feast of hearth and home is the Sabbath (Hebrew *Shabbat*) meal, eaten at home within a family context.[40] The Sabbath has become the most elevated day of Jewish activity, at times described as the "bride," the "queen," the "climax of living," and "spirit in the form of time."[41] Yet it was never something attached to the temple or requiring pilgrimage; in fact, exactly the opposite was (and is) expected. The word *Sabbath* comes from the verb *shabbat,* "cease," and one of the activities that ceased on that day was pilgrimage or long walks.

Although public participation in a synagogue service is the most permissible activity of the Sabbath today, it is the Sabbath meal that is most responsible for us including the Sabbath in the category of feasts of the Bible. Indeed, the most frequently observed feast in ancient Israel was this feast on the seventh day of the week.

Today, Jews typically enjoy three Sabbath meals. Eating them within the family community is one of the most definitive markers of what it means to keep the Sabbath and to be Jewish. The primary Sabbath meal is enjoyed on Friday evening while the Sabbath is ushered in at sunset; the second meal is midday on Saturday; and the third is late afternoon while the Sabbath closes with sunset.

Even though Sabbath meals are not specifically mentioned in the Old Testament, it's not a leap to assume that Israel's weekly Sabbath observance also included a time of feasting. One reason is that the Bible often associates the Sabbath with the term *mo'edim,* "appointed times," of which feasting was an important part. The book of Leviticus, for example, groups the Sabbath with Passover, Firstfruits, Weeks, Trumpets, the Day of Atonement (though not a day to eat), and Booths, calling all of them *mo'edim*—"appointed feasts" as it is sometimes translated (Lev. 23:1–44).[42] The books of Chronicles mention "Sabbaths, new moons and feast days [*mo'edim*]" (1 Chron. 23:31; 2 Chron. 2:4). A second reason to assume that feasting was part of the Sabbath comes from the sacrifices and offerings made on the Sabbath: two lambs, a grain offering, and a drink offering, at least some of which was eaten by the priests (Num. 28:9–10; 1 Chron. 23:31).

Challah, traditional bread baked for the Sabbath meal. (Photo by Paul H. Wright)

The specific ways ancient Israel observed the Sabbath, including its meals, developed over time. Like the sacrifices, we don't have enough detail to see a clear picture, but for sure, the Sabbath was observed in ways that did not always please God or his prophets:

> New moon and Sabbath and the calling of
> convocations—
>
> I cannot endure iniquity and solemn assembly.
>
> Your new moons and your appointed
> feasts [*mo'edim*]
>
> my soul hates.
> (Isa. 1:13–14; see also Isa. 56:1–8; 58:13–14)

Leaving aside Isaiah's larger point that Israel was observing their appointed feasts in ways that God hated (that is, in ways that denied sacrificial and covenant loyalty), we can easily see in the structure of these verses how the Sabbath is equated with the appointed feasts. The word *Sabbath* in the first line parallels *appointed feasts* in the third line, associating Sabbath activity with special meals.

In spite of how the Sabbath may or may not have been kept, the weekly Sabbath meal stood above and beyond ancient Israel's normal daily foods. The meal is especially significant when we notice the pattern and reason for its regularity. Observed every seven days, this is the only recurring communal feast that ancient Israel observed prior to the exile in the sixth century BC that, as we have seen, was not determined by the sun or moon or even seasons. In this, it stands alone, unique, unexplained in the Bible by anything other than the expressed command of God.[43] One day out of seven is infrequent enough to allow a normal, productive life (one's "job") to take place yet often enough to keep the beat of life going.

The Sabbath's defining feature is tied up in the root meaning of the word *Sabbath, shabbat,* "to cease, desist, or rest." It was a day on which no activity that was normal to the other days of the week was to be done (Ex. 16:23–26; 20:8–11; 23:12; 31:15; 35:2–3; Lev. 23:3; Jer. 17:19–27). There is a practical side too: a refreshing break from whatever presses on the body and soul the other six days (Isa. 58:13–14). But the Sabbath is also a holy convocation (*miqra qodesh*), a day separated from the others by its focus on eternity (Lev. 23:3; see also Neh. 9:14).[44] God, after all, "rested [*shabbat*-ed] from all his work that he had done in creation" (Gen. 2:3), providing both the example and the reason for people to do the same.

The Sabbath is a day set apart and different from the rest, but it would be a mistake to say that it is isolated from the week. Quite the opposite! By remembering (Ex. 20:8) and observing (Deut. 5:12) the Sabbath, Jews today look back at the week just completed and forward to the week ahead and rejoice in the ways that their lives are aligned with God. It is this fullness of life—past, present, and future—that the biblical prophets desired for ancient Israel as well.

But this is all a bit of a paradox: What does it mean to cease normal activity but also to eat? To be in the week yet above it? Nothing is more natural than eating a meal—or is it? Torah instruction called for the priests to place twelve fresh loaves of bread on the golden table in the sanctuary of the temple every Sabbath, where they would remain for the coming week (Lev. 24:5–9; 1 Chron. 9:31–32). Usually translated either as "bread of the Presence" or "showbread," the Hebrew word for this bread means, literally, "bread of the face" (*lechem panim;* Ex. 25:30), carrying every bit of intimacy that is typical of a shared meal. Next to the set table with the bread of the Presence was the lampstand (menorah) with its seven lights lit. In the house of the Lord, when the light is on and there is bread on the table, Someone is home. *Indeed!*

NEW MOON AND FULL MOON: THE MONTHLY FEASTS

There are ways to subdivide the month other than using a week of seven days, which, as we have seen, doesn't fit the lunar cycle of 29½ days. The ancient Egyptians divided the month into three weeks of ten days each, a closer mathematical fit. Workers there labored for eight or nine days, with the weekend a time to celebrate and feast.[45] The Egyptians also marked their months by a "New Crescent Day" (day 2) and a "Full Moon Day" (day 15), both of which were feast days.[46] We have, for instance, this incantation the Egyptians uttered to ensure provision for a dead pharaoh in the afterlife:

> Barley is threshed for you,
> Emmer is reaped for you,
> Your monthly feasts are made with it,
> Your half-month feasts are made with it,
> As ordered done for you by [the earth god]
> Geb, your father.[47]

Again, we must ask the question, what impact might these monthly divisions—ten days, new moon, and full moon—have had on the Israelites, given their lengthy stay in Egypt before the exodus? In answering, we must be careful to distinguish the *fact* that the same days of the month were significant for the Egyptians and for ancient Israel from how these special times *functioned* in their societies—what they *meant* to each people group.

A period of ten days is a unit of time in the Bible:

- "at least ten days" (Gen. 24:55)
- "on the tenth day" (Lev. 16:29; Josh. 4:19; 2 Kings 25:1)
- "about ten days" (1 Sam. 25:38)

Yet only once in the Old Testament did a "ten day" marker specifically involve feasting. While still in Egypt, Moses commanded every household to take a lamb *on the tenth day* of the month but wait until twilight on the fourteenth to kill and eat it; this was to be the first Passover (Ex. 12:1–6). In the process, we read that "this month shall be for you the beginning of months" (Ex. 12:2). Of course there is nothing in the book of Exodus about the tenth day also being the Egyptian weekend, nor does the Bible mention that the Feasts of Unleavened Bread and Booths, which begin on the full moon, also happened on Egyptian feast days.

What is clear is that Moses is setting a new calendar for Israel—a new start of the year and a new way of counting the weeks with seven, not ten, days—rather than conforming to the Egyptian calendar under which he and the Israelites had been living all those years. But more importantly, he is giving new meaning to specific days in the month on which the Egyptians were already feasting. By doing so, Moses publicly demonstrated that Israel's feasts were not going to have the same meaning (the same *essence*) as those of Egypt. In the process, Israel was not only being called out of Egypt physically but also called out to form a new identity.

Of these monthly markers, it is the new moon (*rosh hodesh*), signaling the beginning of each month, which appears most frequently in the Old Testament. Even though the Torah mentions the new moon festival only once, it does so in a way that assumes the day is already being celebrated, rather than explaining its origin or singling it out for detailed instruction as with the other feasts:

> On the day of your gladness also, and at your appointed feasts [*mo'edim*] and at the beginnings of your months [*hodeshim*], you shall blow the trumpets over your burnt offerings and over the sacrifices of your peace offerings. They shall be a reminder of you before your God: I am the LORD your God. (Num. 10:10)

The implication seems to be that the new moon festival was one of the oldest (if not the oldest) festival that Israel celebrated, something already well in place by the time that Moses gave instructions for the other appointed feasts. But Moses made sure to say that for Israel, the new moon was a visible and frequent reminder that "I [that is, God and not the Egyptian deities from which you came nor the ones in Canaan where you are going] am the LORD your God" (Num. 10:10). According to the prophets, the new moon was supposed to have been observed like the Sabbath: a day to sacrifice, eat a special meal, and avoid normal activities (Isa. 1:12–17; Hos. 2:11; Amos 8:4–6).

Full moon over the wall of the Old City of Jerusalem, marking the start of Passover. (Photo by Paul H. Wright)

The Israelites also celebrated the full moon (*kese*). It was observed in the same way as the new moon: by blowing the trumpets and feasting. The Old Testament mentions this only once, in a psalm, a celebratory context that suggests that it, too, was normal and expected:

> Blow the trumpet at the new moon, at the full moon, on our feast [*hag*] day. (Ps. 81:3)

Reading between the lines, we have every reason to think that sacrifices and feasts on the new moon and on the full moon were widely celebrated in ancient Israel by priests, royalty, and commoners alike, at home and at local shrines, all before and certainly also after the temple was built in Jerusalem. The story of King Saul, who apparently hosted new moon feasts on a regular basis, and David's expected attendance there, must have been typical rather than exceptional (1 Sam. 20:5–6, 18, 24; see also 2 Kings 4:23).

We also read that Israel tended to celebrate these festivals (and the Sabbath too) in ways that violated both the letter and the spirit of Torah, as if there were nothing distinctive about either the days, the participants, or even God himself:

> Hear this, you who trample on the needy
> and bring the poor of the land to an end,
> saying, "When will the new moon be over,
> that we may sell grain?
> And the Sabbath,
> that we may offer wheat for sale,
> that we may make the ephah small and
> the shekel great
> and deal deceitfully with false balances.
> that we may buy the poor for silver
> and the needy for a pair of sandals
> and sell the chaff of the wheat?"
> (Amos 8:4–6)

But Isaiah saw a better day:

> For as the new heavens and the new earth
> that I make
> shall remain before me, says the Lord,
> so shall your offspring and your name
> remain.
>
> From new moon to new moon,
> and from Sabbath to Sabbath,
> all flesh shall come to worship before me,
> declares the Lord.
> (Isa. 66:22–23)

After the Jews returned from Babylonian exile, the Sabbath, the new moon, and the three annual feast days (Passover with Unleavened Bread, Weeks, and Booths) were all celebrated in Jerusalem (Ezra 3:5; Neh. 10:33). But by the time of the New Testament, the new moon festival no longer remained on equal footing with the other major feasts, giving way to those that, as we will see, had specific connections to Israel's own historic story.

MINOR ANNUAL FEASTS

Many of ancient Israel's minor feasts, whether they were common banquets (*mishteh*) or involved pilgrimage (hence, a *hag*), were celebrated annually.

This Roman-era mosaic from Sepphoris, in Lower Galilee, depicts the fervent motion of grape treaders in a harvest dance with practical results. (Photo by Paul H. Wright)

Again, we see a mixture of occasions, people, and places, with most celebrations happening in the village, though some were celebrated at central regional locations. At least initially, nearly all these annual feasts were linked to the passage of time marked by the seasons. Examples in the Old Testament give us but glimpses of celebrations that were widespread in ancient Israel, the details of which are forever lost in the passage of time.

While farmers had annual harvest festivals, herders had sheep-shearing time.[48] This is best illustrated in the Old Testament story of Nabal, Abigail, and David (1 Sam. 25:2–42).

> [Nabal] was very rich; he had three thousand sheep and a thousand goats. He was shearing his sheep in Carmel.... David heard in the wilderness that Nabal was shearing his sheep. So David sent ten young men. And David said to the young men, "Go up to Carmel, and go to Nabal and greet him in my name. And thus you shall greet him: 'Peace be to you, and peace be to your house, and peace be to all that you have. I hear that you have shearers. Now your shepherds have been with us, and we did them no harm.... Therefore let my young men find favor in your eyes, for we come on a feast day.'" (vv. 2–8)

Sheep were sheared in the spring, with the particular days determined by the shepherd and local weather patterns rather than a fixed calendar. Wool was valuable in the ancient Near East, so this was a festive time—a *yom tov,* literally, a "good day" (v. 8). It was a time worthy of a feast (*mishteh*) that included meat and drink—often too much to drink (v. 36; see also 2 Sam. 13:28). The feast celebrated hard work done, security for the year to come, and a kind of comradery that cut across other bonds or obligations.

We read of a grape harvest festival celebrated by the men of Shechem who used the occasion to revile Abimelech, the odious son of Gideon who had made himself ruler of the city, in the house of their god (Judg. 9:26–27).

> And they went out into the field and gathered the grapes from their vineyards and trod them and held a festival; and they went into the house of their god and ate and drank and reviled Abimelech. (v. 27)

Here the word for festival is *hillul* (from *halal,* "to boast or praise") rather than *mishteh* or *hag. Hillul* implies the kind of drunken merriness that accompanied the uninhibited Bacchanalia festivals later known in the Greco-Roman world. There is nothing in this story to connect this celebration with Israel's annual fall Festival of Booths, but it does suggest that vintage festivals

were common among the towns and villages of ancient Israel, as they were across the ancient world. More appropriate was "the yearly feast [*hag*] of the Lord at Shiloh" (Judg. 21:19), apparently at the time of the grape harvest, which involved the "daughters of Shiloh" (v. 21) dancing in the vineyards. Commentators from the time of the New Testament until today assume that this was the Feast of Booths, but the author of the book of Judges doesn't specifically make that connection, again prompting us to wonder just how early and in what ways the ancient Israelites actually did celebrate the end of summer harvest.

We are left with the same question when we read about King Solomon's festival celebrated in Jerusalem "in the month Ethanim [Tishri], which is the seventh month" (1 Kings 8:2). All Israel was in attendance "from Lebo-hamath to the Brook of Egypt," the far northern and southern ends of Solomon's kingdom (v. 65). The feast lasted seven days, concluding on day eight with a solemn assembly (1 Kings 8:63–66; 2 Chron. 7:5–10). While this description evokes the pilgrimage festival of Booths, which, as we will see, would eventually center in Jerusalem after the return from exile, the reason for the Solomon's feast was quite different: to dedicate the newly built temple.

We are equally in the dark about the details of the annual feast instituted by Jeroboam, first king of the breakaway northern kingdom, who appointed his feast "on the fifteenth day of the eighth month *like* the feast [*hag*] that was in Judah" (1 Kings 12:32–33, emphasis added). What we would like to know is what the word *like* means. What was happening in Judah? How did Jeroboam's feast compare? That he tried to replicate—or surpass—the feast in Jerusalem is clear, though we will never know the specific details. So we turn our attention instead to the better-known great annual feasts of Israel.

PASSOVER, WEEKS, AND BOOTHS: THE GREAT FEASTS

The best-known biblical feasts are those that occur at regular intervals in the calendar. It is these which "run their round" (Isa. 29:1) that most forged Israel's identity. Recurring moments reinforce memory everywhere, but especially within a worldview that sees the passage of time as cyclical rather than linear and that embraces the journey rather than the end, like ancient Israel. A cyclical calendar is relational: memory touches event touches memory touches event, so for an Israelite these feasts were associative rather than singular in character. That is, they were not once-and-done holidays celebrated differently each year ("Let's do a destination Christmas this year, someplace where it's warm and different") but were intentionally repetitive so as to reinforce, year by year by year, Israel's connection to the ways that God had redeemed them in the past and would continue to do so in the future.

The feasts were also accessible to everyone. The act of any given Israelite celebrating the same thing at the same time every year, either with his or her hearth-and-home group or at an appointed pilgrimage site far from home—along with countless others whom he or she didn't know and would otherwise never get to know—is strong glue binding individuals into a community, and a community into a people. Together, such feasts professed what Israel's relationship to God was—or at least what it could be. We have already met some of the strongest of these recurring feasts: the weekly Sabbath and, to a lesser extent, the new moon. But here, we will look at the feasts that "run their round" and have become the most familiar Jewish biblical feasts today. These three annual feasts can be called the "great feasts:"

- Passover (Pesach) with Unleavened Bread
- Feast of Weeks (Shavuot)
- Feast of Booths (Sukkot)

From all the evidence we have, it is clear that these feasts coincided in the calendar with the natural agricultural harvest celebrations of hearth and home observed in the land of ancient Israel. How this agricultural backdrop merged with portions of Israel's great founding story (the exodus, revelation at Mount Sinai, and wilderness wanderings) was a long drawn-out process that had only partially developed by the close of the Old Testament.

The books of Exodus, Leviticus, Numbers, and Deuteronomy provide many details about how the feasts were supposed to have been celebrated. We have already seen that what Israel did and what the prophets said the people should have done are two different things. In addition, when we carefully read the accounts of the feasts in the Torah, one of the first things we notice is how the feasts are described differently in each passage. In fact, some of these differences seem to be rather significant. (See the following charts for a detailed comparison.)

As we read these passages, we need to keep in mind that in spite of the details provided, we just don't have a clear picture of how the festivals were celebrated in the time of the Old Testament. As a result, what we as readers tend to do is to assume that they were celebrated then essentially the same way that they were celebrated in the time of the New Testament, a period from which we have a clearer view. This is understandable but not necessarily accurate; and it prompts us to read carefully, form conclusions humbly, and sometimes allow ourselves to admit, "I just don't know." That being said, we can still make some helpful observations about Israel's three great pilgrimage feasts from the information that we do have.

1. Dealing with Differences

These three feasts are mentioned frequently in the Torah, in what we usually think of as the Bible's legal material (the word *Torah* actually means "instruction"). So it's not surprising that they became ancient Israel's most important annual feasts. But each time one of these feasts is mentioned in the Torah, the instructions about how to celebrate the feast are different. Bible scholars tend to take one of two approaches in dealing with these differences:

- One approach is to group all of the details into a single picture, producing a full or composite description of the ideal (or proper) way that Israel celebrated (or should have celebrated) each feast during the time of the Old Testament.[49]
- Another approach (and this is the majority view) is to assume that the differences indicate that the feasts developed slowly, over time, and among different sections of ancient Israel, coming to resemble the Jewish feasts that we know from the time of the New Testament only late in their history.[50]

We have already seen the gap between what Moses said *should* happen and what actually *did* happen in ancient Israel. Given the ethnic, cultural, and political diversity of the region in which Israel lived throughout the time of the Old Testament, we probably shouldn't expect the on-the-ground process by which these feasts became what we know them today to have been linear or even necessarily very intentional.

2. Grounded in Agriculture

A second observation is that each of these feasts coincides with a natural harvest season in the land of ancient Israel:

- Passover and Unleavened Bread at the beginning of the barley harvest (early spring)
- Feast of Weeks to mark the wheat harvest (late spring)
- Feast of Booths at the harvest of summer fruit (early autumn)

In their earliest mention in the Bible, Weeks was called the Feast of Harvest (Hag HaQatzir) and Booths, the Feast of Ingathering (Hag Ha'Asif; Ex. 23:16). We recall that *qatzir* and *asif* were the terms used in the Gezer calendar for the spring and autumn harvests, respectively. For this reason, some scholars have wondered if Passover and Unleavened Bread, two closely connected festivals, did not also have agricultural origins: Passover among shepherds (hence the emphasis on the lamb) and Unleavened Bread among farmers (emphasizing grain). Israel had deep roots in both livelihoods.[51] It is too much to say that Passover originated as an agricultural feast given the Bible's clear presentation of the Passover event in Egypt. At the same time, it is interesting that the first Passover took place at the same time as the beginning of the grain harvest in Israel. The exodus from Egypt and the start of the annual grain harvest season do have something in common: the start of a new, or renewed, life.

Shepherd tending her sheep in an olive grove between Jerusalem and Bethlehem. (Photo by Lindasj22/Shutterstock)

Passover and Unleavened Bread

	Biblical Reference	What Was the Feast Called?	Why Was the Feast Held?	When Was the Feast Held?
#1	Ex. 12:1–27	The Lord's Passover *Pesach l'Adonai* "a memorial day" *zikaron* Feast of Unleavened Bread *Hag HaMatzot* Days one and seven are a holy convocation (*miqra qodesh*).	To remember that the Lord "passed over" the houses of Israel when he caused the death of the first born in every house in Egypt, and to mark Israel's exodus from Egypt	In the first month ("this month shall be for you the beginning of months") Day 10: each family chose a lamb Day 14: the lamb was slaughtered at twilight Days 14–21: all Israel ate unleavened bread
#2	Ex. 23:14–17	Feast of Unleavened Bread *Hag HaMatzot*	To mark Israel's exodus from Egypt	"For seven days at the appointed time [*mo'ed*] in the month of Abib"
#3	Ex. 34:18, 22–23, 25	Feast of Passover *Hag HaPesach* Feast of Unleavened Bread *Hag HaMatzot*	To mark Israel's exodus from Egypt	For seven days "at the appointed time [*mo'ed*] in the month of Abib"
#4	Lev. 23:4–21; 33–44	The Lord's Passover *Pesach l'Adonai*	Not mentioned	"In the first month, of the fourteenth day of the month, at twilight"
		Feast of Unleavened Bread *Hag HaMatzot* All feasts in this passage are called appointed feasts of the Lord (*mo'ed Adonai*) and holy convocations (*miqra'e qodesh*).	"When you come into the land and reap its harvest"	"On the fifteenth day of the same month," and for seven days The first and last days are holy convocations.
#5	Num. 28:16–31; 29:12–38	The Lord's Passover *Pesach l'Adonai*	Not mentioned	"On the fourteenth day of the first month"
		A feast (*hag*) with days one and seven as a holy convocation (*miqra qodesh*)	Not mentioned	"On the fifteenth day of this month," for seven days
#6	Deut. 16:1–17	Passover to the Lord *Pesach l'Adonai* Feast of Unleavened Bread *Hag HaMatzot*	To mark Israel's exodus from Egypt To mark that "you came out of the land of Egypt in haste"	"In the month of Abib" For seven days The seventh day is a solemn assembly (*atzara*).

	Who Participated?	What Was Eaten or Included in the Feast?	What Was Sacrificed?	Where Was the Feast Held?
	"The whole assembly of the congregation of Israel"	Roasted lamb (sheep or goat) Unleavened bread Bitter herbs	Sacrifice of the Lord's Passover (*zevach Pesach l'Adonai*) at twilight of day fourteen	Within family groups in Egypt
	"All your males"	Unleavened bread	Not mentioned	"Before the LORD your God"
	"All your males"	Unleavened bread	Sacrifice of the Feast of Passover (*zevach Hag HaPesach*)	"Before the LORD your God"
	"The people of Israel"	Not mentioned	Food offering	"In all your dwelling places"
	"The people of Israel"	Unleavened bread	A sheaf (*omer*) of the firstfruits (*reishit*) of your harvest on the day after the Sabbath (Passover) Food offering Burnt offering Grain offering Drink offering	"In all your dwelling places"
	"The people of Israel"	Not mentioned	Food offering Burnt offering Grain offering Sin offering	Not mentioned
	"The people of Israel"	Unleavened bread	Food offering	Not mentioned
	"You"	The Passover lamb that was sacrificed, eaten for seven days	Passover sacrifice (*zevach Pesach*)	"Not within any of your towns ... but at the place that the LORD will choose, to make his name dwell there"
	"You"	Unleavened bread, eaten for seven days	Not mentioned	

Feast of Weeks

	Biblical Reference	What Was the Feast Called?	Why Was the Feast Was Held?	When Was the Feast Held?
#1	Ex. 12:1–27	The Feast of Weeks is not mentioned in this passage.		
#2	Ex. 23:14–17	Feast of Harvest *Hag HaQatzir*	To mark "the firstfruits [*bikkurim*] of your labor, of what you sow in the field"	Not mentioned
#3	Ex. 34:18, 22–23, 25	Feast of Weeks *Hag Shavuot*	To mark "the firstfruits [*bikkurim*] of the wheat harvest"	Not mentioned
#4	Lev. 23:4–21; 33–44	A specific name is not given, but all feasts in this passage are called appointed feasts of the Lord (*mo'ede Adonai*) and holy convocations (*miqra'e qodesh*).	To mark the wheat harvest, implied by "an offering of new grain"	"Seven full weeks from the day after the Sabbath" (that is, the day of Passover)
#5	Num. 28:16–31; 29:12–38	Feast of Weeks *Shavuot* A holy convocation *miqra qodesh*	To mark the wheat harvest, implied by "an offering of new grain"	"On the day of firstfruits" (*yom habikkurim*)
#6	Deut. 16:1–17	Feast of Weeks to the Lord *Hag Shavuot l'Adonai*	"Remember that you were a slave in Egypt"	"Seven weeks from the time the sickle is first put to the standing grain"

	Who Participated?	What Was Eaten or Included in the Feast?	What Was Sacrificed?	Where Was the Feast Held?
	"All your males"	Not mentioned	Not mentioned	"Before the LORD your God"
	"All your males"	Not mentioned	Not mentioned	"Before the LORD your God"
	"The people of Israel"	Not mentioned	Grain offering of loaves as firstfruits (*bikkurim*) Burnt offering Drink offering Peace offering	"In all your dwelling places"
	"The people of Israel"	Not mentioned	Grain offering Burnt offering Sin offering	Not mentioned
	"You, your son and your daughter, your male servant and your female servant, the Levite who is within your towns, the sojourner, the fatherless, and the widow who are among you"	Not mentioned, but told to rejoice	"The tribute of a freewill offering from your hand"	"At the place that the LORD your God will choose, to make his name dwell there"

Feast of Booths

	Biblical Reference	What Was the Feast Called?	Why Was the Feast Held?	When Was the Feast Held?
#1	Ex. 12:1–27	The Feast of Booths is not mentioned in this passage.		
#2	Ex. 23:14–17	Feast of Ingathering *Hag Ha'Asif*	To mark "when you gather in from your field the fruit of your labor"	"At the end of the year"
#3	Ex. 34:18, 22–23, 25	Feast of Ingathering *Hag Ha'Asif*	Not mentioned	"At the year's end"
#4	Lev. 23:4–21; 33–44	Feast of Booths to the Lord *Hag HaSukkot l'Adonai* Feast to the Lord *Hag l'Adonai* All feasts in this passage are called appointed feasts of the Lord (*mo'ede Adonai*) and holy convocations (*miqra'e qodesh*).	"...that your generations may know that I made the people of Israel dwell in booths [*sukkot*] when I brought them out of the land of Egypt"	"On the fifteenth day of the seventh month and for seven days" The first day is a holy convocation (*miqra qodesh*) and a day of solemn rest (*shabbaton*). The eighth day is a holy convocation (*miqra qodesh*), a solemn assembly (*atzara*), and a day of solemn rest (*shabbaton*).
#5	Num. 28:16–31; 29:12–38	A feast to the Lord *Hag Adonai*	Not mentioned	"On the fifteenth day of the seventh month," for seven days The first day is a holy convocation (*miqra qodesh*). The last day is a solemn assembly (*atzara*).
#6	Deut. 16:1–17	Feast of Booths *Hag HaSukkot*	To mark the harvest "when you have gathered in the produce from your threshing floor and your winepress"	For seven days

	Who Participated?	What Was Eaten or Included in the Feast?	What Was Sacrificed?	Where Was the Feast Held?
	"All your males"	Not mentioned	Not mentioned	"Before the LORD your God"
	"All your males"	Not mentioned	Not mentioned	"Before the LORD your God"
	"All native Israelites"	Rejoice with "the fruit of splendid trees, branches of palm trees and boughs of leafy trees and willows of the brook"	Food offering each day for seven days	"You shall dwell in booths for seven days"
	"The people of Israel"	Not mentioned	Food offering Burnt offering Grain offering Sin offering	Not mentioned
	"You, your son and your daughter, your male servant and your female servant, the Levite, the sojourner, the fatherless, and the widow who are within your towns"	Not mentioned, but told to rejoice	Not mentioned	"At the place that the LORD your God will choose, to make his name dwell there"

Both Passover with Unleavened Bread and the Feast of Booths began on a full moon and lasted seven days. (Weeks was a single day just before the first quarter moon.) This was a significant time in the month for agricultural calendars generally, and it was also the length of time appropriate in many cultures for harvest and other life passage celebrations. Given the tendency of people to mark the normal cycles of life and Israel's ancient connection with their land, it is only natural to suppose that Israel would have celebrated these harvests from earliest times, whether they were instructed to do so by the Torah or not.

Since Israel harvested the land, of course that means they also planted and tended it. In the mindset of the ancient Near East (prior to or in the absence of formal title deeds), the practical aspects of land ownership were determined by who actually used it or brought it to life. Because the three great festivals are fixed to the harvest seasons of the land of ancient Israel rather than to those of Mesopotamia or Egypt (out of which Abraham and then Moses came) or even to other parts of the world for that matter, they forged a God + Israel + land bond that rooted Israel *there*. This reality has persisted to link Jews to their ancestral homeland for thousands of years, even when living in parts of the world where harvest periods are at opposite times of the year. The instructions in the Torah, then, are intended to teach Israel *how* to celebrate their harvest festivals, now that they had entered into a special covenant relationship with God.

3. Connected to Our Story

A third observation is that of the three great feasts, it is only for Passover and its seven-day feast called Unleavened Bread that the Bible gives us an actual detailed story specifically connecting it to an event in the history of Israel. Passover is rooted in the exodus story about how God passed over the houses of the Israelites when he caused the death of the firstborn in every house in Egypt; this in turn prompted Pharaoh to relinquish his control over Israel and allow them to leave his land (Ex. 12:1–32). That account includes the line, "This day shall be for you a memorial day [*zikaron*]" (Ex. 12:14). This links the festival to a specific redemptive act in history. This became the founding event in Israel's national epic, and Passover with Unleavened Bread, the most significant of their three annual feasts.

By contrast, the reasons given in the Torah to celebrate Weeks and Booths are primarily agricultural, with but a single short note otherwise in Deuteronomy. According to Deuteronomy 16:12, Weeks was celebrated to "remember that you were a slave in Egypt" (the same reason given by Deuteronomy 5:15 to keep the Sabbath). The connection between slavery and the Feast of Weeks is unclear, and by the time of the New Testament, the Feast of Weeks (called Shavuot or Pentecost) was associated instead with the giving of Torah on Mount Sinai, God's gracious provision of instruction to enable his people to know how to live.

The non-agricultural association of the Feast of Booths is implied by its name: that Israel lived in booths (*sukkot*) during their years of wilderness wandering. This is mentioned nowhere in the Torah's lengthy wilderness wanderings narratives (except only by association in Leviticus 23:42–43). Numbers 10:10 hints at the transition in Israel's thought from focusing on agriculture to focusing on the character of God, who graciously provided daily food and redemption:

> Your appointed feasts [*mo'edim*] and … the beginnings of your months [the new moon] … shall be a reminder [*zikaron*] of you before your God: I am the Lord your God.

These three festivals came to mark three events in Israel's founding history, celebrated each year in sequence, in a way that made them unique to Israel.

We can hear God saying: *You are my people; I am your God. We have a collective identity. So when you celebrate your harvest festivals, make sure you tell our story.*

4. Eventually in Jerusalem

Throughout the Torah instructions (with the exception of Deuteronomy 16:5, 11, 15) the great feasts could be held anywhere: locally, in family or village groupings, and certainly "before the LORD your God" (Ex. 34:24).

Though this hut serves the field needs of an Egyptian village farmer, it calls to mind the booths (sukkot) the Israelites constructed from branches and reeds on their journey through the Sinai. (Photo by Paul H. Wright)

According to Deuteronomy, the feasts were to be held only "at the place that the LORD your God will choose, to make his name dwell in it" (Deut. 16:6) with the added caveat for Passover that "the place" is a single location, "not … within any of your towns" (v. 5). Eventually for the Jews this place became Jerusalem,[52] though Jerusalem by name is mentioned nowhere in the Torah.[53] Solomon, Hezekiah, and Josiah celebrated the Passover in Jerusalem, as did Ezra and Nehemiah the Feast of Booths. As noted at the beginning of this chapter, we have no way of knowing how typical these Jerusalem-oriented feasts actually were in Old Testament times, but all available evidence suggest that they were the exception.

5. Leaving Room for Innovation

Even though the Torah gives many details about these feasts, we are struck by how much is not said (note all of the "not mentioneds" in the great feasts comparison charts in this chapter). Twice in the Torah, the autumn festival is called simply a feast (*hag*), without the formal name "Booths" (Lev. 23:39; Num. 29:12). Similarly, the Feast of Unleavened Bread is identified only as a *hag*, otherwise unnamed, in Numbers 28:17. What must be the Feast of Weeks is described but called by no name, neither Weeks nor even *hag*, in Leviticus 23:15–23. Equally curious is that Passover, the only one of these feasts that is clearly described as a meal (Ex. 12:1–27), is actually called a feast (*hag*) only once in the Torah (Ex. 34:25).

These gaps in what seems to be key information support the idea that the ways that these feasts were celebrated in the time of the Old Testament varied. While we shouldn't assume our modern expectations of consistency to apply to the ways that the Torah instructions are laid out, it does seem that the full nature of each of the feasts was not yet set when the words of the Torah were written down. An important consequence is that this seems to have opened the door for local creativity and innovation, which was necessary to make sure that the feasts would continue to meet the needs of the people from generation to generation (as it still does). It also provides at least some explanation (or even justification) for why the priests of King Hezekiah's day weren't familiar with a single proper way to celebrate the Passover (2 Chron. 30:2–3, 18–19). In fact, it took a royal decree from Hezekiah, sent out by couriers, to tell everyone when and where to celebrate (vv. 1, 5–6, 10); and note that Hezekiah was the king, not a priest or member of the temple leadership.

6. The Time for Firstfruits

Our final observation is that Leviticus and Numbers in particular link these great feasts with formal offerings and sacrifices. Every Israelite who engaged in agriculture (and this was the majority) was instructed to bring their first ripened produce, "firstfruits" (*bikkurim*), as an offering to God (Ex. 23:19; 34:26; Num. 18:13; Deut. 26:1–11). The Feast of Unleavened Bread also included a firstfruits offering, though it was called *reishit,* "first," rather than *bikkurim* (Lev. 23:10). These were acts of thanksgiving—part obligatory, part spontaneous—signaling the farmer's recognition that both land and people belonged to God.[54] It was a family obligation—certainly widespread, ancient, and expected. We can assume that on the village level and from earliest times, such harvest-time offerings were also natural times to have a feast. The most formal firstfruits offering became connected to the Feast of Harvest/Weeks (Shavuot), which marked the all-important wheat harvest.[55] For this reason, Weeks, which was celebrated for only one day, became known also as "the day of firstfruits" (*yom habikkurim*).

Other Descriptions of the Feasts

So we see that the great pilgrimage feasts are described in the Torah in a variety of ways. This shouldn't surprise us, given how they appear in the rest of the Old Testament. This is apparent when we look at the books of the Bible that were written *prior* to Israel's return from Babylonian exile. These are the books of Joshua through 2 Kings and they reflect the priorities of life on the ground during the time of the judges and the monarchy, as Israel struggled to establish a national identity in the midst of a persistent and seductive Canaanite presence.

We have already seen that harvest festivals must have been common at this time, but now we notice how uncommon the three great pilgrimage festivals are in this part of the Bible. They are hardly mentioned by name or otherwise. The only references in the books of Joshua through 2 Kings to any of these feasts *by name* are a brief note that Joshua held a Passover on the western bank of the Jordan River after crossing into Canaan (Josh. 5:10–11) and an equally brief note that King Josiah celebrated Passover as part of his national and religious revival in Jerusalem in the waning days of the kingdom of Judah (2 Kings 23:21–23). These two Passovers appear as bookends in the Joshua-through-Kings narrative, encompassing (but not necessarily describing) Israel's life in Canaan before the exile. In neither instance are any details given about how Passover was actually celebrated. The feasts of Weeks and Booths are not mentioned *by name* in Joshua through 2 Kings, books written prior to the return from exile.[56]

What are mentioned in these books are various feasts that were similar to, but not exactly the same as, the three great festivals:

- The feast at the city of Shiloh at which the young women danced in the vineyards perhaps was an early variation of Feast of Booths, given legitimacy by the presence of the tabernacle in the city (Judg. 21:19–21).
- Solomon celebrated an eight-day autumn feast when the ark of the covenant was brought into the Holy of Holies of the newly constructed Jerusalem temple (1 Kings 8:1–66). The occasion had nothing to do with Israel's dwelling in booths during the years of

wilderness wanderings, but it is reminiscent of the story of Moses receiving Torah from God on Mount Sinai, the portion of Israel's founding epic that became associated with the late spring Feast of Weeks by the time of the New Testament.

- A few years after Solomon, the breakaway king Jeroboam celebrated a "feast [*ḥag*] on the fifteenth day of the eighth month like the feast that was in Judah" (1 Kings 12:32), again, unspecified.

The prophets Amos and Hosea criticized the ways that Israel was keeping their feasts—though again, not mentioning them specifically *by name.* Both lived in the mid-eighth century BC, a couple of generations before King Hezekiah sent word that the Passover properly be kept in Jerusalem (although this was recorded in the Bible only centuries later, in the books of Chronicles, not Kings).

> I hate, I despise your feasts,
> and I take no delight in your solemn assemblies.
>
> Even though you offer me your burnt offerings
> and grain offerings,
> I will not accept them;
> and the peace offerings of your fattened animals,
> I will not look upon them.
>
> Take away from me the noise of your songs;
> to the melody of your harps I will not listen.
> (Amos 5:21–23)
>
> I will put an end to all her mirth,
> her feasts, her new moons, her Sabbaths, and all her appointed feasts.
> (Hos. 2:11 [Hebrew v. 13])

In describing Israel's attitude toward the feasts, Hosea emphasized their agricultural, rather than historical, heritage:

> Threshing floor and wine vat shall not feed them,
> and the new wine shall fail them.
>
> They shall not pour drink offerings of wine
> to the LORD,
> and their sacrifices shall not please him.
>
> It shall be like mourners' bread to them;
> all who eat it shall be defiled;
> for their bread shall be for their hunger only;
> it shall not come to the house of the LORD.
>
> What will you do on the day of the
> appointed festival
> and on the day of the feast of the LORD?
> (Hos. 9:2, 4–5)

In addition to harvest time, Amos and Hosea mention various sacrificial offerings made to the Lord, like the ones described in Leviticus and Numbers. We also see that each celebration included a "solemn assembly," a key component of Passover and Booths in Leviticus 23:36, Numbers 29:35, and Deuteronomy 16:8. To our delight, Amos adds a musical note, "the noise of your songs ... [and] the melody of your harps" (Amos 5:23), providing audio for the command of Deuteronomy 16:14 to "rejoice in your feast."

This festive stand from Ashdod is the only known object from the region of ancient Israel dating to the time of David and Solomon that depicts a musical ensemble. At each window, a player stands with a different instrument: cymbals (profile, right), a lyre (center), a double-pipe (left), a frame drum (around the curve far left), and another double-pipe (behind). The only thing missing is the sound! This musical stand is on display in the Israel Museum, Jerusalem. (Photo by Paul H. Wright)

Because the great feasts were linked to offering and sacrifice, they bound the festivity of celebration and the joys of song and food to the weightiness of covenant, unworthiness, and sin. Hosea and Amos give us just enough information to see that certain feasts were being kept during the time of the monarchy; whether they were intended to be the Passover, Weeks, and Booths of the Torah remains a matter of debate. But in any case, when it came down to it, the "weightier matters of the law" were too often glossed over in favor of the celebratory pleasures of the moment.

When we look at the books of the Old Testament written *after* Israel's return from exile—like Chronicles, Ezra, and Nehemiah—we notice a shift in how the feasts are portrayed. In these books, there is a clear tendency to focus on keeping Torah instruction and calling the feasts by name, that is, Passover, Weeks, and Booths. This was the period when the people of Israel started to be called Jews, and these biblical books were written with the priorities the Jews had in mind as they sought to reestablish their presence in Jerusalem. Gone was the kingdom and the nation. Gone, too, at least for the most part, was the seductive edge of Canaanite culture. What was left were the people, the temple (soon to be rebuilt), Jerusalem, and the land of Judea. It was these great feasts, the *haggim*, that provided the adhesive to bind together God, people, and land in personal, communal, and recurring ways. Israel's agricultural base survived the exile, re-rooting the Jews into their homeland soil, while their grand national epic provided confidence that God again would redeem and bless his people.

- So it is in 2 Chronicles 8:12–13, written after the Jews had returned to Jerusalem from exile, that we read about how King Solomon had offered up sacrifices for Passover, Weeks, and Booths, although the note is brief and lacking any detail.
- It is in 2 Chronicles 30 and 35, not in the books of Kings, that we read of the Passovers of Hezekiah and Josiah, this time in great detail and as a public catalyst to energize their great reforms. Like the first Passover, these were celebrations of redemption on a national level, giving the Jews hope that if Israel *had* continued to keep the great feasts according to the Torah, the exile might not have had to happen.
- For the first time since Deuteronomy, we find the name "Feast of Booths" when this great feast was celebrated by the priest Ezra "as it is written ... according to the rule" (Ezra 3:4). But this is only after the return from exile, when the newly rebuilt temple was dedicated in Jerusalem (recall Solomon's celebration of the unnamed autumn festival as he dedicated the First Temple).
- And with Nehemiah, a bit later (mid-fifth century BC), we have the first detailed description of the Feast of Booths actually being kept as instructed in Deuteronomy

> (Neh. 8:14–18). Yet Nehemiah didn't use the name Booths and simply called the festival "the feast [*hag*] of the seventh month" (v. 14).

But by this point in the biblical record, it is clear that the shift toward some sense of official agreement about the great feasts had begun, so much so that the prophet Zechariah saw a day coming when "everyone who survives of all the nations that have come against Jerusalem shall go up year after year to worship the King, the LORD of hosts, and to keep the Feast of Booths" (Zech. 14:16).

ROSH HASHANAH (NEW YEAR'S DAY)

One holiday missing from the Old Testament calendar is New Year's Day. On the surface, this is surprising, given that New Year's Day celebrations were common among people of the ancient Near East. The phrase *rosh hashanah* means literally "the head of the year," and the festival occurs only in Ezekiel, a book written after the exile, as the opening line of Ezekiel's vision of a rebuilt Jerusalem temple:

> In the twenty-fifth year of our exile, at the beginning of the year [*rosh hashanah*], on the tenth day of the month ... the hand of the LORD was upon me, and he brought me to the city. (Ezek. 40:1)

Ezekiel, a priest, doesn't name the month which begins the year, but it certainly must have been Nisan, the newly adopted name for the month of Abib, the month which Moses declared "shall be for you the beginning of months" (Ex. 12:2). It was on the tenth day of this month that lambs were chosen for Passover sacrifice, making it a most appropriate time for a vision of the new temple to take place.

Today, the new year's celebration of Rosh HaShanah is observed on the first day of Tishri (biblical Ethanim; 1 Kings 8:2), which falls six months after the Old Testament's month of Abib (Nisan). Moses designated the month of Abib, which marks the beginning of the barley harvest, as the first of the year "for you." This implies that Abib was neither the natural or obvious choice, nor the time that Israel (and its neighbors) had already recognized as the beginning of their year. The Egyptian calendar, which Moses would have been living under at the time of the first Passover, began on July 19 or 20 (according to our calendar today) with the rising of Sirius, the Dog Star, at the beginning of the season of the Nile flood.[57]

Meanwhile, Babylon went back and forth between recognizing a new year starting in the autumn and one in the spring. Their New Year's festival (*akitu*) was originally celebrated twice a year: first with the sowing of barley in the autumn and then again with the harvesting of barley in the spring.[58]

From the Gezer calendar, we can assume that the Canaanites celebrated the beginning of their year in the autumn to coincide with the time that the early rains broke the long summer drought and the harvest of the last of the summer fruit gave way to the plow.[59]

Once in Canaan, Israel lived in this natural environment, and were it not for Moses's distinctive instruction "for *you,* this [the spring month of Passover, Abib/Nisan] shall be the beginning of months," Israel's New Year's Day during the time of the Old Testament would have most likely been in the autumn as well.

What is ironic is that even though Israel certainly counted the passage of years, a day specifically labeled New Year's Day is not mentioned in the Old Testament. There must have been one, not only to mark the beginning of the religious calendar with its feasts, but also to regulate civil functions such as determining the time limit of debts, collecting taxes, or marking the length of the reigns of kings. Here we are largely in the dark, although there is evidence—gained by counting and comparing the length of the years in the kings' reigns in Israel and Judah—that there were in fact two beginnings of the year, one to mark the start of the religious calendar and another to start the civil calendar. And to make an already confusing situation even more so, the Southern Kingdom of Judah started their civil year in the autumn while the civil year for the Northern Kingdom of Israel began in the spring, at least during the early decades of the monarchy.[60]

Yet Moses was not as concerned about such civil functions as he was in recognizing Israel's covenantal distinctive: with their exodus from

The high priest carried incense and blood into the Holy of Holies (the Most Holy Place) of the tabernacle behind the curtain on the Day of Atonement. (Art by Balage Balogh)

Egypt, Israel was to be a people set apart, under a set of instructions (Torah) given by the Lord God. All aspects of life (including civil ones) fell under a set of celebrations that marked not only harvest times (everyone has *those*) but also the foundational events of Israel's birth into peoplehood. For this, Passover itself, at the full moon of the first month, was enough to mark the new year. It was an issue of *identity:* who *we* are going to be.

But what about Rosh HaShanah, the New Year's Day of the Jewish calendar today? Leviticus 23:23–25 and Numbers 29:1–6 mention "a day of solemn rest [*shabbaton*], a memorial proclaimed with blast of trumpets, a holy convocation [*miqra qodesh*]" on the first day of the seventh month (Ethanim/Tishri), what we call the beginning of autumn. Nowhere in the Old Testament is a reason for this day given other than to have a holy convocation. This silence made it convenient—sometime after the Babylonian exile and for reasons about which we can only speculate—for the Jews to designate this first day of Tishri, rather than the first day of Nisan, as New Year's Day.

DAY OF ATONEMENT (YOM KIPPUR)

The celebrations of the great feasts and those of the Sabbath—indeed, all of ancient Israel's festivals that include a meal—stand in contrast to an annual day in the calendar that is neither a celebration nor a feast: the Day of Atonement, or Yom Kippur. Marked on the tenth day of the seventh month (Tishri), Yom Kippur has become the most solemn day in the Jewish calendar. It is a day of individual and corporate reflection and penitence before the Lord God, asking that he forgive the sins of the past year and restore his people—individually and collectively—to their covenantal relationship with him, reversing "the world's slow stain" and together restoring it to wholeness.[61]

In the instructions of Leviticus, the high priest made atonement on Yom Kippur by offering sacrifices for his own sin (a bull) and the sin of the people (a goat), sprinkling some of the animals' blood on the mercy seat, the upper surface of the ark of the covenant, behind the curtain that enclosed the Holy of Holies in the tabernacle or temple (Lev. 16:1–19). (In Scripture, the proper Hebrew term for this day is *yom hakippurim,* "day of atonements," plural.) The high priest also confessed the sins of the people while laying his hands on the head of a goat, the "scapegoat," transferring the sins to the animal before it was led away to wander in the wilderness alone. This goat was designated for or to *Azazel,* a word difficult to translate but evoking images and sounds of the howling wasteland, the haunting desert, of life absolutely alone (Lev. 16:8, 10, 26). The contrast with the exuberant sound of the biblical feasts celebrated in community could not be more striking.

Like the three great feasts, the Day of Atonement is a holy convocation (*miqra qodesh*) and a Sabbath of solemn rest (*shabbaton*), with no ordinary work done (Lev. 23:26–32; Num. 29:7–11). But unlike the other celebrations of ancient Israel, it is a day of fasting, not feasting—and even this is not putting it strongly enough. The Torah's repeated command for the Day of Atonement is not "don't eat" but rather "afflict yourselves" (Lev. 16:29, 31; 23:27, 32; Num. 29:7; see also Lev. 23:29). This implies becoming humbled, weak, and lowly, and an absolute denial of physical comfort—the kinds of things that demonstrate genuine sorrow for sin. There were all sorts of conditions in life that afflicted ancient Israel that were not due to individual sin: poor harvests, national calamity, loss of freedom, bodies worn out by hard work, spirits crushed, chance accidents, and illness. These were overcome, at least temporarily, by celebrating its feasts and festivals, regular reminders that in spite of too many of the nasty, brutish, and short realities of life (to borrow a phrase from Hobbes), the equation of the Lord God + people + land was security enough. But the Day of Atonement took matters right to the heart, recognizing that the most significant barrier to life lived the way that God intended it to be was not misfortune but sin.

As important as the Day of Atonement was, there is no mention of it in the Old Testament outside of the detailed instructions in Leviticus and Numbers. Certainly there was a recognition of sin and its consequences, there were calls for national repentance and revival, and there was an awareness that sacrifices without a clean heart were not only worthless but also profane (2 Chron. 7:14; 29:6–11; 34:22–33; Neh. 9:1–2; Ps. 51:1–19; Isa. 1:10–20, Jer. 4:14). But a specific Day of Atonement, let alone one fixed to the calendar, is not mentioned anywhere in the Old Testament outside of the Torah, leaving us in the dark about its development and practice during the time of Israel's settlement and the period of the judges, the monarchy, or the return from exile.

PURIM

Only twice does the Bible include a narrative that explains the historical origins of a feast. One, as we have mentioned, is Passover that is founded in the redemptive events leading up to Israel's exodus from Egypt. The other is the Feast of Purim, which celebrates God's deliverance of the Jews from the edict of Ahasuerus, king of Media and Persia, and his coldly calculating vizier Haman, who together conspired to condemn to death all of the Jews

Esther Denouncing Haman to King Ahasuerus (Ernest Normand, 1888)

in the empire (Est. 9:20–32). Both Passover and Purim commemorate acts of deliverance from an enemy in a foreign land. Even though they were celebrated locally (for Purim, this was in each of the towns across the 127 provinces of Ahasuerus's empire; Est. 9:19, 30), both were done with the full peoplehood, or nation, of Israel in mind.

The event of Purim happened very late in ancient Israel's history, after the exile, so it is natural that the Old Testament does not contain any further comments about how the feast was actually celebrated after the time of Esther. In this sense, Purim belongs more properly to the period between and after the Old and New Testaments, when the Jews lived under foreign domination, even in their homeland—except for the brief period of the Hasmonean dynasty in the second to first centuries BC.

By all accounts, Purim was not one of the great religious festivals of ancient Israel: the name of God is absent from the book of Esther; the storyline, though redemptive, is wrapped around royal court politics; the feast is a *mishteh* (Est. 9:18, 22) rather than a *hag* (Ahasuerus's decadent feast opening the book was also a *mishteh*; Est. 1:3); the word used to designate the appointed time to celebrate the feast was *zaman* (Est. 9:27, 31), a generic term for "arrangement of time" taken from Aramaic, rather than *mo'ed*, which as we have seen is the standard Hebrew term for a feast that Israel held "before the LORD."

We note as well that Purim was celebrated on the fourteenth day of Adar (Est. 9:19), one full moon prior to the full moon of Passover, making these two redemptive feasts bookends to the year.[62] Passover, which began the ancient Israelite year with the memory of redemption, is framed by holy assemblies on days one and seven. Purim, a late addition to the calendar, ended the year with delightful and earthy expressions of relief felt when the clouds of evil had passed. But because ancient Israel thought of time as cyclical rather than linear, Purim and Passover weren't so much a conclusion and a beginning as much as they were points of time in which the grace of God redeeming people from all sources of evil was evident year-round.

CONCLUDING THOUGHTS

These are the feasts of ancient Israel as described in the Old Testament. They are many and varied, earthy and divine, and rather elusive when we compare them to the ways that Jewish festivals are celebrated today. Some mirrored the festivals of Israel's neighbors (often, like the marzeah, a bit too much). This was to be expected, given the tight living spaces in the region where the Israelites lived. We know just enough about ancient Israel to see that their celebratory life was full but not enough to take a detailed photograph. Rather, as we look through a glass darkly, we can just make out image and outline; sometimes it is sharp, but too often it is blurry.

Comparing the feasts can help us see what Israel's observances had in common with each other. We see the value of eating together, of hospitality that extends beyond the family, of taking time to celebrate and remember, to recognize the reality of God's control over our natural environment, and to honor our mutual responsibilities to our world and to God. We can recognize similarities between Israel's feasts and the feasts of their neighbors. These similarities are interesting and to be expected, but they shouldn't be threatening when we remember their different motives and beliefs.

Throughout the time of the Old Testament, a period of more than a millennium, the feasts of ancient Israel were enriched by many traditions. Some of these filled out the instructions of Moses while others were in spite of them. This process gained steam in the centuries leading up to the time of the New Testament and in early Judaism, and it is to that which we now turn.

Notes for Chapter 1

1 There remains some debate as to the exact chronology of the reign of Hezekiah. We are following Edwin R. Thiele, *The Mysterious Numbers of the Hebrew Kings*, rev. ed. (Grand Rapids, Mich.: Academie Books, Zondervan, 1983), 174–176.

2 Although the Northern Kingdom of Israel had fallen to Assyria in 722 BC, a significant remnant of Israelites remained in the land.

3 The Hebrew word *Torah,* usually translated "Law," more properly means "direction" or "instruction."

4 Carl Ortwin Sauer, "Forward to Historical Geography," in *Land and Life: A Selection from the Writings of Carl Ortwin Sauer*, ed. John Leighly (Berkeley: University of California Press, 1963), 362.

5 This term was first used in C. S. Lewis, *Surprised by Joy: The Shape of My Early Life* (New York: Harcourt, Brace and Co., 1955), 206.

6 This list of the ancient biblical world and modern Western world is adapted from Victor H. Matthews and Don C. Benjamin, *Social World of Ancient Israel 1250–587 BCE* (Peabody, Mass.: Hendrickson, 1993), xiv–xx.

7 Paul H. Wright, *Holman Illustrated Guide to Biblical Geography: Reading the Land* (Nashville, Tenn.: B&H, 2020), 32–41.

8 Paul H. Wright, *Heart of the Holy Land: 40 Reflections on Scripture and Place* (Peabody, Mass.: Rose Publishing, 2020), 20–26.

9 Paul H. Wright, "Famines in the Land," in *Lexham Geographic Commentary on Acts through Revelation,* ed. Barry J. Beitzel (Bellingham, Wash.: Lexham, 2019), 279–289.

10 The wonderfully descriptive phrase identifying the land of ancient Israel as a "land between" is that of James M. Monson with Steven P. Lancaster, *Regions on the Run: Introductory Map Studies in the Land of the Bible* (Rockford, Ill.: Biblical Backgrounds, 2019), 6.

11 I am borrowing the term *hungry gap,* which was used for the same phenomenon that occurred during July in Medieval England, from Robert Lacey and Danny Danziger, *The Year 1000: What Life Was Like at the Turn of the First Millennium* (London: Little, Brown and Co., 1999), 101.

12 John N. Oswalt, *The Bible among the Myths* (Grand Rapids, Mich.: Zondervan, 2009), 57–62.

13 Cynthia Shafer-Elliott, "Food Preparation in Iron Age Israel," in *Behind the Scenes of the Old Testament: Cultural, Social, and Historical Contexts,* eds. Jonathan S. Greer, John W. Hilber, and John H. Walton (Grand Rapids, Mich.: Baker Academic, 2018), 456–463; Oded Borowski, *Daily Life in Biblical Times* (Leiden: Brill, 2003), 63–74; and Philip J. King and Lawrence E. Stager, *Life in Biblical Israel* (Louisville, Ky.: Westminster John Knox, 2001), 64–68. Note as well *Table 1: Environmental Zones of the North-Central Highlands* which lists foodstuffs most suitably grown in individual micro-environments of Israel during the days of the Judges, in Robert D. Miller II, "Modeling the Farm Community in Iron I Israel," in *Life and Culture in the Ancient Near East,* eds. Richard E. Averbeck, Mark W. Chavalas, and David B. Weisberg (Bethesda, Md.: CDL, 2003), 301–306.

14 Margaret Visser, *The Rituals of Dinner* (New York: Penguin, 1991), 79–136.

15 Kraters were common at the time of the Israelite monarchy.

16 Christine D. Pohl, *Making Room: Recovering Hospitality as a Christian Tradition* (Grand Rapids, Mich,: Eerdmans, 1999), 73–75.

17 Matthews and Benjamin, *Social World of Ancient Israel,* 82–95.

18 Janling Fu, "Feasting in the Biblical World," in *Behind the Scenes of the Old Testament: Cultural, Social, and Historical Contexts,* eds. Jonathan S. Greer, John W. Hilber, and John H. Walton (Grand Rapids, Mich.: Baker Academic, 2018), 465.

19 Fu, "Feasting in the Biblical World," 467.

20 We note a similar word in Arabic, *hajj,* which designates the pilgrimage to Mecca incumbent on every adult Muslim at least once in their lifetime.

21 During the divided monarchy, the Northern Kingdom of Israel and the Southern Kingdom of Judah each had their

own civil calendar, reckoning the number of years that their kings reigned according to different sets of criteria. For details, see Thiele, *The Mysterious Numbers of the Hebrew Kings,* 43–60.

22 Oded Borowski, *Agriculture in Iron Age Israel* (Boston: American Schools of Oriental Research, 2002), 31.

23 The lunar calendar remains the basis of the calendar in Islam.

24 The translation is that of John Sailhamer, *The Pentateuch as Narrative: A Biblical-Theological Commentary* (Grand Rapids, Mich.: Zondervan, 1992), 93.

25 Shmuel Ahituv, *Echoes from the Past: Hebrew and Cognate Inscriptions from the Biblical Period.* A Carta Handbook (Jerusalem: Carta, 2008), 252–257; Borowski, *Agriculture in Iron Age Israel,* 32–38.

26 Ahituv, *Echoes from the Past,* 254.

27 Wilfred G. E. Watson, "Daily Life in Ancient Ugarit (Syria)," in *Life and Culture of the Ancient Near East,* eds. Richard E. Averbeck, Mark W. Chavalas, and David B. Weisberg (Bethesda, Md.: CDL Press, 2003), 139–140.

28 Alex Strashny, "Modern Searches for *Aviv* Barley in the Context of the Hebrew Calendar: A First Description of the Israeli Barley Observational Data" *Jewish Bible Quarterly* 45/3 (2017): 182.

29 Roland de Vaux, *Ancient Israel* (New York: McGraw-Hill, 1961), 470.

30 de Vaux, *Ancient Israel,* 186–187.

31 Oswalt, *The Bible among the Myths,* 85–107; Christopher J. H. Wright, *Walking in the Ways of the LORD: The Ethical Authority of the Old Testament* (Downers Grove, Ill.: InterVarsity, 1995), 59–60.

32 Philip J. King, "The Marzeah Amos Denounces," *Biblical Archaeology Review* 14/4 (1988): 34–44; King and Stager, *Life in Biblical Israel,* 355–357; Elizabeth Bloch-Smith, "The Cult of the Dead in Judah: Interpreting the Material Remains," *Journal of Biblical Literature* 3/2 (1992): 213–224.

33 Amos Kloner and David Davis, "A Burial Cave of the Late First Temple Period on the Slope of Mount Zion," in *Ancient Jerusalem Revealed,* ed. Hillel Geva, rev. ed. (Jerusalem: IES, 2000 repr.), 107–110.

34 Richard E. Averbeck, "Sacrifices and Offerings," in *Dictionary of the Old Testament: Pentateuch,* ed. T. Desmond Alexander and David W. Baker (Downers Grove, Ill.: InterVarsity, 2003), 706–733.

35 William G. Dever, *What Did the Biblical Writers Know and When Did They Know It?* (Grand Rapids, Mich.: Eerdmans, 2001), 173–198.

36 I use the word *weightiness* intentionally. The Hebrew word *kavod,* "honor" or "glory," derives from the verb *kaved,* "to be weighty." The act of sacrifice recognizes the glory due to God alone.

37 "Fellowship offering" as translated by the New International Version; see Lev. 3:1, etc.

38 A. F. Rainey, "The Order of Sacrifices in Old Testament Ritual Texts," *Biblica* 51 (1970): 498.

39 A. Leo Oppenheim, *Ancient Mesopotamia: Portrait of a Dead Civilization,* rev. ed. (Chicago: University of Chicago Press, 1977), 183–198.

40 *Shabbat* (sha-BAHT) is the biblical Hebrew spelling and the way that the word is pronounced by modern Israelis and Sephardi Jews. Ashkenazi Jews pronounce the word as *Shabbos* (SHAB-ahs), its Yiddish form.

41 Abraham Joshua Heschel, *The Sabbath* (Boston, Mass.: Shambhala, 2003), 2, 47, 51, 70.

42 For instance, as in the English Standard Version.

43 Heschel, *The Sabbath,* xviii. For a discussion—and rejection—of the idea that the biblical Sabbath developed from the Babylonian belief that every seventh day was a "bad omen" day during which certain normal activities were forbidden, see de Vaux, *Ancient Israel,* 476–478.

44 Heschel, *The Sabbath,* 59–77.

45 A. G. McDowell, *Village Life in Ancient Egypt: Laundry Lists and Love Songs* (Oxford: Oxford University Press, 1999), 7.

46 Richard A. Parker, *The Calendars of Ancient Egypt, Studies in Ancient Oriental Civilizations* 26 (Chicago: University of Chicago Press, 1950): 9–23.

47 Miriam Lichtheim, *Ancient Egyptian Literature,* vol 1, *The Old and Middle Kingdoms* (Berkeley, The University of California Press, 1973), 42.

48 John A. Beck, *The Baker Illustrated Guide to Everyday Life in Bible Times* (Grand Rapids, Mich.: Baker, 2013), 234–235.

49 For example, Abraham E. Millgram, *Jewish Worship* (Philadelphia: Jewish Publication Society, 1971), 199–205.

50 For example, de Vaux, *Ancient Israel,* 484–502; Theodore H. Gaster, *Festivals of the Jewish Year* (New York: Morrow Quill, 1953); Borowski, *Agriculture in Iron Age Israel,* 38–44; Bernard R. Goldstein and Alan Cooper, "The Festivals of Israel and Judah and the Literary History of the Pentateuch," *Journal of the American Oriental Society* 110/1 (1990): 19–31.

51 de Vaux, *Ancient Israel,* 489, 491.

52 For the Samaritans, the place was, and remains, Mount Gerizim. See Husney Wasef, *The Israelite Journey through the Wilderness in the Sinai Peninsula* (Mount Gerizim, Nablus: Centre of the Good Samaritan, 2012), 273.

53 Melchizedek's Salem (Gen. 14:18) is widely recognized to have been Jerusalem, even though it is not called that specifically.

54 The Hebrew word *bikkurim* ("firstfruits") is a form of *bikur,* a word designating the "firstborn" child or animal. These were living beings that held a special relational significance to their parent throughout the biblical world.

55 Barley, ripe at Passover, is a rougher grain, not quite as suitable for bread or fine flour but excellent for donkeys.

56 The prophet Jeremiah, a contemporary of Josiah, may have made an allusion to the festivals of Weeks and Booths: "They do not say in their hearts, 'Let us fear the LORD our God, who gives the rain in its season, the autumn rain and the spring rain, and keeps for us the weeks [*shavuot*] appointed for the harvest [*qatzir*]" (Jer. 5:24). Whether Jeremiah's reference to "weeks" is the Feast of Weeks or just a reference to the period of harvest cannot be known for sure, although the latter seems more likely.

57 Rosalie David, *Handbook to Life in Ancient Egypt,* rev. ed. (Oxford: Oxford University Press, 1998), 261–262.

58 Jean Bottéro, *Religion in Ancient Mesopotamia,* trans. Teresa Lavender Fagan (Chicago: University of Chicago Press, 2001), 158–164; Wolfram von Soden, *The Ancient Orient: An Introduction to the Study of the Ancient Near East,* trans. Donald G. Schley (Grand Rapids, Mich.: Eerdmans, 1994), 189, 191–192, 197–198.

59 Ahituv, *Echoes from the Past,* 254.

60 Thiele, *The Mysterious Numbers of the Hebrew Kings,* 43–60.

61 Theodore Gaster, *Festivals of the Jewish Year,* 136.

62 See also 2 Maccabees 15:36.

CHAPTER 2

Feasts of the Bible During the New Testament and in Early Judaism

Moshe Silberschein

The Second Temple period spans over half a millennium, from the rebuilding of the Jerusalem temple in the sixth century BC to its destruction by the Romans in AD 70. The centuries following are closely tied to this period, as the rabbis produced a large volume of literature that codified, or formalized, what it meant to be Jewish now that the temple, which had been the focal point of Jewish life, no longer existed. This long era was a very diverse time in Jewish history, one which saw significant changes in the ways that the biblical feasts were celebrated.

Unlike the period of the Hebrew Scriptures (the Old Testament) when the First Temple was still standing, in the Second Temple period the majority of Jews lived in the Diaspora, in places far from the Land of Israel. How did these Jews observe the biblical feasts when they lived outside of the land to which the feasts were so tightly tied? The psalmist understood the issue when he lamented, "How shall we sing the LORD's song in a foreign land?" (Ps. 137:4). And if Jews did decide to travel to the temple in Jerusalem for one of the pilgrimage festivals, what was it like? According to the first-century historian Josephus, the number of pilgrims making the trip to Jerusalem to celebrate Passover numbered over two and a half million.[1] The Talmud speaks of an amount "twice those that came out of Egypt," that is, twice the roughly 600,000 mentioned in Numbers 1:46.[2] Even if both estimates are exaggerations (and they probably are), the number was still immensely large. How did a multitude of pilgrims—a number far in excess of the number of people who celebrated the feasts in the time of the Hebrew Scriptures—impact the way the biblical feasts were observed? What would Jesus and his disciples have experienced when they went to Jerusalem to celebrate the feasts? The answer is not as clear as it may seem.

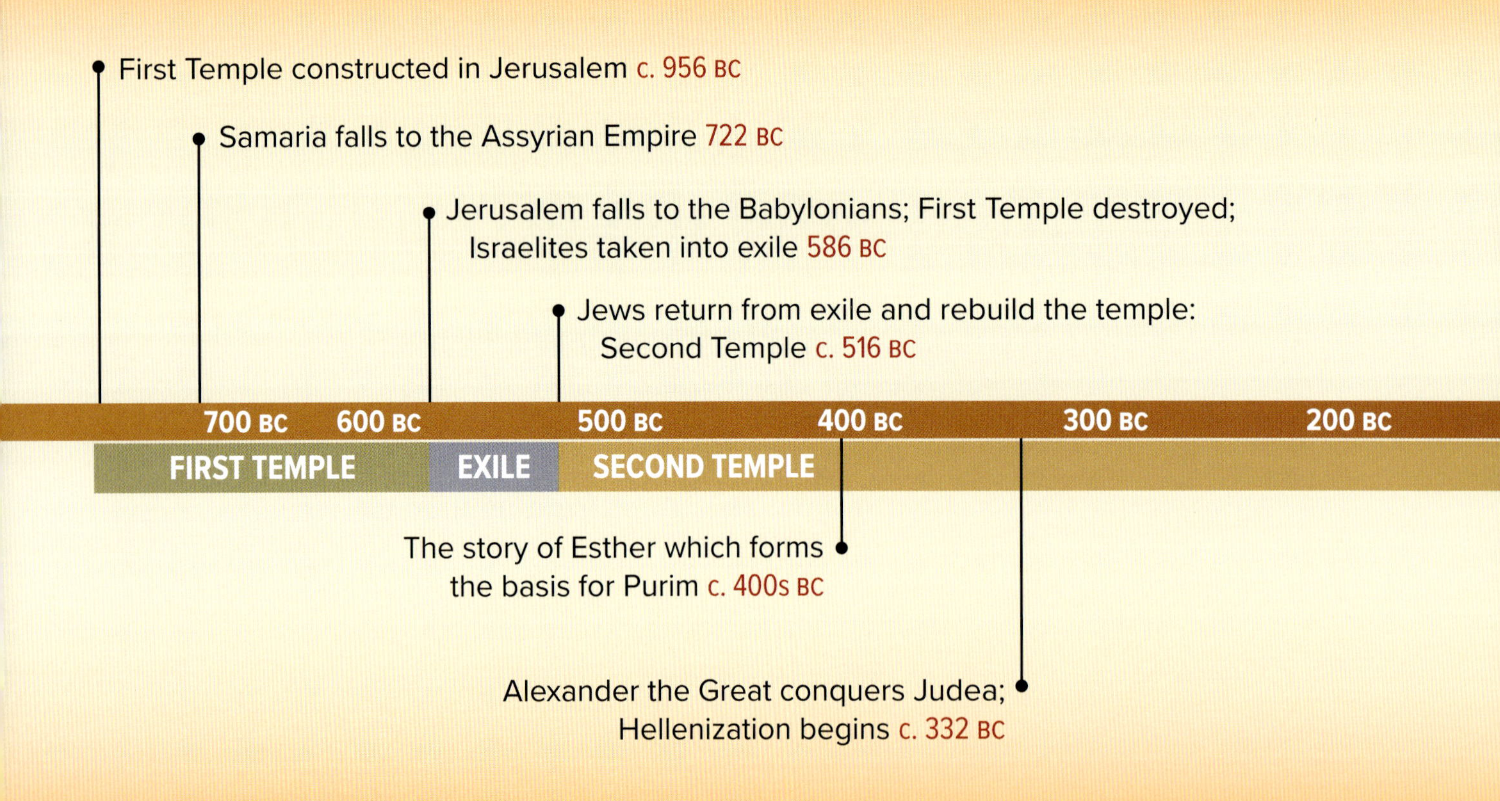

How people observed the feasts in the Second Temple period changed considerably to fit their new circumstances. In part, this was because different strands of Judaism interpreted the Torah's instructions about the feast days quite differently. Were the variety of approaches accepted, or at least tolerated, by the majority Jewish community? The Mishnah, a written codification of Jewish oral tradition compiled around the year AD 200, gives detailed explanations of how to celebrate the biblical feasts. But to what extent did Jews follow (or even know of) these instructions in the Diaspora, let alone in Jerusalem during the time of Jesus' ministry over a century and a half before the instructions were written down?

In this chapter, we will explore these questions and more by looking at sources from rabbinic literature, New Testament books, and other historical writings to piece together a picture (though often a very limited picture) of what celebrating the biblical feasts looked like for people in the Second Temple period.

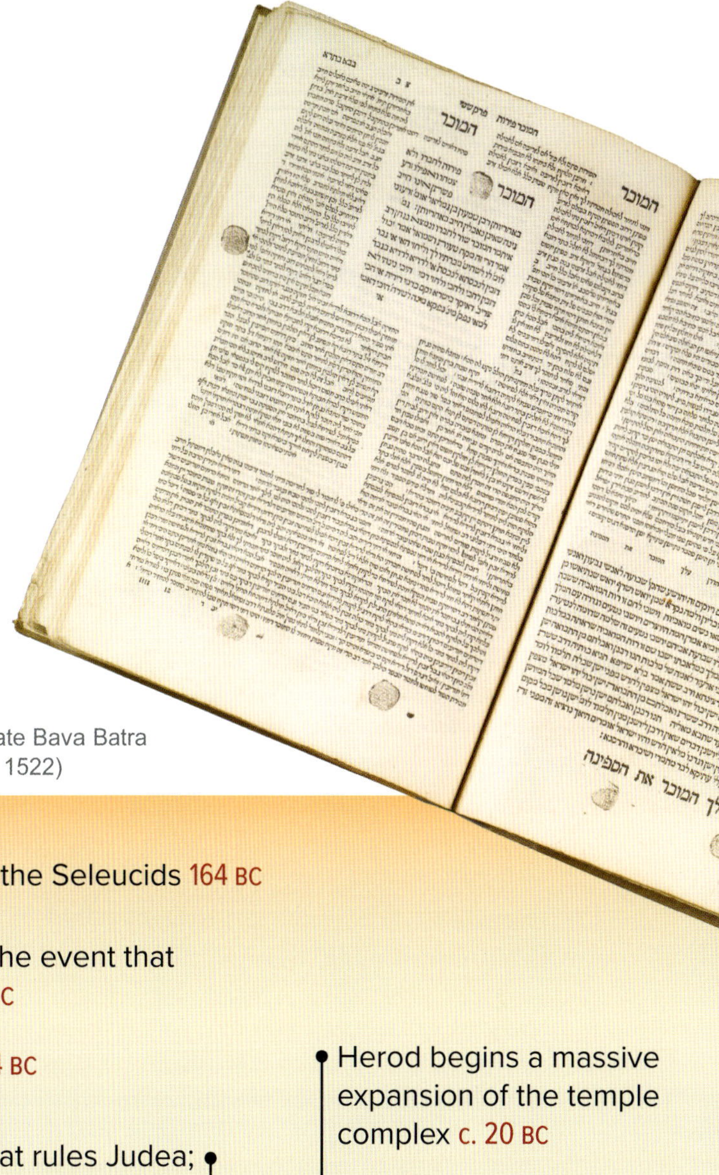

Babylonian Talmud, Tractate Bava Batra (Daniel Bomberg, Venice, 1522)

- Maccabees reclaim Jerusalem from the Seleucids 164 BC
- Temple cleansed and rededicated, the event that forms the basis for Hanukkah 164 BC
- Hasmonean dynasty established 164 BC
- Pompey conquers Jerusalem for Rome 63 BC
- Herod the Great rules Judea; end of the Hasmonean dynasty 37 BC
- Herod begins a massive expansion of the temple complex c. 20 BC
- Ministry of Jesus of Nazareth c. AD 27–30
- First Jewish Revolt against the Romans AD 66–70
- Romans plunder and set fire to the temple AD 70

100 BC | AD 1 | AD 100

CLASSICAL RABBINIC LITERATURE

Much of what we know about Judaism in the Second Temple period comes from classical rabbinic literature.[3] This literature consists of books written and preserved by Jews that complement and complete the Hebrew Scriptures. (You'll find many references in this chapter to this literature.) In a way, how Christians see the Old Testament and the New Testament as parts of one unit is similar to how Jews view the Hebrew Scriptures and classical rabbinic literature as one Torah, the Word of God. However, unlike the New Testament, classical rabbinic literature consists of many volumes of written collections of oral rabbinic traditions that span the first century BC through the sixth century AD.

These collections can be divided into two main groups:

- The first includes works from the period of the sages of Israel (rabbis), who are called Tana'im, from the first century BC through AD 200.
- The second contains works of the sages called Amora'im, from AD 200 through the sixth century.

From the Jewish perspective, the teachings of the Tana'im and Amora'im are one. The rabbis are collectively referred to in Jewish circles as Chazal, a Hebrew acronym for "Our Sages of Blessed Memory." Classical rabbinic literature is then called, for short, the literature of Chazal.

The following works from classical rabbinic literature are cited and quoted in this chapter.[4]

The Literature of Tana'im:

- Mishnah (*m.*)
- Tosefta (*t.*)
- Mekhilta
- Sifrei Deuteronomy
- Seder Olam Rabbah
- Avot De-Rabbi Natan

The Literature of Amora'im:

- Jerusalem Talmud (Talmud Yerushalmi) (*y.*)
- Babylonian Talmud (Talmud Bavli) (*b.*)
- Genesis Rabbah
- Leviticus Rabbah
- Pesikta Rabbati
- Midrash Tehillim (Psalms)

Classical rabbinic literature's original language is either Hebrew or Aramaic, or both. Some of these works have accessible translations in English, while others do not. Many of the texts preserve oral traditions from, or about, the period of the Second Temple.

This chapter also cites some Jewish Hellenistic works that are not part of classical rabbinic literature: the book of Jubilees (c. 150 BC), the writings of Philo (25 BC–AD 50) and Josephus (c. AD 37–100), and the Apocryphal books of Tobit, Judith, and 1 and 2 Maccabees. These writings, like the New Testament, were never considered sacred texts in the synagogue but remain an important source for understanding the religion of Jews during the first century.

The New Testament and classical rabbinic literature are different types of literature, written in different languages, and follow different organizational principles. Yet because they overlap in cultural, geographical, and historical contexts, they supplement each other as we try to understand the Second Temple period.

One important challenge, however, is how to date these sources and place each in its correct historical, social, and religious context. To what extent can this literature be read backward into the Second Temple period, including the decades of the New Testament? Many times (probably most of the time), it is not clear if any given oral tradition describing the feasts comes before or after the destruction of the Second Temple in AD 70.[5] Thankfully, the New Testament can help verify dates for some Jewish festive traditions prior to AD 70. A case in point: although there is no source in classical rabbinic literature for the practice of waiting to name a Jewish baby boy until he is eight days old at the feast of his circumcision, the custom clearly goes back to the time of the Second Temple, as evidenced by the circumcision of both John the Baptist and Jesus mentioned in the New Testament (Luke 1:59; 2:21).

When read carefully, the New Testament and classical rabbinic literature complement each other in their descriptions of how the biblical feasts were observed. As much as they may differ on important theological issues, classical rabbinic literature and the New Testament share a common culture and are part of the same world of ideas. Jesus is called "rabbi" in three of the four gospels (for example, Matt. 26:25; Mark 9:5; John 3:2), a title that indicates his training. The apostle Paul considered himself a disciple of one of the great sages of Israel, Rabban Gamaliel (Acts 22:3). While the Second Temple was still standing in Jerusalem, the sages of Israel (Chazal), the rabbis and their disciples, and Jesus with his followers were all part of the same Jewish society, celebrating the same festive days as prescribed by Scripture.

How do we make the commands of the Torah relevant for today? This was a real question during the Second Temple period and the centuries following. Synagogues were bustling centers of Jewish learning and life, bringing practical Torah instruction to the people. This stone capital from the fifth-century synagogue in Capernaum bears the image of a menorah (branched candlestick), like one that would have been found in the Jerusalem temple. By incorporating images like this, the temple which no longer stood became a present reality for Jews everywhere. (Photo by Paul H. Wright)

 SHABBAT (SABBATH)

Shabbat (Hebrew for *Sabbath*) is chief among the feasts of the Bible. It was clearly the central focus of the week in Jewish society during the Second Temple period, as it is for Jews today. This is illustrated by the following recollection of Shammai, one of the sages of Israel (c. 30 BC) in classical rabbinic literature. He was a contemporary of Herod the Great—who also enjoyed feasting but not necessarily according to Torah regulations.[6] Shammai made sure that the best food was always set aside for Shabbat and planned his weekly menu accordingly:

> Shammai only ate food to honor Shabbat. If he came upon a choice animal to eat, he would say, "Let it be for Shabbat." And if he came upon another even more choice animal, he would then set that animal aside for his Shabbat table, and only afterward would he eat the first animal he found.[7]

When Did Shabbat Begin?

Did Shabbat begin on Friday night in the Second Temple period, or Saturday morning? Based on a careful examination of the Hebrew Scriptures, many biblical scholars conclude that throughout the time of the First Temple (c. 956–586 BC), Shabbat began at sunrise on Saturday morning and ended at sunset.[8] According to this view, it was only sometime after the return from exile that the Jews adopted a lunar calendar that measured all days, including Shabbat, from sunset to sunset. There were, however, some traditionalists who wanted to go back to a solar calendar system, but these diehards are remembered in classical rabbinic literature as heretical fringe groups.[9] Changing the calendar doesn't happen overnight, but just as the Sabbath as a day of rest was formally transferred to Sunday in Christianity by the fourth century AD,[10] so the start of Shabbat in Second Temple times was eventually transferred to Friday night, beginning in the fourth century BC. We can, therefore, assume that by the time of Shammai (and the New Testament), Shabbat began on Friday night.

What Did People Eat and Drink on Shabbat?

When the Second Temple was still standing, people traditionally ate only two meals per day:

- *pat shacharit,* food eaten on the morning pita bread, and
- *pat arvit*, food eaten on the evening pita bread.[11]

This was (and remains in some parts of the world today) a kind of everyman's meal where pita bread served as both plate and cutlery.

But once Shabbat came, the festivities required more meals and more food. Classical rabbinic literature includes a discussion among the rabbis as to whether an observant Jew should have three meals or even four in honor of the Sabbath.[12] Traditionally, a person began his or her daily activities with the sunrise and went to bed with the sunset after a hard day's work. But once a week, come the start of Shabbat on Friday evening, people could stay up late since no one worked the next day. Everyone had time to enjoy a festive family meal, friendly conversation, and the commanded leisure of God's Torah. It is important to note that the most natural way of marking this break in the weekly routine was by eating a shared meal and doing so in a way that was different from all other meals of the week. Moreover, an entire chapter of Mishnah Shabbat is dedicated to the lighting of the Shabbat lamp (this was something new, not found in the Hebrew Scriptures). The chapter ends with a Friday evening checklist of things to do before the start of Shabbat at sunset, concluding with the command, "Light the lamp!"[13] Thanks to the Shabbat lamp, once a week even commoners had a late-night banquet in their home. We can think of the Shabbat Friday night dinner like having a Thanksgiving or Christmas dinner every week!

The Friday night feast ushered in the Sabbath day with wine and blessings. A very early rabbinic expansion of the fourth commandment, "Remember the Shabbat to sanctify it" (Ex. 20:8 JPS[14]), set the

Sunset over Hula Valley, an agricultural region in northern Israel

tone: "sanctify it over wine."[15] Later generations connected the last words of the fourth commandment, God "rested on the seventh day. Therefore the LORD blessed the Sabbath day and made it holy" (Ex. 20:11) with a verse from Esther, "on the seventh day [of the king's feast], when the heart of the king was merry with wine" (Est. 1:10). This was done to clarify that the role of wine on Shabbat was to help make the meal festive, though not to the extent of drunkenness:

> It was the Sabbath day, a day when Israel would eat and drink, beginning with words of Torah and songs of praise to the Holy One, but idolaters [like those at the king's feast] when they eat and drink, they commence their activity with only words of insipid licentiousness.[16]

How Did People Prepare for Shabbat?

Everything on the menu for the Shabbat festive meals was prepared during the daylight hours of Friday, well in advance of sundown, according to the reading of Exodus 16:5 in classical rabbinic literature: "On the sixth day, when they prepare what they bring in, it [the manna from heaven] will be twice as much as they gather daily."[17] The practice of Friday being the day of preparation for Shabbat seems to have been universally accepted by all groups of Jews throughout the Second Temple period. This is found in the description of the day of Jesus' crucifixion in the gospel of John:

> Since it was the day of Preparation, the Jews did not want the bodies left on the cross during the sabbath, especially because that sabbath was a day of great solemnity. ... And so, because it was the Jewish day of Preparation, and the tomb was nearby, they laid Jesus there. (John 19:31, 42 NRSV)[18]

And as early as the mid-second century BC, the book of Jubilees states:

> You shall do no work whatever on the Sabbath day save that you have prepared for yourselves on the sixth day, so as to eat, and drink, and rest, and keep Sabbath from all work on that day, and to bless the Lord your God, who has given you a day of festival, and a holy day: and a day of the holy kingdom for all Israel is this day among their days for ever.[19]

The "work" that could not be done on Shabbat included the clear command in Exodus 35:3: "You shall kindle no fire in all your dwelling places on the Sabbath day." This means that the food of Shabbat—certainly what was consumed from sunrise Saturday until the end of Shabbat—was likely eaten cold. The Shabbat lamp could be lit before Shabbat began to provide light on Friday night, but the oven would still be cold come Saturday.

A lamp typical of daily life—and the Sabbath—in the first century lights a simple meal. The dish and decanter are objects from the time of the New Testament. (Photo by Paul H. Wright)

Yet cold food did not in any way detract from the festive atmosphere of the holy day. This we see in a tale about Rabbi Yehudah, president of the Sanhedrin, and his guest for the Shabbat meal, the Roman emperor Antoninus (second century AD):

> When our Rabbi entertained Antoninus on Shabbat, he served him cold dishes, which Antoninus ate and liked. On another occasion, our Rabbi entertained him on a weekday, when he served him hot dishes. Antoninus said, "I found the cold dishes more tasty than the hot." Our Rabbi replied, "The hot dishes lack one seasoning." To which Antoninus said, "Can there be anything at all lacking in the emperor's pantry?" Said our Rabbi to him, "The hot dishes lack Shabbat. Does your pantry have Shabbat?"[20]

Even the pagan emperor Antoninus realized that the feast and the food he experienced with Rabbi Yehudah meant nothing without the special aura of Shabbat![21] Whether fact or fiction, the tales of the sages show us that as early as the first century AD, what made the Shabbat meals festive was more than the food: it was the very day itself.

A weaver demonstrates how textiles were created in the first century AD, the kind of task that would have been prohibited on the Sabbath, at Nazareth Village, an open-air musem with historical recreations in Old Nazareth, Israel. (Photo by Kobby Dagan/Shutterstock)

How Did People Keep Shabbat Holy?

Throughout the Second Temple period, different Jewish groups took up the spiritual challenge of Scripture to "observe the Shabbat and keep it holy," and they arrived at a variety of opinions about how to do just that. *Holy* is an abstract concept, but in the Hebrew Scriptures there is only one clear, practical commandment, repeated again and again, about how to keep Shabbat holy: the general prohibition of doing work on the Sabbath day; and the only clear, specific example of work prohibited in the Torah is that of kindling fires in one's home (Ex. 35:3). But are there other work activities that also should be prohibited to keep the day holy?

We have a few examples from the first half of the Second Temple period that illustrate the struggle to clarify and codify Scripture's general prohibition of work on Shabbat. The book of Jubilees, for instance, prohibited marital relations on Shabbat among the adherents of its community.[22] According to Josephus, the Essenes, a strict religious group, forbade any elimination of bodily wastes on the Sabbath.[23] The first book of Maccabees tells us that there were communities of Jews that forbade any warfare on the Sabbath, even to defend themselves from attacking forces.[24] There is even a hint in classical rabbinic literature that there were once among the sages of Israel some who refrained from eating and drinking on the Sabbath, dedicating themselves solely to sitting and studying the Torah.[25] But by the time of Jesus' ministry, these specific prohibitions were no longer observed by most Jews. As we might expect, a clear and definitive agreement of what makes Shabbat a special day was still in the making.

Rabbi Akiva's Thirty-Nine Prohibitions

Midrash is, literally, a "searching out" of every nuance, every jot and tittle, of Hebrew Scripture to better understand the word of God and hence what God desires of his people. Through this very careful "midrashic" reading of the Bible, Rabbi Akiva and his disciples in the early second century AD spoke of thirty-nine categories of activity (*melakhah*) prohibited on Shabbat:

> The principal categories of labor [*melakhah*] prohibited on Shabbat are forty-less-one: sowing; plowing; reaping; gathering sheaves into a pile; threshing; removing the kernel from the husk; winnowing threshed grain in the wind; separating the inedible waste from the edible; grinding; sifting the flour in a sieve; kneading dough; baking; shearing wool; bleaching, combing, straightening, and dyeing wool; spinning wool; stretching the threads of the warp in the loom; and constructing two meshes; tying the threads of the warp to the base of the loom; weaving two threads; severing two threads for constructive purposes; tying a knot; untying a knot; sewing two stitches with a needle; tearing a fabric in order to sew two stitches; hunting a deer, slaughtering, flaying, salting, curing, [and] tanning [the deer's] hide; smoothing, scraping, [and] cutting the hide into measured parts; writing two letters; erasing in order to write two letters; building a structure; dismantling a structure; extinguishing a fire; lighting a fire; striking with a hammer to complete the production process of a vessel; [and] carrying from one domain to another. All these are the principal categories of labor, forty-less-one.[26]

Melakhah is a specialized Hebrew term that the Torah uses whenever it speaks of activities prohibited on the Sabbath.[27] But it is also specifically used when speaking of work done to build the tabernacle. Exodus 35 opens with the prohibition of *melakhah* on Shabbat and then continues through the rest of the chapter—indeed, through the rest of the book—to use *melakhah* for all the specialized activities that were needed to build God's sanctuary. In this way, we can think of the sanctuary of space (the tabernacle) pointing us toward the sanctuary of time (Shabbat). What then is forbidden when the Torah commanded that on Shabbat a person shall not do any *melakhah* (Ex. 20:9)? All of the thirty-nine types of *melakhah* used to construct God's sanctuary! Indeed, during the second half of the Second Temple period, these thirty-nine kinds of *melakhah* came to define not only what was and was not proper behavior for the festive atmosphere of Shabbat but also for the three pilgrimage holidays.[28]

We can also see a connection between God's sanctuary and Shabbat in the teachings of Jesus, when the Pharisees caught Jesus' disciples eating grain plucked from the fields on the Sabbath:

> When the Pharisees saw it, they said to him, "Look! Your disciples are doing what is not lawful to do on the Sabbath." He said to them, "Have you not you read what David did when he was hungry, and those who were with him: how he entered the house of God and ate the bread of the Presence, which it was not lawful for him to eat nor for those who were with him, but only for the priests? Or have you not read in the Law how on the Sabbath the priests in the temple profane the Sabbath and are guiltless?" (Matt. 12:2–5)

Though these verses do not mention the thirty-nine categories later specified by Rabbi Akiva, they are the earliest Jewish texts from the Second Temple period that make a connection between the temple (God's sanctuary) and activities prohibited on the Sabbath. In this story, we can sense that a century before Rabbi Akiva, there was a real rabbinic debate about the relationship between Shabbat and *melakhah*.

In the wars of the Maccabees in the mid-second century BC, some Jews initially did choose to die rather than violate Shabbat by defending themselves. But by the latter half of the Second Temple period, those days were long over. It became clear that Jews should live by the commandments on Shabbat, not die by (or because of) them. Self-defense in warfare was permissible on Shabbat, with classic rabbinic literature clearly stating that saving a human life overrides the prohibitions of *melakhah*.

> Rabbi Shimon Ben Menassia [c. AD 200] teaches, "And you shall keep the Sabbath, for it is holy to you" [Ex. 31:14]. The Sabbath is given to you and you are not given to the Sabbath.[29]

Almost two centuries earlier, however, this principle is found in the teachings of Jesus in the New Testament: "The Sabbath was made for man, not man for the Sabbath" (Mark 2:27).[30]

Shabbat in the Greco-Roman World

At the beginning of the first millennium AD, the Sabbath was not just a festive day for Jews; it also found resonance among God-fearers. These were non-Jews throughout the Roman Empire attracted to the faith of Israel. Josephus reports the following:

> The masses have long since shown a keen desire to adopt our religious observances; and there is not one city, Greek or barbarian, not a single nation, to which our custom of abstaining from work on the seventh day has not spread, and where the fasts and the lighting of lamps and many of our prohibitions in the matter of food are not observed.[31]

Josephus's observation is confirmed by the Roman philosopher Seneca (c. 4 BC–AD 65), who critiqued the strange habit of Jews who "by introducing one day of rest in every seven they lose in idleness almost a seventh of their life, and by failing to

The activities used in constructing the tabernacle in the wilderness became the basis for defining what was and was not permitted on the Sabbath. This life-sized model of the tabernacle is located in Israel's Timna Park in the Negev Desert. (Photo by ChameleonsEye/ Shutterstock)

This mosaic depicts well-to-do banqueters in Roman dress feasting at a triclinium, a three-sided arrangement by which the participants recline at a table. The mosaic graced the floor of an actual triclinium in the so-called House of Orpheus in Sepphoris, Galilee, in the third and fourth centuries AD. The Greek god Orpheus was often associated with both David and Christ in Byzantine art. Forms of feasting in the Greco-Roman world eventually made their way into Jewish practices, including the Sabbath meal. (Photo by Paul H. Wright)

act in times of urgency they often suffer loss."[32] While Josephus saw the spread of Sabbath observance in the Roman Empire as a positive development, Seneca saw it in quite a different light. "Meanwhile," Seneca bemoaned, "the customs of this accursed race have gained such influence that they are now received throughout all the world. The vanquished have given laws to their victors."[33] Seneca is commenting on a process—already four centuries old in his day—in which Jews, especially those living in urban centers or the Diaspora, were becoming part and parcel of the larger Greco-Roman world. And, it seems, that the cultural handoff went both ways.

Seneca saw the Sabbath as the direct opposite of Greco-Roman culture. He would have been appalled by some of the habits of Sabbath feasting. For instance, it was typical to end a Greco-Roman banquet by burning incense to cleanse the palate and senses.[34] A Shabbat meal could not end this way because of the prohibition to kindle a fire. Some Jews shaped their Shabbat meals around this practice anyway, using spices, herbs, or aromatic flowers as an alternate way to arouse the senses.[35] Eventually, classical rabbinic literature would go even further by transforming any secular feast eaten by Jews into a surrogate altar, its activities offered to God, by mandating special home liturgies to be said at each meal. (It remains unclear, however, whether these liturgies were already being practiced in the lifetime of Seneca, during the time of the New Testament.)[36]

Shabbat and the End of Days

Mishnah Tamid 7:4 lists the psalms that were sung on each day of the week in the temple in Jerusalem.

On Shabbat, it was, of course, Psalm 92, which opens with the heading "A Psalm: a Song for the Sabbath." The Mishnah expands:

> A Psalm: a Song for the Shabbat Day; a Psalm, and song for the time to come, for the day that shall be entirely Shabbat and rest for life everlasting.[37]

At the End of Days, when the Messiah comes, Shabbat will never end and the banquet, the Shabbat feast, in God's revealed kingdom will never cease. In the only example in the Gospels of Jesus attending a Shabbat feast, we hear a similar message. Luke 14 recounts the Shabbat meal where Jesus was hosted by a leader of the Pharisees. One of the dinner guests, inspired by Jesus' teachings, said to Jesus: "Blessed is everyone who will eat bread in the kingdom of God!" (Luke 14:15). Jesus responded by telling the parable of the great banquet, reflecting the imagery of the world to come as an everlasting Shabbat banquet (Luke 14:16–24).

 ROSH HODESH (NEW MOON)

References to Sabbaths, new moons, and appointed feasts appear throughout Hebrew Scripture, the Apocrypha, and the New Testament, for example here in the reforms of Nehemiah:

> We also take on ourselves the obligation to give yearly a third part of a shekel for the service of the house of our God: for the showbread, the regular grain offering, the regular burnt offering, the Sabbaths, the new moons, the appointed feasts, the holy things, and the sin offerings to make atonement for Israel, and for all the work of the house of our God. (Neh. 10:32–33 [Hebrew v. 34])

(Other examples include: Hos. 2:11 [Hebrew v. 13], Isa. 1:13–14; 1 Chron. 23:31; 2 Chron. 8:12–13; 1 Macc. 10:34; Judith 8:6; Col. 2:16; see also Gal. 4:10.)

Sabbaths occurred weekly, new moon celebrations monthly, and appointed feasts yearly. From the weekly Sabbath, we now turn our attention to the monthly new moon festival, *Rosh Hodesh,* a term that means literally "head, or beginning, of the month." Rosh Hodesh marks the renewal of each 29½-day segment of the lunar cycle.

Trying to reconstruct how the celebration of Rosh Hodesh, the appearance of the new moon, was celebrated during the Second Temple period is especially difficult because it is not even clear in the Hebrew Scriptures how it was celebrated in the time of the First Temple. The Torah does not expressly prohibit work (*melakhah*) on Rosh Hodesh, as it does for Shabbat and the appointed feasts of Pesach (Passover), Shavuot (Weeks), and Sukkot (Booths). In fact, unlike Shabbat and the three pilgrimage festivals, there are no commandments in the Torah whatsoever instructing the people how to observe the new moon, such as refraining from leaven or dwelling in booths for seven days. Rather, the event of the new moon in the Torah is a national or public event in which it was the priests who officiated over set animal sacrifices and the blowing of trumpets (Num. 10:10; 28:11–15). What might this have meant in the life of the average citizen during biblical times, especially for someone who did not live in Jerusalem or visit the temple?

What Did People Do on Rosh Hodesh?

There are hints at ways that individuals observed the new moon in the books of Samuel and Kings.

David fails to attend King Saul's feast on Rosh Hodesh (1 Sam. 20:5–29). Was this only a royal feast held in the palace? And was it a onetime event or a monthly occurrence? David tries to excuse himself from attending the king's feast because he has a yearly family sacrifice in his hometown of Bethlehem at the same time (1 Sam. 20:6)—but this is not a family Rosh Hodesh feast marking the start of the month.[38]

Rosh Hodesh may have been a typical time to visit a seer or prophet, based on the question of the Shunamite's husband to his wife when she announced that she was going to visit Elisha: "Why will you go to him today? It is neither new moon nor Sabbath" (2 Kings 4:23). Was it a general practice to visit the seer on these days or just a local custom? Once again, the evidence is not enough to determine any standard set of Rosh Hodesh observances or customs.

There are several Rosh Hodesh customs mentioned in classical rabbinic literature, traditions which may have been in practice as early as the first century AD. Instead of family feasts, we read of communal feasts held on the new moon in synagogues or Torah study academies of the Land of Israel.[39] Because there were no synagogues[40] or Torah study academies during the time of the First Temple, this was a new practice in Second Temple times, though it built on the hints about new moon observances in the Hebrew Scriptures.[41] The full menu for these communal meals is not mentioned in classical rabbinic literature, but sources do reveal a special, final course for dessert—boiled lupine beans.[42] According to the Mishnah, these poisonous, bitter beans could only be edible as a favored dessert if they were first boiled and rinsed in water seven times.[43] These beans, then and now, were found in the pods of the purple lupine wildflowers that grow to this day in fields and on hillsides in Israel.

Another innovation described in classical rabbinic literature seems to come from the story of the Shunamite's visit to the prophet Elisha. According to Leviticus Rabbah 18:1, on every Rosh Hodesh, Rabbi Shimon Ben Halafta would visit his mentor Rabbi Yehudah, president of the Sanhedrin.[44] In the Talmud, later generations of scribes would quote the question of the Shunamite's husband as a proof text that on holidays in general, a person should make a pilgrimage to his rabbi to invigorate his

The blue lupine (*Lupinus pilosus*), a protected species, blankets hillsides and fields on foothills throughout Israel every February and March. A stalk of seed pods rises center front. (Photo by Paul H. Wright)

study of Torah.[45] In this regard, we recall that in the mindset of the sages, the rabbis followed in the footsteps of the prophets:

> Since the time that the First Temple was destroyed, prophecy has been taken from the prophets and given to the Sages of Israel.[46]

Even while the Second Temple stood, we can assume that most Jews would not be in attendance every month while the new moon animal sacrifices were offered on behalf of the nation for renewal, but a pilgrimage on Rosh Hodesh to a teacher of Torah to renew one's yearning for the Word of God was always a possibility.

Just as the Sabbath was a day of rest for weekly renewal, was Rosh Hodesh also considered a monthly day of rest and renewal? Although the Torah does not contain prohibitions of *melakhah* (work) for new moon, the prophet Amos suggests that at least by his day the observance was marked in ways similar to those of keeping the Sabbath:

> Hear this, you who trample on the needy and bring the poor of the land to an end, saying, "When will the new moon be over, that we may sell grain? And the Sabbath, that we may offer wheat for sale, that we may make the ephah small and the shekel great and deal deceitfully with false balances, that we may buy the poor for silver and the needy for a pair of sandals and sell the chaff of the wheat?" (Amos 8:4–6)

Was this prohibition of commerce something that was largely voluntary or established by custom? Was it enacted by ordinance, as when Nehemiah closed the gates of Jerusalem so as to ban commerce on the Sabbath (Neh. 13:15–21)? We have evidence in classical rabbinic literature that some Jews saw Amos 8:4–6 as a legal precedent and did indeed

A new moon over Jerusalem, signaling Rosh Hodesh, the start of a new month. (Photo by Paul H. Wright)

observe the same prohibitions of Shabbat, including acts of commerce, on Rosh Hodesh.[47]

In spite of the call of Amos, the practice of equating Rosh Hodesh to Shabbat in terms of *melakhah* prohibitions never became the norm for the entire Jewish community in the Second Temple period. Indeed, in the face of all of the strong warnings found in Scripture against any idolatrous worship of the moon, it is understandable why the Jewish sages would not want to expand new moon celebrations.

> And beware lest you raise your eyes to heaven, and when you see the sun and the moon and the stars, all the host of heaven, you be drawn away and bow down to them and serve them, things that the LORD your God has allotted to all the peoples under the whole heaven. (Deut. 4:19; see also Jer. 8:2)

The lack of evidence of any fully sanctioned celebrations on Rosh Hodesh during the Second Temple period may reflect an intentional effort to counter the widespread new moon festivities found in pagan cultures.

How Was Rosh Hodesh Announced?

During the Second Temple period, the major custom associated with the new moon was indicating exactly when it first appeared, namely, when the new month began. This was a national rather than a private event, since it was crucial for determining the days of the feasts.[48] After the Jews returned from exile in the sixth century BC, they shifted their calendar to a lunar rather than solar emphasis. This resulted in a change in the way that the first day of each new month was calculated. Instead of indicating the start of each new month by set dates throughout the year according to the seasons, as is typical with a solar calendar, the months were now determined by the appearance of the new moon.

All eyes were to the skies, with witnesses coming before the Sanhedrin to testify to the first sighting of each new moon. From the temple court, the Sanhedrin would declare that a chain of fire beacons, or torches, be lit in sequence on certain mountaintop stations to signal the new moon's arrival. The Mishnah mentions five of these stations, with the first being on the Mount of Olives overlooking Jerusalem.[49] Once that torch was lit and its signal seen by the second station, a fire beacon would be lit there to alert the next, then on to the third, fourth, and fifth stations. At the fifth one, the person lighting the torch would continuously wave his fire beacon up and down until all the land as far as Babylonia looked like one big bonfire, since once the Jews saw his signal, they all went up on their rooftops and lit their own torches in response.

How did the average person experience this monthly chain of torch signaling? Was it a powerful national ceremony showing how human beings (in this case, the Sanhedrin) could partner with God, even to the extent of determining the calendar dates for the holidays that God had ordained? Or was it just the Second Temple's version of smoke signals or the Pony Express and taken for granted? Regardless of how the fire beacons were perceived, we can assume that they were effective in announcing to all Jews living in the Land of Israel, as well as to an even greater number living in the Diaspora, the exact dates of their upcoming holy days.

The authority of the Sanhedrin to determine the appearance of the new moon and the start of each month was apparently accepted among Jews living along the Mediterranean Sea and in Asia Minor, not just in the Land of Israel. Perhaps Paul's statement to the Colossians reflects something about this relationship, distant in miles though it was to Jerusalem:

> Therefore let no one pass judgment on you in questions of food and drink, or with regard to a festival or a new moon or a Sabbath. (Col. 2:16)

Paul may be encouraging the Colossians to become independent and not beholden to the Sanhedrin in Jerusalem. His motivation could also reflect the same concern he expressed to the Galatians, which echoed from the time of Jeremiah against any type of celebration that might suggest a pagan worship of the heavenly bodies:

> But now that you have come to know God, or rather to be known by God, how can you turn back again to the weak and worthless elementary principles of the world, whose slaves you want to be once more? You observe days and months and seasons and years! I am afraid I may have labored over you in vain. (Gal. 4:9–11; see Jer. 7:18; 44:17–19)

During the first century AD, some Jews may have seen the new-moon fire beacons sent by the Sanhedrin as a celebration for renewal, while for others, they were only a reminder of moon-worship idolatry and no longer needed.

PESACH (PASSOVER)

Passover (the Hebrew word is *Pesach*) is the first of the three annual pilgrimage holidays mentioned in the Torah and the first in the year according to the biblical calendar. Passover commemorates the exodus from Egypt and freedom from slavery to Pharaoh, the first great event in the story of the founding of ancient Israel. But already quite early in the book of Exodus, in chapter 12, we read of more than one description of how to celebrate Passover.

Two Passovers

In their reading of Exodus 12, the sages of classical rabbinic literature noted different instructions for two different types of Passover ceremonies:

A modern table set for the Passover of generations. (Photo by Brian Negin)

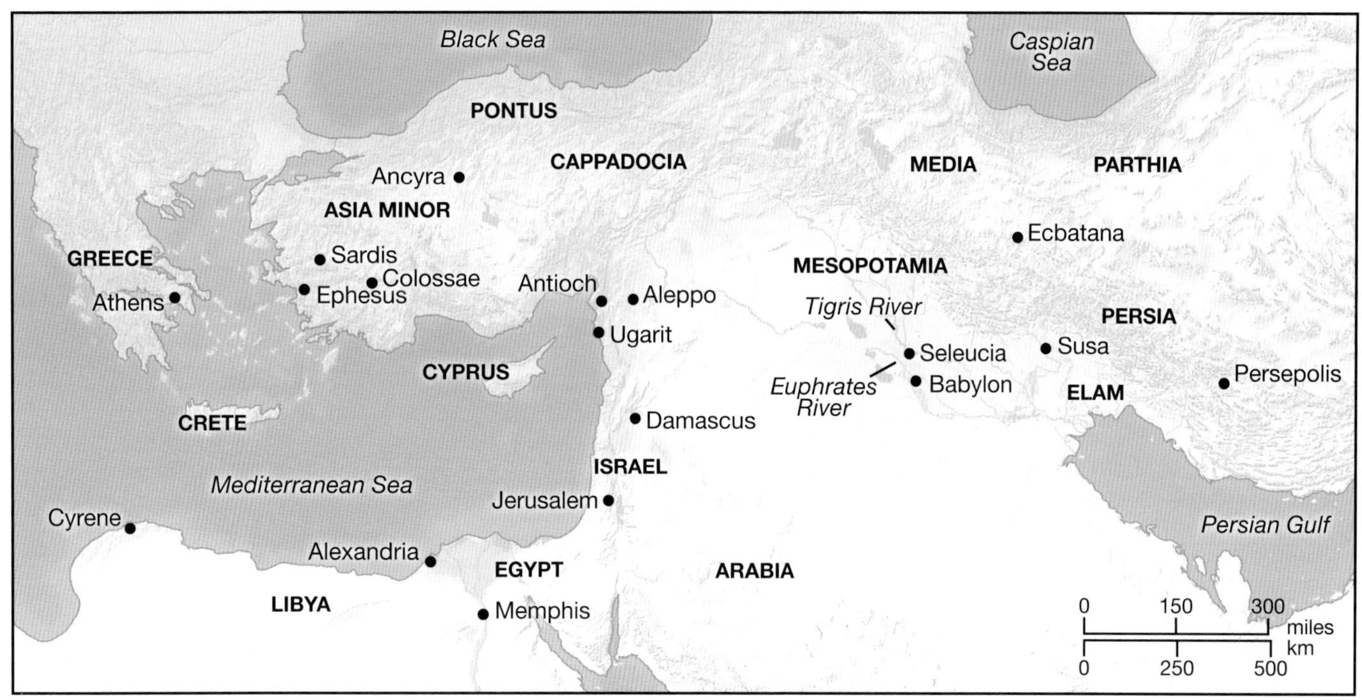

By the first century AD, Jewish communities in the Diaspora, the cities and lands outside of Israel, stretched across the known world.

- those for the first-ever Passover, the **Passover of Egypt** (Ex. 12:1–13, 21–23, 29–41); and
- those for how Passover should be celebrated in the years following, what we can call the **Passover of generations** (Ex. 12:14–20, 24–28, 42–49).[50]

The instructions for these two Passover celebrations are intertwined in the text of Exodus 12. It seems that when the first Passover event was recorded, there was already a concern about how it would be remembered and reenacted in the future.

The first Passover, the Passover of Egypt, was a home event shared by family and friends who slaughtered and ate the Passover lamb together. But the Passover of generations has a very different orientation. Only twice do the Hebrew Scriptures record how it was celebrated once the Israelites left Egypt, and both follow a provision added in Deuteronomy:

> You may not offer the Passover sacrifice within any of your towns that the Lord your God is giving you, but at the place that the Lord your God will choose, to make his name dwell in it, there you shall offer the Passover sacrifice, in the evening at sunset, at the time you came out of Egypt. And you shall cook it and eat it at the place that the Lord your God will choose. And in the morning you shall turn and go to your tents. (Deut. 16:5–7)

Here, we see how the yearly event was no longer home-centered but temple-centered, in Jerusalem, "at the place that the Lord your God will choose, to make his name dwell in it." Not only that, but in the two accounts of the Passover celebrated once Israel was in their land—one during the reign of Hezekiah (2 Chron. 30:1–27) and the other during the reign of Josiah (2 Chron. 35:1–19)—the priests and Levites took complete charge. They slaughtered the lambs, they dashed the lamb's blood on the altar, they roasted the lamb at the temple, and only then was it distributed to be eaten by the people who presumably were there, waiting in the precincts (2 Chron. 30:13–17; 35:10–13). Passover was no longer a home affair, in Egypt or anywhere else.

The Pilgrimage

After the return to the Land of Israel and the rebuilding of the temple, the power of Passover returned to the people. This was due in part to the rapid growth of the Jewish nation; the temple precincts could not easily accommodate the number of pilgrims arriving for the festival. But it was also in response to a challenge posed by Scripture from the very beginning of the holiday:

> At the end of 430 years, on that very day, all the hosts of the LORD went out from the land of Egypt. It was a night of watching by the LORD, to bring them out of the land of Egypt; so this same night is a night of watching kept to the LORD by all the people of Israel throughout their generations. (Ex. 12:41–42)

The challenge was to ensure that the significance of these events remained relevant for all the generations that followed. The solution was to remember the exodus events on every anniversary of the day that the first Passover took place with an annual "night of watching." In the first Passover in Egypt, Scripture tells us what happened during the all-night vigil: the lamb's blood put on the doorposts, the slaying of the Egyptian first born, and the preparations to leave Egypt at a moment's notice. But how was Israel to observe this vigil a year later, or centuries later, as they celebrated the Passover of generations? Was there a special liturgy to enhance the annual celebration? Scripture seems to assume that a dialogue between children and adults would take place during Passover:

> You shall observe this rite as a statute for you and for your sons forever. And when you come to the land that the LORD will give you, as he has promised, you shall keep this service. And when your children say to you, "What do you mean by this service?" you shall say, "It is the sacrifice of the LORD's Passover, for he passed over the houses of the people of Israel in Egypt, when he struck the Egyptians but spared our houses." (Ex. 12:24–27)

"Then they shall take some of the blood and put [the lamb's blood] on the two doorposts and the lintel of the houses.... And when I see the blood, I will pass over you, and no plague will befall you to destroy you, when I strike the land of Egypt" (Ex. 12:7, 13). *(The Signs on the Door* by James Tissot, c. 1896–1902)

This declaration became even more important during the Second Temple period when the majority of Jews lived outside the Land of Israel. For them, Passover became a significant way to express their Jewish identity while they were living as a minority among other peoples.

Whatever number we accept for how many people lived in Jerusalem before AD 70 or how many pilgrims worldwide came to Jerusalem on

Passover—the estimate of Josephus, Tacitus, or the Talmud, as previously mentioned—Jerusalem was in its heyday at the time.[51] How did the city and temple personnel cope with a large influx of pilgrims, each with their Passover lamb, in numbers never imagined during the Passovers of Hezekiah or Josiah? Primary sources from this period suggest a Passover celebration with more people participating and greater creative interaction during the night-long vigil not seen since the original exodus from Egypt.

The Passover Lamb

The Mishnah describes a kind of slaughterhouse production line manned by priests to handle the large number of lambs sacrificed for Passover:

> The Israelite killed the lamb; and the priest caught the blood. He would hand it to his colleague and his colleague would hand it to his colleague. And he would receive the full basin and give back the empty one. The priest nearest the altar would sprinkle it once over against the altar.[52]

During the Passover in the days of Hezekiah (seventh century BC), many participants had not properly consecrated themselves before offering their sacrifice, prompting the Levites to perform the duty (2 Chron. 30:17–19). But by the Second Temple period, this was no longer a concern. Archaeological evidence has uncovered several public ritual baths (*mikva'ot*) in the immediate vicinity of the temple. These ensured that the people, not the priests, could slaughter the lambs in a state of ritual purity themselves, after having been cleansed in the ritual baths. Philo of Alexandria (c. 20 BC–AD 50) justified this return to a hands-on observance:

> Now at other times the daily priests chosen from the people, being appointed for the slaughtering and taking care of them, performed the sacrifices. But at the Passover, here spoken of, the whole people together is honored with the priesthood, for all of them act for themselves in the performance of the sacrifice.[53]

Philo goes on to explain that "each house is at that time invested with the character and dignity of a temple" as all are properly purified; and the reason they gather is "not as they do to other entertainments, to gratify their bellies with wine and meat, but to fulfil their hereditary custom with prayer and songs of praise."[54]

Classical rabbinic literature adds details about the location of the meal: although the lambs were sacrificed in the temple precincts, they were cooked and eaten with the full Passover meal elsewhere: "Passover lamb sacrifices are slaughtered anywhere in the temple courtyard ... and are eaten anywhere in the city by any person together with any food."[55] Special Passover ovens for use by pilgrims could be found on the rooftops of all the lodgings in Jerusalem: "No one ever said to his fellow, 'I couldn't find an oven for roasting the Passover lamb in Jerusalem.'"[56]

Honi the Circle Maker (second century BC), the legendary rainmaker of classical rabbinic literature, implied that these ovens, which were made of clay, were out in the open when he boasted to the people of Jerusalem after they had begged him to pray for rain: "Bring in your Passover ovens so that they won't dissolve [in the rainstorm]."[57]

The Mishnah stipulates that the Passover lamb be eaten only on a full stomach after a full meal so that participants eat their portion in fulfillment of God's commandment and not because of their own hunger cravings. The minimum amount of the Passover lamb that one has to eat is a *kzayit*, the amount equal to the volume of a small olive.

One colorful description of the feast in Jerusalem is found in a folk saying recorded in the Jerusalem Talmud: "The Passover lamb is a *kzayit,* but the Hallel breaks roofs."[58] This saying implies that on Passover night everyone on their rooftops ate only the most miniscule amount of the Passover lamb, but the amount of Hallel—their praises of thanksgiving—that they rambunctiously sang to God was so outrageously huge that it could bring the house down!

The Last Supper

The description of Jesus' Last Supper recorded in the gospels of Matthew, Mark, and Luke is clearly in accord with sources found in classical rabbinic literature about Passover.

> On the first day of the Festival of Unleavened Bread, the disciples came to Jesus and asked, "Where do you want us to make preparations for you to eat the Passover?" He replied, "Go into the city to a certain man and tell him, 'The Teacher says: My appointed time is near. I am going to celebrate the Passover with my disciples at your house.'" So the disciples did as Jesus had directed them and prepared the Passover. (Matt. 26:17–19 NIV)[59]

Jesus and his disciples and other visitors to Jerusalem ate their Passover lambs outside the temple precincts. Preparations for the meal likely included using a special Passover oven on the rooftop, used only for this event. Two of the gospels emphasize that the setting for the Last Supper was in "a large upper room" (Luke 22:12; Mark 14:15). Therefore, after the feast, Jesus and his disciples easily could have climbed from there to the rooftop to eat their lamb on a full stomach, joining the rest of Jerusalem in celebrating their rooftop barbecues and singing Hallel to the heavens.

This portion of the Second Temple model at the Israel Museum in Jerusalem shows large houses with flat roofs on the upper, western part of the city. Tradition holds that this was the area where Jesus ate his last Passover meal. (Photo by Paul H. Wright)

In classical rabbinic literature, Hallel refers specifically to Psalms 113–118, with appropriate blessings to God before and after. The association of these psalms with Passover is found in the opening verses of Psalms 113 and 114:

- "Praise the Lord! Praise, O servants of the Lord" (Ps. 113:1)—that is, you were once servants (or slaves) of Pharaoh, but now you are servants of the Lord.
- "When Israel went out from Egypt, the house of Jacob from a people of strange language" (Ps. 114:1)—a clear reference to the exodus.

Even though there is no mention of songs of praise in connection with the Passover instructions in the Torah, singing did accompany the Passover celebrations of Hezekiah and Josiah (2 Chron. 30:21; 35:15). Hallel was recited not only on the rooftops of Jerusalem but also by the Levitical choir in the temple while the Passover lambs were slaughtered.[60] The book of Jubilees, a text dating to the mid-second century BC, also alludes to some type of praise and blessing on the first Passover:

> And all Israel was eating the flesh of the Passover lamb, and drinking the wine, and was lauding, and blessing, and giving thanks to the Lord God of their fathers, and was ready to go forth from under the yoke of Egypt, and from the evil bondage. And remember thou this day all the days of thy life, and observe it from year to year all the days of thy life, once a year, on its day, according to all the law.[61]

The New Testament records giving thanks and singing with the Last Supper:

> Then [Jesus] took a cup, and when he had given thanks, he gave it to them, and they all drank from it. "This is my blood of the covenant, which is poured out for many," he said to them. "Truly I tell you, I will not drink again from the fruit of the vine until that day when I drink it new in the kingdom of God." When they had sung a hymn, they went out to the Mount of Olives. (Mark 14:23–26 NIV)

The question quickly arises, was the Last Supper meal a Passover Seder?[62] The Seder is a set liturgy recited at the Passover Feast in a family setting. Its origins are in the Mishnah, an anthology of rabbinic traditions compiled around AD 200.[63] Most (if not all) of the material about the Seder, as it appears in the Mishnah, seems to have been an innovation of the sages after the year AD 70 following the destruction of the temple (though dating material in the Mishnah about the Seder is notoriously difficult).[64] Without a temple, so the reasoning goes, the sages created a liturgy to take the place of the sacrifice of the Passover lamb, something previously inseparable from the sacred temple service (Deut. 16:5–7). No temple, then no Passover lamb. And with no lamb, the Seder became the substitute.

On the other hand, both the New Testament and sources in classical rabbinic literature suggest that even while the temple was standing, different Jewish groups has already developed their own set liturgies for Passover. Some even used Greco-Roman symposium techniques to fulfill the commandment of an all-night Passover vigil. The descriptions of Passover night both in the gospel of Matthew and the Mishnah share the same basic elements which eventually developed into the rabbinic Seder of the home and the Communion ceremony of the Christian church. While Jesus' Last Supper meal certainly contained elements of the Passover Seder, it was an early variation of what we see in the Mishnah.

Let's consider this passage from the Mishnah about Rabban Gamaliel's observance of Passover:

> Rabban Gamaliel used to say, "Whoever does not make mention of these three things on Pesach does not fulfill his duty. And these are they: the Pesach, matzah, and bitter herbs. The Pesach/Passover sacrifice, because the Almighty passed over the houses of our fathers in Egypt. The matzah, because our fathers were redeemed in Egypt. The bitter herbs because the Egyptians embittered the lives of our fathers in Egypt."[65]

Here, the three symbolic foods of the Seder mentioned are:

- the Passover lamb,
- matzah (unleavened bread), and
- bitter herbs.

But who is this Gamaliel who taught that these Seder foods need to be understood as symbols? Scholars who believe the Mishnah reflects practices after AD 70 say that he was Rabban Gamaliel of Yavneh, president of the Sanhedrin who was only a young boy when the Second Temple was destroyed. Other scholars identify him as that Gamaliel's grandfather who lived while the Second Temple still stood—the same Gamaliel who defended the apostles before the Sanhedrin and whom Paul saw as one of his mentors (Acts 5:33–40; 22:1–3). If this latter view is correct, we would expect that Gamliel's description of the Seder and the description of the Last Supper in the gospels would complement each other, helping us to better understand how the Passover was celebrated during the Second Temple period. And they do indeed:

> And [Jesus] took a cup, and when he had given thanks he said, "Take this, and divide it among yourselves. For I tell you that from now on I will not drink of the fruit of the vine until the kingdom of God comes." And he took bread, and when he had given thanks, he broke it and gave it to them, saying, "This is my body, which is given for you. Do this in remembrance of me." And likewise the cup after they had eaten, saying, "This cup that is poured out for you is the new covenant in my blood." (Luke 22:17–20)

The account of Luke follows the basic Seder outline of Mishnah Pesachim: opening the feast by sanctifying the day with blessings over wine, followed by a blessing thanking God for bread, and then ending the meal with a cup of wine lifted up while saying "Grace After Meals," a liturgy of classical rabbinic literature, thanking God for food, the land of Israel, and Jerusalem. But more important is the use of wine and bread as symbols.

In the time of the Gospels, Jews preferred to eat and drink from vessels made from soft limestone. This was because limestone was deemed to remain ritually pure, while pottery could become impure. Stone vessels dating to the first century have been found in excavations throughout the land of ancient Israel, attesting to vibrant Jewish communities in Judea and Galilee. It is reasonable to assume that stone vessels were used for Passover meals and that the Cup of Blessing in the time of the New Testament may well have looked like these, now on display in Jerusalem's Rockefeller Museum. (Photo by Paul H. Wright)

What both Jesus and Rabban Gamaliel are doing at their respective Seders is not an exposition of Scripture (a midrash), as might be expected in a Jewish context, but teaching by using foods like the lamb, matzah, and bitter herbs, as well as wine and bread, as symbols that point toward a higher significance. Both these Seders should be seen as Jewish examples of Greco-Roman banquets where at times the food eaten was elevated to symbolic significance in the midst of philosophic discussions.[66]

On the other hand, lifting up what is called the Cup of Blessing in classical rabbinic literature for the "Grace After Meals" blessings is definitely a uniquely Jewish practice at the close of a feast and can be dated to as early as the first century AD, as evidenced in a letter written to the Corinthians by Paul, Gamaliel's former disciple:

> Therefore, my beloved, flee from idolatry. I speak as to sensible people; judge for yourselves what I say. The cup of blessing that we bless, is it not a participation in the blood of Christ? The bread that we break, is it not a participation in the body of Christ? (1 Cor. 10:14–16)

In fact, another passage by Paul in this same letter clarifies and complements the use of food as symbols by his teacher, Rabban Gamaliel. The rabbi would point to the matzah (the unleavened bread) and declare that its significance is "because our fathers were redeemed from Egypt."[67] How does matzah represent our redeemed fathers? Unleavened bread is without yeast, so it lacks an ingredient which rises or bloats the bread. Symbolically, then, matzah lacks something which bloats the ego; it's humble and redeemed. In the words of Paul:

> Cleanse out the old leaven that you may be a new lump, as you really are unleavened. For Christ, our Passover lamb, has been sacrificed. Let us therefore celebrate the festival, not with old leaven, the leaven of malice and evil, but with the unleavened bread of sincerity and truth. (1 Cor. 5:7–8)

SHAVUOT (FEAST OF WEEKS, PENTECOST)

Of the three pilgrimage holidays mentioned in the Torah, Shavuot, or the Feast of Weeks, seems to be the least important. It has no independently set date like the holidays of Passover and (as we will see later) Sukkot, the Feast of Booths. Rather, its date is calculated from seven weeks following the day after Passover, making the date of its celebration dependent on that of Passover.

This mosaic panel from the Dionysus mosaic in Sepphoris, Galilee, depicts a festive procession, its participants wearing leafy crowns and carrying baskets of fruit. Though pagan, the scene provides a visual echo of other festive processions in the ancient world, including the Shavuot and Sukkot pilgrimages to Jerusalem. (Photo by Paul H. Wright)

Also, Shavuot is only one day long, while Passover and Sukkot are each celebrated for seven days. Finally, the Torah connects Passover and Sukkot to events in the salvation history of Israel: Passover to the exodus and Sukkot to the forty years of wilderness wandering before entering the promised land. But the Hebrew Scriptures make no mention of any similar historical event whatsoever in connection with the feast day of Shavuot.

This lack of emphasis continues into the Second Temple period. In the time of the New Testament, Jerusalem was packed with pilgrims at Passover, each offering their sacrificial lamb. During the entire week of Sukkot, the streets of Jerusalem were filled with festivities on the holiday, which is often referred to in the Hebrew Scriptures and in the Mishnah as simply *HeHag*, "the pilgrimage holiday," that is, the holiday of rejoicing par excellence. Josephus relates that when the Roman general Cestius Gallus marched with his hordes from Antipatris to Lydda (AD 66), he found "the entire city deserted, for the whole population had gone up to Jerusalem for [Sukkot]."[68] No such reports exist for Shavuot.

But there is an event on Shavuot recorded in the New Testament book of Acts that suggests that as early as the fourth decade of the first century a historic significance had already been added to the holiday:

> When the day of Pentecost [Shavuot] arrived, [the disciples] were all together in one place. And suddenly there came from heaven a sound like a mighty rushing wind, and it filled the entire house where they were sitting. And divided tongues as of fire appeared to them and rested on each one of them. And they were all filled with the Holy Spirit and began to speak in other tongues as the Spirit gave them utterance. (Acts 2:1–4)

Why was this revelation of the Holy Spirit to the disciples specifically recorded as occurring on Pentecost? (*Pentecost* is the Greek name for the Feast of Shavuot.) Classical rabbinic literature suggests that Shavuot commemorates the revelation of God's presence at Sinai in the book of Exodus.[69] If this connection between Sinai and Shavuot was already well established by the time of the apostles, it seems very fitting that the revelation of the Holy Spirit should occur on the holiday of the revelation at Sinai.

But even when the sages, through careful reading of Scripture, were able to deduce a date connecting God's revelation at Sinai to Shavuot on the sixth day of the month of Sivan (the third month in the Jewish calendar), still the crowds did not flock to Jerusalem in droves specifically for the holiday. Rather, they came to Jerusalem throughout the following weeks and months over the four-month period between Shavuot and Sukkot. Shavuot is also called Yom HaBikkurim, "the day of the

David playing a lyre, depicted on a mosaic from the sixth-century synagogue in Gaza. In the words of 2 Samuel 23:1, David was "the sweet psalmist of Israel." (Photo by Paul H. Wright)

firstfruits" (Num. 28:26), and during those four months, delegation after delegation from different parts of the Land of Israel brought their baskets of firstfruits offerings to the temple in Jerusalem.[70] In this light, we should probably think that the crowds that were in Jerusalem for Pentecost (described in Acts 2) were composed of people from the Diaspora who were already living in the city (based on the phrase "Now there were dwelling in Jerusalem Jews, devout men from every nation under heaven" in Acts 2:5), plus early-bird visitors who arrived at the start of the months-long pilgrimage process.

The Mishnah reports that people of each specific region within Israel brought their firstfruits to Jerusalem as a group, camping out in the public square of that region's capital city the night before their pilgrimage, from places as far as Galilee or the Golan (Gaulanitis).[71] Early the next morning, as they began their journey together toward Jerusalem, their appointed leader would proclaim, "Arise, and let us go up to Zion, to the LORD our God" (Jer. 31:6). Once they entered the gates of the temple in Jerusalem, a Levitical choir greeted them with a rendition of Psalm 30, beginning with "I will extol you, O LORD, for you have drawn me up and have not let my foes rejoice over me" (Ps. 30:1 [Hebrew v. 2]).

Why were these particular verses chosen to enhance the pilgrims' trek to the temple? What do they have to do with bringing firstfruits to Jerusalem? The answer is in their biblical context:

> Again I will build you, and you shall be built,
>
> O virgin Israel!
>
> Again you shall adorn yourself with tambourines
>
> and shall go forth in the dance of the merrymakers.
>
> Again you shall plant vineyards on the mountains of Samaria;
>
> the planters shall plant
>
> and shall enjoy the fruit.
>
> For there shall be a day when watchmen will call
>
> in the hill country of Ephraim:
>
> "Arise, and let us go up to Zion,
>
> to the LORD our God." ...
>
> Then shall the young women rejoice in the dance,
>
> and the young men and the old shall be merry.
>
> I will turn their mourning into joy;

A cluster of grapes, a bunch of pomegranates, and a palm heavy with dates adorn lintel stones from the fifth-century synagogue at Capernaum. Pilgrims brought summer fruit such as these to the temple as firstfruits offerings. (Photos by Paul H. Wright)

I will comfort them, and give them gladness
for sorrow.

I will feast the soul of the priests with
abundance,

and my people shall be satisfied with my
goodness, declares the LORD."

Thus says the LORD:

"A voice is heard in Ramah,

lamentation and bitter weeping.

Rachel is weeping for her children;

she refuses to be comforted for her children,

because they are no more."

Thus says the LORD:

"Keep your voices from weeping,

and your eyes from tears,

for there is a reward for your work,
declares the LORD,

and they shall come back from the land
of the enemy.

There is hope for your future,
declares the LORD,

and your children shall come back to their own
country." (Jer. 31:4–6, 13–17)

A Psalm of David. A song at the dedication of
the temple.

I will extol you, O LORD, for you drawn me up

and have not let my foes rejoice over me....

You have turned for me my mourning into
dancing;

you have loosed my sackcloth

and clothed me with gladness,

that my glory may sing your praise and not
be silent.

O LORD my God, I will give thanks to you
forever! (Ps. 30:1, 11–12)

Both of these passages were well known to those firstfruits pilgrims who lived during the glory days of the Second Temple period. Predicting the destruction of Jerusalem and the First Temple, Jeremiah had promised that one day there would be an end to the exile, Jerusalem would be rebuilt, and the products of renewed agricultural activities in the Land of Israel would be brought up to Jerusalem. This was following the watchmen's proclamation: "Arise, and let us go up to Zion, to the LORD our God" (Jer. 31:6). When the pilgrims began their journey and heard that wake-up verse from Jeremiah, they would have considered themselves as the living fulfillment of his prophecy! More soberly, they also would have been reminded that Jerusalem was not a gift to be taken for granted; as a people, they had lost it once and could lose it again. Then, when the pilgrims were finishing their journey, they heard the Levitical choir singing the words of Psalm 30, a song for the dedication of the temple, a temple that they had once lost but where now God had "turned ... mourning into dancing." Again, they were reminded of how they themselves were living proof of these words. They were truly living the dream: "When the LORD restored the fortunes of Zion, we were like those who dream" (Ps. 126:1).

SUKKOT (FEAST OF BOOTHS)

What most clearly connects the three pilgrimage feasts of the Bible is not historical events but the agricultural year of the Land of Israel. Passover coincides with the barley harvest and Shavuot falls during the time of the wheat harvest. In the months between Shavuot and Sukkot, the firstfruits of the various kinds of fruit trees throughout Israel would ripen at different times, with Sukkot marking the end of the agricultural year. Clearly, it was a time when "you will be altogether joyful" (Deut. 16:15). Already in the Torah, we find Sukkot blessed with joyous commandments: take "the fruit of splendid trees, branches of palm trees and boughs of leafy trees and willows of the brook" and "dwell in booths [*sukkot*] for seven days" (Lev. 23:40, 42).

Ceremonies of Water and Light

During the time of the Second Temple, new rituals were added to the celebration of Sukkot. One of these was that each morning following the first day of the week-long festival, water was drawn from the pool of Siloam in Jerusalem and then offered as a libation in a ceremony of pouring the water on the altar at the temple. This was something new, since the only liquid poured on the altar mentioned in Scripture was wine (Lev. 23:13).

Another new ritual was that each evening there was an all-night outdoor celebration called Simchat Beit HaSho'evah, "Joy of the House of the Drawing of Water." According to the Mishnah, "He who never has seen the joy of the Beit HaSho'evah has never in his life seen joy."[72] At night, the city was so brightly lit that there was not a courtyard in Jerusalem that did not reflect its light.[73] It was said that a woman could even sort her wheat grain by this light![74] Even the wise sages of Israel let their hair down and danced ecstatically before the Lord:

> It was related of Rabban Shimon Ben Gamaliel (the president of the Sanhedrin) that when he would rejoice at the Celebration of the Place of the Drawing of the Water, he would take eight

"The next day the large crowd that had come to the feast [of Passover/Unleavened Bread] heard that Jesus was coming to Jerusalem. So they took branches of palm trees and went out to meet him" (John 12:12). The crowd shouted lines from the Hallel, which is sung on Israel's three great pilgrimage feasts. (*Christ's Entrance to Jerusalem* by Hippolyte Flandrin in Saint-Germain-des-Prés, Paris, 1842–1848) (Onyshchenko/Shutterstock)

flaming torches and toss one and catch another, juggling them, and, though all were in the air at the same time, they would not touch each other.[75]

The biblical associations were powerful:

> With joy you will draw water from the wells of salvation. (Isa. 12:3)
>
> Behold, how good and pleasant it is
>   when brothers dwell in unity!
>
> It is like the precious oil on the head,
>   running down on the beard,
> on the beard of Aaron,
>   running down on the collar of his robes!
>
> It is like the dew of Hermon,
>   which falls on the mountains of Zion!
>
> For there the LORD has commanded
>   the blessing,
>   life forevermore. (Ps. 133:1–3)

Water was central to the holiday of Sukkot because, ideally, in the Land of Israel the rainy season would begin right after the feast. But in reality, more often than not, the rains were late and the summer drought continued after the holiday. And in the Land of Israel, rainfall was often a matter of life and death.

Jesus and Sukkot

The pool of Siloam, where the waters for the ceremony were drawn, is also featured in Jesus' miraculous healing of the blind man in the gospel of John:

> As he passed by, he saw a man blind from birth. And his disciples asked him, "Rabbi, who sinned, this man or his parents, that he was born blind?" Jesus answered, "It was not that this man sinned, or his parents, but that the works of God might be displayed in him. We must work the works of him who sent me while it is day; night is coming, when no one can work. As long as I am in the world, I am the light of the world." Having said these things, he spat on the ground and made mud with the saliva. Then he anointed the man's eyes with the mud and said to him, "Go, wash in the pool of Siloam" (which means Sent). So he went and washed and came back seeing. (John 9:1–7)

According to an earlier chapter in the gospel, Jesus expanded the imagery of the waters of God's salvation with a bold pronouncement:

> On the last day of the feast, the great day, Jesus stood up and cried out, "If anyone thirsts, let him come to me and drink. Whoever believes in me, as the Scripture has said, 'Out of his heart will flow rivers of living water.'" (John 7:37–38)

The "feast" in this verse is the great feast, Sukkot (John 7:2), and the phrase "the great day" most likely refers to Hoshana Rabbah, "the Great Hosanna," which in classical rabbinic literature is the name for the last day of Sukkot.[76] Jesus' message is especially fitting on Sukkot, for this occasion is not only the most joyous holiday on the Jewish calendar but, according to the Hebrew Scriptures, will also become a joyous event for all of humanity at the end of days: "Then everyone who survives of all the nations that have come against Jerusalem shall go up year after year to worship the King, the Lord of hosts, and to keep the Feast of Booths" (Zech. 14:16).

The Hallel

Another innovation of the sages of classical rabbinic literature for Sukkot was to sing the Hallel (Psalms 113–118). Indeed, the sages taught that the Hallel was to be sung on each of the three pilgrimage feasts: at the Passover Seder and on the first day of the Feast of Unleavened Bread; in the morning of Shavuot; and on Sukkot. But only on Sukkot was the Hallel chanted on all eight days of the festivities, including on the final day, known as Shemini Atzeret, "Eighth Day of Assembly."[77]

One of the many examples of the world of ideas shared by classical rabbinic literature and the New Testament is how both understand certain verses found at the end of the Hallel as a fulfillment of the messianic line of David. According to the gospels of Matthew, Mark, and Luke, when Jesus entered Jerusalem as a pilgrim, he was greeted as an heir of the house of David the son of Jesse by crowds of people shouting out Psalm 118:26.[78] The rabbis typically read this verse in the context of the earlier verses 22 and 23, and it is likely that the crowds who so enthusiastically welcomed Jesus had these in mind as well:

> The stone that the builders rejected
> has become the cornerstone.
>
> This is the LORD's doing;
> it is marvelous in our eyes....
>
> Blessed is he who comes in the name
> of the LORD!
>
> We bless you from the house of the LORD.
> (Ps. 118:22–23, 26)

In a parallel passage in the Talmud, these verses from Psalm 118 are recited by David himself, by members of his family, and by Samuel the prophet.[79]

Talmud	Hallel: Psalm 118
"I will give thanks to you, for you answered me" was said by David.	verse 21
"The stone which the builders have rejected has become the chief cornerstone" was said by Jesse.	verse 22
"This is from the Lord; it is wondrous in our eyes" was said by David's brothers.	verse 23
"This is the day which the Lord has made; let us rejoice and be happy" was said by Samuel.	verse 24
"We beseech you, Lord, save now" was said by David's brothers.	verse 25
"We beseech you, Lord, make us prosper now" was said by David.	verse 25
"Blessed be he who comes in the name of the Lord" was recited by Jesse.	verse 26
"We bless you out of the house of the Lord" was said by Samuel.	verse 26
"The Lord is God, and has given us light" was said by all of them.	verse 27
"Order the festival procession with boughs, even to the horns of the altar" was said by Samuel.	verse 27
"You are my God, and I will give thanks to you" was said by David.	verse 28
"You are my God, I will exalt you" was said by all of them.	verse 28

The House of David, the waters of Siloam, and Sukkot were thoroughly connected in the minds of the Jews in the Second Temple period as they waited in expectation of the final redemption prophesied long ago: "In that day I will raise up the booth [*sukkah*] of David that is fallen and repair its breaches, and raise up its ruins and rebuild it as in the days of old" (Amos 9:11).

YOM TERUAH (ROSH HASHANAH) AND YOM KIPPUR

The Torah mentions five annual occasions in the biblical calendar that are holy convocations for which the *melakhah* (work) prohibitions of Shabbat apply (Lev. 23:1–44; Num. 28:16–29:39). Three of these are grouped together elsewhere in the Torah as pilgrimage feasts (Ex. 23:14–17; Deut. 16:1–16) and occur at times spread out over the first seven months of the year:

- Passover (Pesach)
- Shavuot (Weeks)
- Sukkot (Booths)

The remaining two occasions fall just nine days apart, in the seventh month and just prior to Sukkot:

- Yom Teruah (Day of Blasting)
- Yom Kippur (Day of Atonement)[80]

There is no indication in the Hebrew Scriptures as to how these are related to each other or to the pilgrimage feasts, nor does Scripture mention all the details about how and why they are to be observed.

What Scripture does say is that the first day of the seventh month is the day of the blowing of trumpets, believed to be *shofars*, rams' horns (Num. 29:1; Lev. 23:24). Scripture provides no other information about any other activity for that day other than that which is designated by its name: sound the ram's horn.

The tenth day of the same month is the Day of Atonement, Yom Kippur (Lev. 23:27). On this day, the high priest performed an annual cleansing of the sanctuary of God and of the people; about this day, the Torah speaks in great detail. On this same day, according to Scripture, all Israel was to "afflict yourselves" (Lev. 16:29–30; 23:27, 32; Num. 29:7).

By the Second Temple period, the mysteries about these two special events leading up to Sukkot were clarified. The Mishnah tells us that the first day of the seventh month was now called Rosh HaShanah, "the first day of the year" and it commemorated

Although the instrument that was sounded on the first day of the seventh month is not mentioned by name in Leviticus or Numbers, most scholars assume that it was the shofar, a ram's horn. The shofar was also trumpeted on the Day of Atonement in the Jubilee year, once every fifty years (Lev. 25:9). (Photo by Paul H. Wright)

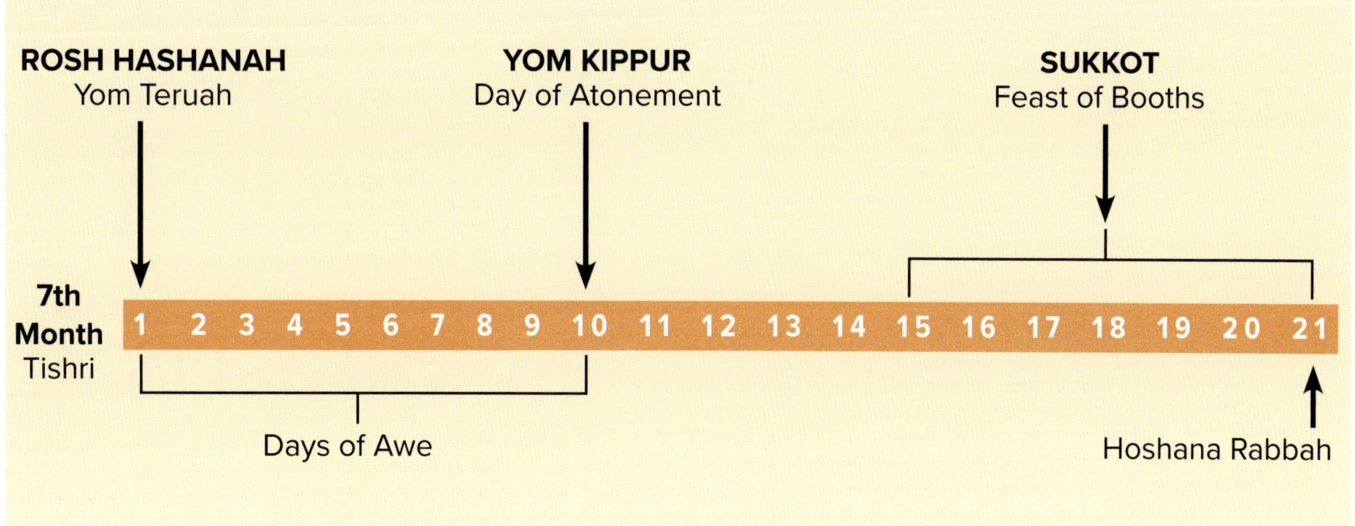

the day the world was created.[81] Every year, on the anniversary of creation, the shofar was blown to announce Judgment Day, the day when God the creator reviews his works and decides whether we, and our planet, are still worthy of existence.[82] This began a ten-day period of intense repentance and penitence called the Days of Awe. These Days of Awe lasted through Yom Kippur, a day of self-affliction and fasting that ended with God's pronouncement of judgment for the year to come.[83] The sages of classical rabbinic literature defined the biblical command "to afflict yourselves" as refraining from several common activities: eating and drinking, bathing, anointing one's body with oil, wearing sandals, and marital intercourse.[84]

Only five days later came the most festive holiday on the calendar, Sukkot! Observing an intensely somber day of judgment so close to an exuberant celebration ending the agricultural year might certainly seem unusual, until we realize that the themes of these holy days overlap in more than one way. If, according to the rituals of Leviticus, the high priest was able to cleanse the temple and the people of Israel from all sin on the Day of Atonement, everyone would begin the new year with a clean slate. This makes a joyous festival less than a week later more than appropriate. But there is more. The overarching concern of Sukkot is that rainwater in the upcoming weeks will begin to fall, the land will be replenished, and people can live. For ancient Israel, water was both the symbol and reality of life and death, a constant reflection of the consequences of Judgment Day. The prayers for rain at Sukkot were considered worthy and effective only after the preceding ten-day period of introspection and penitence from Rosh HaShanah through Yom Kippur.

Tu b'Av, Yom Kippur, and the Grape Harvest

Tu b'Av, the fifteenth day of the month of Av (the fifth month in the Jewish calendar), was a minor Jewish holiday that marked the beginning of the grape harvest. The end of the grape harvest was marked by Yom Kippur two months later. This agricultural cycle was a natural link that connected the two days, highlighting the love of God for his people in the process. Two very practical questions about what people actually did on Yom Kippur will help us see this connection.

First, how long did it take for the high priest to complete the rituals for the Day of Atonement that are described in Leviticus 16? Probably a few hours at most. Classical rabbinic literature suggests that many Jews came to the temple precincts on the morning of Yom Kippur to encourage their high priest on his way to the Holy of Holies, the inner sanctum of the temple.[85]

Second, what did the people do in the afternoon on this, the most holy day in the calendar? One popular event is described in Mishnah Ta'anit:

> Rabban Shimon Ben Gamaliel taught: There were no more festive days in Israel than Tu b'Av and Yom Kippur, for on those [two] days [two months apart] the daughters of Jerusalem [Song 2:7] would go out to the vineyards in borrowed white dresses in order not to embarrass those who did not own their own white dresses.... The daughters of Jerusalem would go out and dance in the vineyards and what would they say? "Young man, lift up your eyes and discern what you're choosing for yourself. Do not look for beauty but for family. 'Grace is deceptive, beauty is illusory; it is for her fear of God that a woman is to be praised. Extol her for the fruits of her hands' work and let her deeds praise her in the gates' [Prov. 31:30–31]. And it is also written: 'O maidens of Zion, go out and gaze on King Solomon wearing the crown that his mother gave him on his wedding day and on the happiest day of his heart'" [Song 3:11].
>
> "On his wedding day"—that is the building of the Temple. May it be rebuilt speedily in our day. Amen.[86]

"Again you shall plant vineyards on the mountains of Samaria" (Jer. 31:5). Unlike neatly trellised vineyards common in most parts of the world today, vines in ancient Israel grew close to the ground, their leaves full and tendrils long. This vine is in the hill country of Samaria, east of the site of ancient Shiloh. (Photo by Paul H. Wright)

The original social mixer for the opposite sexes initiated by "the daughters of Jerusalem" happened not just once but twice a year. Tu b'Av occurs on the Hebrew calendar two months before Yom Kippur. As any good vintner in the northern hemisphere will tell you: grapes are harvested twice a year, once in the month of August and two months later in October, corresponding on the Hebrew calendar to Tu b'Av and Yom Kippur. According to the Mishnah, grapes and wine were among the firstfruits one brought in a basket to the temple between Shavuot and Sukkot.[87] These grapes were harvested during the biannual "daughters of Jerusalem dancing in the vineyards" wine festival. Vineyards are an idyllic, romantic setting for matchmaking in any era, but classical rabbinic literature in the Second Temple period, commenting on the Song of Songs, also shows that they were the setting of God's love for his people, as this selection of verses makes clear:

> I am my beloved's,
> and his desire is for me....
>
> Come, my beloved,
> let us go out into the fields
> and lodge in the [henna plants];
> let us go out early to the vineyards
> and see whether the vines have budded,

> whether the grape blossoms have opened
> and the pomegranates are in bloom.
>
> There I will give you my love.
> (Song 7:10–12)

And the imagery of maidens of Israel dancing in the vineyards with tambourines in their hands, like Miriam and the women of Israel at the Red Sea, was the embodiment of God's redemptive power promised by Jeremiah:

> Again I will build you, and you shall be built,
> O virgin Israel!
>
> Again you shall adorn yourself with tambourines
> and shall go forth in the dance of the merrymakers.
>
> Again you shall plant vineyards
> on the mountains of Samaria;
> the planters shall plant
> and shall enjoy the fruit.
>
> For there shall be a day when
> watchmen will call
> in the hill country of Ephraim:
> "Arise, and let us go up to Zion,
> to the LORD our God." …
>
> Then shall the young women rejoice in the dance,
> and the young men and the old shall be merry.
> (Jer. 31:4–6, 13)

NEW FESTIVE DATES

In addition to Tu b'Av, the Second Temple period saw many other new festive dates added to the calendar, to a large extent under the influence of the Hasmonean dynasty founded by the Maccabees. For almost a century (mid-second to mid-first centuries BC), the Hasmoneans were able to create a semi-independent Jewish state in the Land of Israel. One document preserved from this time is Megillat Ta'anit, "the Scroll of Fasting," which lists thirty-five calendar dates that the Maccabees declared as public holidays and on which it was forbidden to fast. Personal days of fasting, which were a common practice of piety, gave way to the public days of feasting.[88]

Many of the new dates commemorated military victories of the Maccabees, but these were forgotten over time. Two holidays, however, Purim and Hanukkah, became popular, eventually developing special customs and practices that remain part of their celebration to this day. Both received extra attention in the Scroll of Fasting because the scroll forbade public mourning (eulogizing the dead) on the days of Purim and Hanukkah.

Queen Esther by Andrea del Castagno (c. 1450)

PURIM

Purim, celebrated on the fourteenth day of the month of Adar (the twelfth month), did not receive general acceptance right away, according to classical rabbinic literature. The sages debated whether the book of Esther, which relates the story of Purim and the command to celebrate the day (Est. 9:16–32), was written through the inspiration of the Holy Spirit and as a result deserved to be part of the biblical canon.[89] Moreover, the story of the book of Esther was centered in Susa, the capital of Persia, far from the Land of Israel, and this fact needed to be tweaked a bit for the book to be accepted as Scripture in Jerusalem. The solution was ingenious: Esther 9:18 clearly states that the city of Susa and Susa alone had its own special feast day to celebrate Purim, the fifteenth day of Adar, while everyone else celebrated the day prior. The Mishnah, however, expands the celebration on the fifteenth to include not just Susa but "all cities walled during the time of Joshua son of Nun."[90] Because Jerusalem was chief among all walled cities, Purim became an important holiday for its residents as well.

Today's well-known and beloved custom of Purim as a drinking feast doesn't appear in classical rabbinic literature until well after AD 200,[91] and the tradition of dressing up in masquerade costumes is an even later (medieval) invention. So how was Purim celebrated in the Second Temple period? The main observance on Purim prior to AD 70 was the public reading of the Scroll of Esther in every town and village where possible. As a result, an entire volume of the Mishnah, one out of sixty-three, is dedicated to the public reading of *Megillat Esther*, the Scroll of Esther. Its name is *Megillah*, "the Scroll," par excellence.

HANUKKAH (FEAST OF DEDICATION)

Hanukkah, which means "dedication," commemorated the cleansing and rededication of the temple in Jerusalem after the Maccabean victory in the second century BC over the Seleucid (Greek) Empire that had defiled the sacred site. Interestingly, Hanukkah is nearly ignored in classical rabbinic literature. The only significant mention is a long afterthought about lighting the Hanukkah lamp in an otherwise detailed discussion about lighting the lamp on Shabbat:[92]

> For when the Greeks entered the temple, they defiled all the oil found there; but when the kingdom of the Hasmonean dynasty prevailed and defeated them, they searched throughout the entire temple until just one cruse of oil was found bearing the seal of the high priest. However, the cruse had only enough oil to light for one day. Yet a miracle occurred: they were able to light from it for eight days. The year after, these days were established as festive days with [the recitation of] Hallel and thanksgiving.[93]

The miracle of the Hanukkah lights, which most people associate with Hanukkah today, is in fact not mentioned in any of the books of the Maccabees. All discussions about these lights in classical rabbinic literature appear in passages that are dated only after the Hasmonean dynasty.[94] The Maccabees may never have even celebrated the rededication of the temple by lighting a special lamp. And the Hasmoneans probably knew nothing about the miracle of the small vial of oil found in the temple that lasted for eight days, as mentioned in classical rabbinic literature.

How then was Hanukkah celebrated during most of the Second Temple period? What might the celebration have looked like when Jesus was in Jerusalem for Hanukkah (John 10:22–23)? The

Mosaic of a synagogue menorah

These large stones from the Second Temple complex fell onto a street running parallel to the temple compound wall, a result of Rome's destruction of Jerusalem in the year AD 70. (Photo by Seth Aronstam/Shutterstock)

element that made the holiday special for the Maccabees and their descendants living in the first century AD was the Maccabees' radical decision to recite the Hallel for the eight-day period of Hanukkah. Up to that time, the Hallel was only part of the liturgies of the three pilgrimage feasts that prohibited *melakhah* (work). But the Maccabees' urgent need for a return to normalcy after a long and bloody war for independence led them to a liturgical innovation that would have been unthinkable in prior generations:

> The Jews celebrated [Hanukkah] joyfully for eight days as on the feast of Booths, remembering how, a little while before, they had spent the feast of Booths living like wild animals in the mountains and in caves. Carrying rods entwined with leaves, beautiful branches and palms, they sang hymns of grateful praise [Hallel] to him who had successfully brought about the purification of his own place.[95]

So the first Hanukkah was a make-up date for the ultimate joyous holiday of Sukkot that the Maccabees had missed two months prior while they were still at war and Jerusalem and the temple were in the hands of their enemies. When the Maccabees liberated the temple, they celebrated as if it were Sukkot. While palm branches were never again brought to Jerusalem as part of Hanukkah celebrations, a precedent was set of reciting the Hallel for eight days of thanksgiving—as it was on the seven days of Sukkot plus Shemini Atzeret, the Eighth Day of Assembly.[96]

DAYS OF FASTING

The only set day of fasting mentioned in the Torah is the Day of Atonement, Yom Kippur. But with the return to the Land of Israel following the Jews' exile in the sixth century BC, there was cause for more days of fasting. Zechariah 8:19 lists four separate fast days that apparently were observed throughout the seventy years of exile.[97] Because they marked stages of Babylon's destruction of Jerusalem, these fasts were not part of Israel's prior history and so do not appear elsewhere in the Hebrew Scriptures.

- **The fast of the tenth month**—the tenth of Tevet. This fast marked the date on which the Babylonian siege of Jerusalem began (2 Kings 25:1).
- **The fast of the fourth month**—the seventeenth of Tammuz. This fast came six months after the tenth-month fast and marked the date on which the walls of Jerusalem were breached and a three-week battle ensued (2 Kings 25:3–4).
- **The fast of the fifth month**—the ninth of Av (which is a translation of the more common Hebrew term *Tisha b'Av*). This fast marked the date on which Jerusalem fell to Babylon and the temple was destroyed (2 Kings 25:8–10).
- **The fast of the seventh month**—the fast of Gedaliah. This fast was observed on the third day of Tishri, the date on which Gedaliah, the Jewish governor appointed by King Nebuchadnezzar to rule Israel, was assassinated, putting an end to any hope of Jewish independence under the Babylonians (2 Kings 25:25–26).

Taking the words of the psalmist seriously, for seven decades the Jewish exiles in Babylonia refused to forget Jerusalem:

> How shall we sing the LORD's song
> in a foreign land?
>
> If I forget you, O Jerusalem,
> let my right hand forget its skill!
> (Ps. 137:4–5 [Hebrew vv. 5–6])

But once the temple was rebuilt and Jerusalem was once again a reality, a serious discussion arose about continuing these particular days of fasting.

> Now the people of Bethel had sent Sharezer and Regem-melech and their men to entreat the favor of the LORD, saying to the priests of the house of the LORD of hosts and the prophets, "Should I weep and abstain in the fifth month, as I have done for so many years?" Then the word of the LORD of hosts came to me: "Say to all the people of the land and the priests, 'When you fasted and mourned in the fifth month and in the seventh, for these seventy years, was it for me that you fasted? And when you eat and when you drink, do you not eat for yourselves and drink for yourselves?'" (Zech. 7:2–6)

The rhetorical question leaves it up to the people to decide whether they needed to continue fasting once their temple was rebuilt and Jerusalem was in their hands. Their answer is implied by the fact that we have no evidence that any of these four fast days were canceled in the Second Temple period. Indeed, classical rabbinic literature suggests that the fast of the Ninth of Av was observed while the Second Temple was still standing.[98] In the centuries following, the Ninth of Av (Tisha b'Av) became equal in status to the Day of Atonement, with fasting from sunset to sunset; it, too, was—and still is—a time of national soul searching, parallel to personal repentance and cleansing. The other three fasts became minor fast days, observed from sunrise to sunset only.

A different type of public fast also appears in the Second Temple period, one without any set date on the calendar. All too frequently, the Land of Israel faced drought during the expected rainy season between Sukkot and Passover. In the face of impending disaster when the drought was severe, public fast days were declared. The seriousness of the situation and the desperation of the people is clear, for an entire volume of the Mishnah is dedicated to this type of fast:

> What is the order of service for fast days? The Holy [Torah] Ark [with its scrolls] is taken out to the open square of the city. And ashes are placed on the Ark, on the head of the president of the Sanhedrin and on the head of its chief justice. And everyone else then puts ashes on his own head. The elder among them addresses them with words of admonition: "Thus, our brethren, Scripture does not say of the people of Nineveh, 'And God saw their sackcloth and their fasting,' but, 'and God saw their deeds, how they were turning back from their evil ways' [Jonah 3:10]. And in the Prophets it is said, 'And rend your heart and not your garments.'"[99]

From 586 BC, the year of the estruction of the First Temple, fast days as public memorials for past

The Jerusalem temple complex in the first century AD, built by Herod the Great, as viewed from the Mount of Olives. (Art by Balage Balogh)

national tragedies were added to the Jewish calendar, as well as fast days for impending national disasters like droughts. The mood was similar to that of the Day of Atonement, with prayer and fasting helping the individual and the entire community reconnect to themselves, their tradition, their history, and their God.

During festive times the presence of God was tangible and exhilarating: celebrating the Passover lamb, dancing during Sukkot, or marching to Jerusalem with overflowing baskets of firstfruits. But while the Second Temple was still standing—and certainly after it was gone—there were times when the people of the land felt disconnected to their Father in heaven and needed to fast. Fasting and feasting are two sides of the same coin. The quietude and contemplation of the four Jerusalem fast days, the Judgment Days of Rosh HaShanah, and Yom Kippur could bring people closer to their Creator than the exuberant, even raucous, gatherings of the three pilgrimage feasts.

Could someone mourn meaningfully on the Ninth of Av (Tisha b'Av), marking the date of Jerusalem's fall, when Jerusalem was again a thriving city and the Second Temple was still standing? The answer is yes. But for those who were uncomfortable doing so, Zechariah had a reassuring prophecy. A time was coming at the end of days when God's people would love both truth and peace, when tolerance would fill the land, and when fasts would become feasts:

> Thus says the Lord of hosts: The fast of the fourth month and the fast of the fifth and the fast of the seventh and the fast of the tenth shall be to the house of Judah seasons of joy and gladness and cheerful feasts. Therefore love truth and peace. (Zech. 8:19)

Notes for Chapter 2

1 Josephus, *Jewish War* vi.423–26.

2 *b. Pesachim* 64b. See also *Tosefta Pesachim* 4:15. For an analysis of the sociological and legislative implications of this huge influx of pilgrims to Jerusalem, see Daniel Sperber, "Social Legislation in Jerusalem during the Latter Part of the Second Temple," *Journal for the Study of Judaism* 6/1 (1975), 86–95.

3 For a summary of texts, see David Instone-Brewer, *Traditions of the Rabbis from the Era of the New Testament*, vol. 1: *Prayer and Agriculture* (Grand Rapids, Mich.: Eerdmans, 2004), 1–27.

4 The Mishnah, Tosefta, Jerusalem Talmud, and Babylonian Talmud are all organized according to the sixty-three volume names of the Mishnah. When citing these works, therefore, the individual volumes, or tractates, are preceded by the following italicized letters: *m.* for the Mishnah; *t.* for the Tosefta; *y.* for the Jerusalem Talmud; and *b.* for the Babylonian Talmud.

5 Instone-Brewer, *Traditions of the Rabbis*, 28–40, suggests guidelines for ascertaining the date of various customs or traditions mentioned in classical rabbinic literature.

6 Avner Ecker, "Dining with Herod," in *Herod the Great: The King's Final Journey*, ed. by Silvia Rozenberg and David Mevorah (Jerusalem: The Israel Museum, 2013), 66–79; Adam Kolman Marshak, *The Many Faces of Herod the Great* (Grand Rapids, Mich.: Eerdmans, 2015), 284–294.

7 *b. Beitzah* 16a; author's translation.

8 Julian Morgenstern, "The Calendars of Ancient Israel," *Hebrew Union College Annual* 19 (1934), 15–28; Roland de Vaux, *Ancient Israel* (New York: McGraw-Hill, 1961), 183. See also Shemaryahu Talmon, "Reckoning the Sabbath in the First and the Early Second Temple Period—From the Evening or the Morning?" in *Sabbath: Idea, History, Reality*, ed. by Gerald J. Blidstein (Beer Sheva: Ben Gurion University of the Negev Press, 2004), 9–32.

9 This is evidenced in the books of Enoch (c. 400 BC) and Jubilees (c. 150 BC). Solomon Buber, ed., *Midrash Psalms* (Vilnius, 1891; repr. Jerusalem: Vahshal, 1977), 230.

10 The change, which was already present as early as the late first century AD, was codified in Canon 29 of the Council of Laodicea (363–364): "Christians must not judaize by resting on the Sabbath, but must work on that day, rather honoring the Lord's Day; and, if they can, resting then as Christians. But if any shall be found to be judaizers, let them be anathema from Christ;" *Nicene and Post-Nicene Fathers*, Second Series, vol. 14: *The Seven Ecumenical Councils,* ed. Philip Schaff and Henry Wace (New York: Charles Scribner's Sons, 1900), 148. See also Philip Schaff, *History of the Christian Church*, vol. 2: *Ante-Nicene Christianity* (New York: Charles Scribener's Sons, 1930), 201–205; and Jacques B. Doukhan, *Israel and the Church: Two Voices for the Same God* (Peabody, Mass.: Hendrickson, 2002), 41–45.

11 *m. Peah* 8:7; *m. Eruvin* 8:2; *b. Shabbat* 118a.

12 *b. Shabbat* 117b.

13 *m. Shabbat* 2:7.

14 Jewish Publication Society Bible translation.

15 *Mekhilta, Yitro.*

16 *b. Megillah* 12b; cf. *Esther Rabbah* 3:11; author's translation. By comparison, we note as well the criticism by the apostle Paul against those who took the Lord's Supper while drunk (1 Cor. 11:20–22) or "in an unworthy manner" (1 Cor. 11:27–28).

17 *Beitzah* 2b; *Shabbat* 117b; *Eruvin* 38b.

18 Note the phrases: "the day of Preparation, that is, the day before the Sabbath" in Mark 15:42 and "the day of Preparation, and the Sabbath was beginning" in Luke 23:54. New Revised Standard Version Bible, copyright © 1989 National Council of the Churches of Christ in the United States of America. Used by permission. All rights reserved worldwide.

19 Jubilees 50:11–12.

20 *Genesis Rabbah* 11:4; author's translation.

21 Another version of this story involves Rabbi Yehoshua Ben Hananiya, a sage who lived a good century before Rabbi Yehudah, while the temple was still standing in Jerusalem (this time the Roman emperor isn't named): The emperor said to Rabbi Yehoshua Ben Hananya, "Why does a cooked Shabbat dish have such a fragrant odor?" He replied, "We have a certain seasoning called the Shabbat,

which we put into it, and that gives it a fragrant odor." The emperor asked, "Give us some of it." Rabbi Yehoshua Ben Hananya replied, "To him who keeps the Shabbat it is efficacious, but to him who does not keep the Shabbat it is of no use" (*b. Shabbat* 119a; author's translation).

22 Jubilees 50:8–10.

23 *Jewish War* ii.147–149.

24 1 Maccabees 2:31–38.

25 *b. Pesachim* 68b; *b. Brachot* 31b; and see Y. D. Gilat, "On Fasting on the Sabbath," *Tarbiz* 5/1 (1982), 1–15 (Hebrew with English summary).

26 *m. Shabbat* 7.2; author's translation

27 The more common word in biblical Hebrew for work is *avodah*, yet Scripture uses *melakhah* when discussing what is prohibited on Shabbat. The only other word in biblical Hebrew sharing the same triliteral root (*l-'-k*) with *melakhah* is *malakh,* "agent" or "messenger," suggesting that what is prohibited on Shabbat isn't necessarily physical labor but specialized activities normally performed by an agent or artisan.

28 There was, however, a major difference between the *melakhah* observance on the three pilgrimage holidays and that of Shabbat. Based on Exodus 12:16, "No work shall be done on those days [i.e., the first and last days of Passover]. But what everyone needs to eat, that alone may be prepared by you," Chazal concluded that unlike on Shabbat, one may transfer fire and carry it from one domain to another on Passover, Shavuot, and Sukkot.

29 *Mekhilta De-Rabbi Ishmael*, Tractate Ki Tissa; author's translation.

30 This is another example from the New Testament that suggests that Shabbat traditions spoken in the name of certain sages such as Rabbi Shimon Ben Menassia may actually go back one or two centuries prior to their formulation in classic rabbinic literature, to a time prior to the destruction of the temple in AD 70.

31 *Against Apion* ii.282.

32 Menachem Stern, ed., *Greek and Latin Authors on Jews and Judaism*, vol. 1 (Jerusalem: Israel Academy of Sciences and Humanities, 1974), 431.

33 Stern, *Greek and Latin Authors*, vol. 1, 431.

34 This practice is well documented in the Mishnah; see for instance *m. Brachot* 6:6.

35 Jacob Z. Lauterbach, "The Origin and Development of Two Sabbath Ceremonies," *Hebrew Union College Annual* 15 (1940), 367–424.

36 According to classic rabbinic literature, all standard Jewish liturgy was codified by the Sanhedrin as they convened at Yavneh following the destruction of Jerusalem in AD 70. Scholars are divided as to exactly what, if anything, happened at Yavneh and how that reflects Jewish life prior to AD 70. One school of thought holds that that Yavneh meeting created new authoritative liturgies to replace the void created with the loss of the temple, while another proposes that the assembly at Yavneh based their liturgy on patterns of prayer that existed earlier. See Ruth Langer, "Revisiting Early Rabbinic Liturgy: The Recent Contributions of Ezra Fleischer," *Prooftexts* 19/2 (1999), 179–194; and Stefan C. Reif, "Prayer in Early Judaism," in *Prayer from Tobit to Qumran,* ed. Renate Egger-Wenzel and Jeremy Corley (Berlin: de Gruyter, 2004), 439–464. Note the discussion on the Last Supper in this chapter about the term "Cup of Blessings" (1 Cor. 10:16), which suggests that home liturgical practices such the "Grace After Meals" in the Mishnah may go back as early as the first century AD.

37 *m. Tamid* 7:4; author's translation.

38 Rather than providing evidence that New Moon was a time for family feasts during the time of the First Temple, as scholars sometimes suggest, the event of 1 Samuel 20 gives us only enough information to suggest the opposite.

39 *y. Megillah* 1:4, 60a; *b. Beitzah* 16a; *Leviticus Rabbah* 30:1; *y. Pesachim* 1:1, 27b; *y. Sanhedrin* 8:2, 26b.

40 Synagogues, literally "places of gathering," first appear during the Second Temple period. For more on the possible origins and original function of the synagogue, see Lee I. Levine, "The Nature and Origin of the Palestinian Synagogue Reconsidered," *Journal of Biblical Literature* 115/3 (1996), 425–448; Lee I. Levine, *The Ancient Synagogue: The First Thousand Years* (New Haven, Conn.: Yale University Press, 2005); and Eric M. Meyers, "Early Judaism and the Rise of the Synagogue," in *Archaeology of the Land of the Bible*, vol. 3, *Alexander to Constantine*, ed. Eric M. Meyers and Mark A. Chancey (New Haven, Conn.: Yale University Press, 2012), 203–238.

41 The midrashic mindset valued scriptural bases for all innovations.

42 *y. Brachot* 6:1, 10a; *y. Pesachim* 2:5, 29c.

43 *b. Beitzah* 25b; *b. Brachot* 38b.

44 Rabbi Shimon Ben Halafta, late first to early second centuries AD.

45 *b. Rosh HaShanah* 16b.

46 *b. Baba Batra* 12a; author's translation.

47 These included acts of commerce, even though the thirty-nine categories of prohibited *melakhah* defined in classic rabbinic literature do not include the specific activities of buying and selling. But in any case, such activities clearly fall outside activities which are "conducive to rest:" 'Above all you shall keep My Sabbaths' [Exodus 31:13]. Why is this said, seeing that it states earlier 'You shall not do any Melakhah' [Exodus 20:10]? From this earlier verse I would only know about Melakhah [prohibitions], but how would I know about resting? This is what it means when it says 'Above all you shall keep My Sabbaths:' to include activities which are conducive to rest" (Mekhilta De-Rabbi Ishmael, Shabbata I:3–9; author's translation). *Pesikta Rabbati* 1, 1b; *m. Megillah* 4:2.

48 By *national,* I mean in the sense of "peoplehood," rather than a function of political independence.

49 *Rosh HaShanah* 2:4.

50 *m. Pesachim* 9:5.

51 Josephus gives the population of Jerusalem as 2.7 million (*Jewish War* vi.423–427). Tacitus says the number was 600,000 (*Histories* 5.11). The Talmud cites the population as 1.2 million (*b. Pesachim* 64b).

52 *m. Pesachim* 5:6; author's translation.

53 Philo, *Questions and Answers*, Ex. 1:10.

54 Philo, *The Special Laws* 2, 27:148.

55 *m. Zevachim* 5:8; author's translation.

56 *Avot D'Rabbi Natan,* chapter 35; author's translation.

57 *m. Ta'anit* 3:8.

58 *y. Pesachim* 35b; author's translation.

59 The Holy Bible, New International Version®, NIV®. Copyright © 1973, 1978, 1984, 2011 by Biblica, Inc.™ Used by permission of Zondervan. All rights reserved worldwide. www.zondervan.com The "NIV" and "New International Version" are trademarks registered in the United States Patent and Trademark Office by Biblica, Inc.®

60 *t. Pesachim* 3:11.

61 Jubilees 49:6–7.

62 Scholarly opinion is divided, with a majority concluding that the Last Supper was not a Seder. For example, Joseph Tabory. "Towards a History of the Paschal Meal," in *Passover and Easter: Origin and History to Modern Times,* ed. by Paul F. Bradshaw and Lawrence A. Hoffman (Notre Dame, Ind.: University of Notre Dame Press, 1999), 62–80; and Joel Marcus, "Passover and the Last Supper Revisited," *New Testament Studies* 59 (2013), 303–324. For a summary view of scholars who say yes, see Eckhard J. Schnabel, *Jesus in Jerusalem: The Last Days* (Grand Rapids, Mich.: Eerdmans, 2018), 206–207.

63 *Pesachim* 10.

64 An example of the difficulty of dating the Seder material in the Mishnah is this passage which relates to the Passover meal: "They bring it in front of him. He dips lettuce until he reaches the appetizer that precedes the bread. They bring before him matzah, lettuce, and haroset, although the haroset is not mandatory. Rabbi Elazar son of Rabbi Zadok says, 'It is mandatory.' And in the Temple they would bring before him the Passover lamb" (*m. Pesachim* 10.3; author's translation). How should we understand the words "and in the Temple they would bring before him the Passover lamb?" If the Mishnah represents a situation after AD 70, was this line created by the sages to remind Jews, when reciting their home liturgy, what was lost when the temple was destroyed? Or, if the Mishnah represents life prior to AD 70, is it documenting the practice of the majority of Jews, whether living in Israel or in the Diaspora, who were not able to make the pilgrimage to Jerusalem and so reminding them of what was happening in the temple? We can read the Mishnah either way.

65 *m. Pesachim* 10.5; author's translation.

66 These Hellenistic symposiums were festive meals held by the affluent in society and at times included serious discussion while eating, often led by a philosopher. The most famous Hellenistic symposium recorded in Western literature is the Symposium of Plato. See Blake Leyerle, "Meal Customs in the Greco-Roman World," in *Passover and Easter: Origin and History to Modern Times,* ed. by Paul F. Bradshaw and Lawrence A. Hoffman (Notre Dame, Ind.: University of Notre Dame Press, 1999), 29–61.

67 *m. Pesachim* 10.5.

68 *Jewish* War ii.515.

69 *Seder Olam Rabbah* 5; *b. Yoma* 4b.

70 The commandment to bring one's firstfruits to Jerusalem is found in Deuteronomy 26:1–11, though it is described there only in very general terms. An entire volume of the Mishnah, *Bikkurim*, portrays in vivid detail how this commandment was observed and celebrated during Second Temple times.

71 *m. Bikkurim* 3:2–12; *m. Ta'anit* 4:2. The land of Israel was divided into twenty-four regions, or courses, with regard to the temple affairs for priests and laity. People of the same region would have their firstfruits ripen at the same time, so naturally they brought them together.

72 *m. Sukkah* 5:1.

73 *m. Sukkah* 5:3.

74 *b. Sukkah* 53a.

75 *b. Sukkah* 53a; author's translation.

76 Special names were given to the final day of Sukkot in classical rabbinic literature, which apparently go back to the Second Temple period: the "Day of Hosanna" (*Leviticus Rabbah* 37:2) and Hoshana Rabbah, the "Great Hosanna." The name *Hoshana Rabbah* appears only in one rare manuscript tradition of Midrash Psalms, *Midrash Psalms*, ed. by Solomon Buber, and Psalm 17 (Vilnius, 1891); reprinted by Vagshal (Jerusalem, 1977), 128 (Hebrew).

77 The Eighth Day of Assembly (Num. 29:35; 2 Chron. 7:9; Neh. 8:18) is technically a separate holiday: the commandments to dwell in a sukkah and to gather the four species no longer apply, but like the first day of Sukkot, *melakhah* is prohibited and the Hallel is chanted.

78 Matthew 21:9; Mark 11:9–10; and Luke 19:38.

79 *b. Pesachim* 119a; author's translation in the accompanying table.

80 Yom Kippur appears as Yom Kippurim, Day of Atonements, plural, in the Bible and as Yom HaKippurim, *The* Day of Atonements, in classical rabbinic literature. The name Yom Kippur first appears only in the sixth century in a Hebrew liturgical poem.

81 *b.Rosh HaShanah* 10b–11a; *Leviticus Rabbah* 29:1.

82 *m. Rosh HaShanah* 1:2.

83 *t. Rosh HaShanah* 1:13.

84 *m. Yoma* 8:1.

85 *m. Yoma* 6:2.

86 *m. Ta'anit* 4.8; author's translation.

87 *m. Bikkurim* 1:3; *m. Trumot* 11:3; *Sifrei Deuteronomy* 297.

88 For example: "[Judith] fasted all the days of her widowhood, except sabbath eves and sabbaths, new moon eves and new moons, feastdays and holidays of the house of Israel" (Judith 8:6 NABRE). New American Bible, revised edition © 2010, 1991, 1986, 1970 Confraternity of Christian Doctrine, Washington, D.C.

89 *b. Megillah* 7a; *b. Chullin* 139b.

90 *m. Megillah* 1:1.

91 *b. Pesachim* 68b; *b. Megillah* 7b.

92 *b. Shabbat* 21a–24a.

93 *b. Shabbat* 21b; author's translation.

94 *M. Benovitz*, "Herod and Hanukkah," Zion 68 (2003), 5–40 (Hebrew with English abstract on iv-v).

95 2 Maccabees 10:6–7 NABRE.

96 *t. Sukkah* 3:2.

97 *Sifrei Deuteronomy* 31; *t. Sotah* 6:7; *y. Ta'anit* 4:5/68c.

98 *m. Rosh Hashanah* 1:3.

99 *m. Ta'anit* 2:1; author's translation.

Jewish Feasts and Holidays Today

Ophir Yarden

A common Jewish saying you'll hear around holiday times is this: "Our enemies sought to destroy us, but God saved us. God is great! Let's eat!" These two statements followed by two exclamations capture two notable threads that weave throughout the Jewish holidays today: deliverance and food!

As Jews, we observe special days, weeks, and seasons of time throughout the year to remember and retell the narratives of divine deliverance in the Bible, such as the exodus on Pesach (Passover) and the story of Esther on Purim. For those of us who observe the holidays in synagogues, the rituals and traditions experienced there are enriched with readings from the Torah, shared recitations of liturgical poems, and an atmosphere of either penitence or celebration—or both.

The Jewish festival of Sukkot is a week-long celebration of the harvest, a holiday of special gladness and joy. Pictured here is a Sukkot synagogue service with "boughs of leafy trees and willows of the brook" (Lev. 23:40). (Photo by Brian Negin)

The ritual of reading the Torah is especially important on holidays. We read biblical passages in prayer services with a certain amount of pomp and circumstance; they are the crescendo of worship! We might say that Jewish holy days are not only in the Bible, but the Bible is in them as well.

But just as central to Jewish life as rituals performed in the synagogue are family meals at home. These are often shared with guests. From Shabbat meals to specially prepared foods infused with symbolism eaten at certain times of the year, gatherings around a shared table are opportunities to celebrate and enjoy the provisions of God.

On the flip side of feasting are periods of fasting, and these, too, are important elements in the Jewish holiday calendar. Sacred days such as Yom Kippur and Tisha b'Av are times to reflect on weighty matters: repentance, judgment, and penitence. Yet they are also occasions for confidence in God's mercy. In fact, our holidays of joyous celebration and feasting outnumber the sorrowful days.

Contemporary Judaism owes more to the teachings of the rabbis in the centuries following the Bible (the Hebrew Scriptures, or Old Testament) than it does to the Bible itself, because traditions and customs surrounding the holidays have been adapted to fit changing circumstances over time and place. Even so, some Jews today do not observe the religious aspects of the feasts. For many who live in North America or in Europe, Judaism is more of an ethnic than a religious identity. For most Israeli Jews, it is also a national identity. For this reason, the topic of Jewish feasts has many facets and, to be sure, is both rich and complicated.

In this chapter, I will present the holidays as they are traditionally observed, choosing to focus on their religious character as a way of "setting the table" (to use a festal idiom) for other ways of understanding them within the diverse world of Judaism today. In doing so, I will emphasize their biblical, rather than rabbinic, elements in order to find common ground with a wide reading audience. My own holiday celebration is that of a Jew born in the United States who has lived most of his life in Israel. My observance is traditional yet respectful of other forms of Jewish practice and derives from a sense that Judaism is as much about belonging (to the Jewish people) as it is about believing.

BIBLICAL ROOTS AND MODERN SHOOTS

The feasts and fasts marked by Jews today originate overwhelmingly, but not exclusively, in the Bible. The majority of those are mentioned in the Torah, specifically the books of Exodus, Leviticus, Numbers, and Deuteronomy. They include the following:

- Shabbat (Sabbath)
- Pesach (Passover)
- Shavuot (Weeks, Pentecost)
- Day of Trumpets, which has become Rosh HaShanah (New Year's Day)
- Yom Kippur (Day of Atonement)

The Torah also mentions a minor feast, the new moon festival, Rosh Hodesh. Beyond these are Purim, which is anchored in the book of Esther, and Hanukkah, the feast celebrating the rededication of the Second Temple described in 1 and 2 Maccabees (the books of Maccabees stand outside the Jewish biblical canon). Several fast days also have biblical origins.

Jews who live in Israel (as well as many who do not) also commemorate a number of recent memories, some of which are happy and others sad. While most of these are connected to the State of Israel,

Pictured here is a Bar Mitzvah boy's first Torah reading on a weekday when tefillin (phylacteries, Deut. 6:8) are worn. Bar Mitzvah ceremonies for thirteen-year-old boys—and in the last century also Bat Mitzvah ceremonies for twelve-year-old girls—usually take place during the Shabbat service. They involve the boy or girl reading from the Scriptures and sometimes leading the service. These rites of passage are relatively young in the rich history of Judaism and have no biblical basis. (Photo by Ophir Yarden)

they are significant enough in modern Jewish experience worldwide to include them in this chapter alongside the biblical feasts and festivals.

Jewish festival traditions vary across three major cultural groups:

- **Ashkenazi Jews** hail mostly from the historically Christian lands of northern and eastern Europe.
- **Sephardi Jews** are descendants of Jews exiled from Spain and Portugal in the fifteenth century.
- **Mizrahi Jews** are those whose ancestors lived in the Muslim areas of the Middle East and North Africa.[1]

Because Ashkenazi Jews are the dominant Jewish population in North America, their practices will be the basis of this chapter. To this, I will add information about non-Ashkenazi practices as well as Jewish observances in Israel to complete the picture. (The majority of Jews today live in Israel or in North America.) It is also important to recognize non-traditional observances of the holidays. For instance, some Jews in modern Israel—particularly those who have returned to the land in kibbutz collective communities—have reinterpreted the biblical holidays in ways that highlight the holidays' agricultural aspects and downplay their theological elements. These we will discuss toward the end of this chapter.

THE JEWISH CALENDAR

Christians and Jews define the week similarly, as a period of seven days that ends with Saturday; for Jews, this is the Sabbath, or Shabbat.[2] Christians and Jews differ though in how they mark days, months, and years. For Jews, the day begins with sunset, not midnight.[3] This means that the first worship service of the day is in the evening. On Shabbat, this service is called *Qabbalat Shabbat*, "Welcoming the Sabbath."

The Jewish year is lunisolar, differing from the Christian year which is solar and from the Muslim year which is lunar. In a lunisolar year, both the moon and the sun play a role in fixing the calendar. The Jewish year is synchronized with the sun, but the months follow the phases of the moon, with each month beginning at the new moon, Rosh Hodesh. In ancient times, a new month began when eyewitnesses saw the first crescent of the moon. In the fourth century CE, the rabbis ordained a mathematically calculated calendar that is still followed to this day. Because the moon revolves

A mosaic of a zodiac with images representing the twelve months of the Jewish calendar in Old City Jerusalem. (Photo by Yan Simkin/Shutterstock)

around the earth in approximately 29½ days, months calculated by the moon are, alternately, 29 and 30 days in length. Twelve lunar months give a year of 354 days. Because the earth circles the sun every 365¼ days, the solar year is 11 days longer than the lunar year. To synchronize the lunar calendar with the seasons of the sun, an extra "leap month" is added about every three years, when the lunar year has fallen about one month behind the solar year.[4] The extra month is added just before Nisan because the Bible specifies that Passover must fall in the month of Nisan—or Abib, as it's called in the Torah (Ex. 23:15)—when the barley first ripens in the Land of Israel.[5] Without the extra month, Nisan would creep backward into the winter, then to the autumn, and continue through summer before returning to the spring in a thirty-three-year cycle. (Indeed, this is the case of the Muslim calendar.) This extra month, added between Adar and Nisan, is called Second Adar or Adar II. In the years when Adar is doubled, the holiday Purim, which occurs in Adar, is observed in Adar II, along with any Adar birthdays as well.[6] We see, then, that the lunisolar calendar is an ingenious way of ensuring that the biblical holidays keep their agricultural connection to Israel wherever in the world they are celebrated, tying the Jews to that land in the process.

Jews also count the years differently. A conservative Jewish tradition holds that the world is close to 6,000 years old, and the traditional Jewish calendar numbers the years accordingly. For example, the Jewish New Year's Day that falls in September of the year 2022 marks the beginning of the Jewish year 5783. Numbering the years by, before, or after the birth of Jesus is naturally not a Jewish practice, though Jews will use dates of the Christian era for convenience, replacing AD (*anno Domini,* Latin for "in the year of our Lord") with CE (common era), and BC (before Christ) with BCE (before the common era). In this chapter, I follow this practice and use CE and BCE.

The Name of God

In this chapter, I use YHWH to represent the four-letter, Hebrew proper name of God (the Tetragrammaton). In most English Bible translations, it is not rendered as a name but as "the LORD." In Jewish tradition, God's holy name is not pronounced. Rather, when reading a religious text or praying, one says *Adonai*, which means "my Lord." When reading a text other than in prayer, even then, God's name is not pronounced and many substitute *HaShem*, which means "the name." While we are not certain how the name YHWH was pronounced in ancient times, an English reader scanning the letters YHWH today probably gets a rough idea.[7]

SHABBAT (SABBATH)

Shabbat occurs every week, but even though it happens so frequently, it is not devalued. Jews have a special place of honor for God's holy day, calling it "a delight" (Isa. 58:13).[8] The entire week revolves around Shabbat. In fact, Hebrew doesn't use names for the days of the week but rather calls them by number: for example, the fifth day or the sixth day, in anticipation of the seventh day, Shabbat (see Gen. 1:23, 31; Ex. 31:17).[9]

We are commanded to "remember/observe the Shabbat day and make it holy" (Ex. 20:8; Deut. 5:12).[10] Much of what we do for the six days that we work is prohibited on Shabbat: "The seventh day is Shabbat.... You shall do no task [*melakhah*[11]]" (Deut. 5:14). Shabbat is a day of rest, leisure, and prayer. But Shabbat does not happen by itself (well, it does, when the sun sets). We must prepare for Shabbat if we are to enjoy the day. All shopping, cooking, and cleaning must be completed before Shabbat begins. As one rabbinic saying from the

Talmud points out, "If one toils on Shabbat eve, one is able to eat on Shabbat."[12]

The centerpieces of Shabbat are the evening and morning synagogue services and the celebratory meals in the evening and at lunchtime. (There is an afternoon service and third meal as well, but they are less central.) These are meals that the whole family eats together, even if they do not join each other for meals during the rest of the week. There may be guests as well; indeed, with the celebration of Shabbat, the Jewish family has a dinner party every week! Before the meal itself, the participants recite a sanctification blessing called *kiddush*. In the evening, this prayer includes Genesis 2:1–3 and a rabbinic formula that recognizes Shabbat as commemorating both creation and the exodus. The blessing reads, in part, "Blessed are you God who in love and favor gave us his holy Sabbath as a heritage, as a remembrance of the work of creation, a remembrance of the exodus from Egypt." The table is set with two loaves of bread recalling the double portion of manna that the Israelites collected on Fridays, as such activity was forbidden on Shabbat (Ex. 16:22–26). Before the Shabbat meal, parents bless their children with the words of the "Priestly Blessing:"[13]

> [May] YHWH bless you and protect you!
> [May] YHWH deal kindly and graciously with you!
> [May] YHWH bestow His favor upon you and grant you peace! (Num. 6:24–26)

The Shabbat meal is concluded with the "Grace After Meals" prayer, as commanded in Deuteronomy 8:10, which begins by reciting Psalm 126.[14]

We light candles in the home before sunset on Friday. This is traditionally a woman's role. In the synagogue, the ceremony welcoming Shabbat is the most beautiful moment of the week. Some traditions liken the weekly reunion of Shabbat and the Jewish people to a wedding: Shabbat is the bride and the people the groom.[15] The couple has a long-distance relationship for six days each week and reunites on Friday evening. During the ceremony for welcoming Shabbat, the bride is serenaded with psalms[16] and a *piyyut,* a liturgical poem:

> Come my beloved, towards the bride,
> Let us welcome the countenance of Shabbat!

Likewise, *Midrash Genesis Rabbah* describes Shabbat as the betrothed of Israel who once had no partner:

> Sunday has Monday; Tuesday has Wednesday; Thursday has Friday, but Shabbat has no partner.... Rabbi Shimon bar Yohai taught: Shabbat pleaded with the Holy One, blessed

We mark the conclusion of Shabbat and holidays with the Havdalah ceremony using a multi-wicked candle, wine, and fragrant spices.

On Shabbat and all Torah holidays, we light candles before sunset to welcome the holiday. (Photo by Ophir Yarden)

> be God, saying: "Master of the universe! Every other [day] has a partner, but I have none!" God answered saying: "The community of Israel will be your partner. [Hence,] when Israel stood at Mount Sinai I commanded 'Remember the Shabbat so you may sanctify/betroth her.'"[17]

The central Shabbat liturgy takes place in the morning. This service is expanded with several items:

- Reading additional Psalms[18]
- The ceremonial reading of the week's Torah portion
- A reading from the Prophets called *haftarah*[19]
- An additional service called *Musaf* ("additional"), which refers to the supplementary sacrifices that were offered in the temple for Shabbat and holidays[20]

Not only is the liturgy longer on Shabbat than it is for the daily, weekday service, but most communities sing much more as well.

Shabbat ends at dark on Saturday night. The ceremony signaling its conclusion is called *Havdalah* ("distinction") and marks the transition from the sanctity of Shabbat to the remaining days of the week.

ROSH HODESH (NEW MOON)

Rosh Hodesh (new moon) is only a marginal holiday today, despite being mentioned in the Bible in the same breath as Shabbat and other feasts: "Festivals, new moons, and Shabbat—all Israel's festive seasons" (Hosea 2:11 [Hebrew v. 13]). While its synagogue celebration includes liturgical additions, none of the prohibitions of *melakhah* apply as they do on Shabbat and other festivals.[21]

Rosh Hodesh is the first day of a lunar month and means, literally, "head of the month." We recall that a lunar month may have either twenty-nine or thirty days. If a month has thirty days, Rosh Hodesh is celebrated twice, on the thirtieth day of the concluding month and on the first day of the following month. Since we are no longer dependent upon actual sightings of the new moon to determine its date, Rosh Hodesh is known in advance and announced after the Torah reading on the previous Shabbat. At the conclusion of the Shabbat following Rosh Hodesh, there is an outdoor ceremony sanctifying the new moon, lit by the new crescent.

Because the lunar cycle is similar to the biological cycle experienced by women, Rosh Hodesh has become a women's holiday. After their menstrual cycle, women immerse in a ritual bath, as prescribed by the rabbis based on Leviticus 15:19–24. Some women try to abstain from *melakhah* on this day (although it is only a custom and not prescribed) and some attend Rosh Hodesh assemblies to mark the day with study and celebration.

A mikvah is a stepped ritual pool for whole-body immersion. According to Jewish law, it must contain forty *seahs* of water. The *seah* is a biblical measure of volume equivalent to three or four gallons (Gen. 18:6; 2 Kings 7:1). Immersion is also permissible in natural bodies of water. At left is a twelfth-century bath in Speyer, on the Rhine River, and at right is a modern day mikvah. (Photos by Chris 73/Wikimedia [left] and David Cohen 156/Shutterstock [right].)

THE HIGH HOLIDAYS

Given the special role of the seventh day (Shabbat) and of the seventh year (the Sabbatical year; Lev. 25:1–7) in the Torah, it is not surprising that the seventh month is also special in the Jewish calendar. The seventh month is the month of Tishri (September/October). In this month, we observe an intense series of holidays: Rosh HaShanah, Yom Kippur, Sukkot, and Shemini Atzeret (Simchat Torah). The High Holidays, or as they are known in Hebrew *Yamim Nora'im*,[22] the "Days of Awe," are Rosh HaShanah and Yom Kippur. (We will return to Sukkot and Shemini Atzeret in the context of the pilgrimage festivals.)

Like other holy days, the High Holidays are embedded in a season, and the season's themes are connected to the holy days. In this way, the High Holidays are similar to how Easter is connected to the period of Lent and Christmas to the season of Advent. The High Holidays' themes are repentance and judgment. This generates a period during which we recite prayers of penitence.[23] Mizrahi and Sephardi Jews start these prayers at the beginning of the previous month, Elul (August/September), while Ashkenazi Jews start them in the last week of Elul. These prayers are recited at night, either toward midnight or before dawn, as Jewish mysticism teaches that divine mercy is awakened at this time:[24] "I arise at midnight to praise you" (Ps. 119:62) and "YHWH! At daybreak hear my voice" (Ps. 5:3 [Hebrew v. 4]). The liturgy includes what the rabbis called God's Thirteen Attributes:

> YHWH! YHWH!... God compassionate and gracious, slow to anger, abounding in kindness and faithfulness, extending kindness to the thousandth generation, forgiving iniquity, transgression, and sin. (Ex. 34:6–7)[25]

These prayers declare the ways God harkened to the prayers of Israel in the past, even as we entreat God's forgiveness today.[26] An excellent example is the popular *piyyut* "Anenu," which means "Hear us!" or "Answer our prayers!"

> Answer us, YHWH, answer us!
> Answer us, Refuge of our mothers, answer us![27]
> May the One who answered Abraham on Mount Moriah, answer us! (Gen. 22)
> May the One who answered Isaac when he was bound on the altar, answer us! (Gen. 22)
> May the One who answered Jacob at Bet El, answer us! (Gen. 28)
> May the One who answered Joseph in the prison, answer us! (Gen. 39–41)[28]

This prayer continues with a set of biblical references to such people from the Bible as Moses, Aaron, Phinehas, Joshua, Samuel, David, Solomon, Elijah, Elisha, Jonah, Hezekiah, Hannaniah, Mishael, Azariah, Daniel, Ezra, Mordecai, and Esther. The *shofar* (ram's horn) is blown either during our prayers of repentance or during the morning service in preparation for Rosh HaShanah.[29]

With this, the community is ready for the High Holidays and the Ten Days of Repentance from Rosh HaShanah through Yom Kippur.

ROSH HASHANAH

The holiday we know today as Rosh HaShanah developed from a rather generic "sacred occasion" falling on the new moon (the first day) of the seventh month mentioned in the Bible. This was also the date on which Ezra read the Torah before the congregation (Neh. 8). Leviticus 23:24 commands, "You shall observe complete rest, a sacred occasion commemorated with loud blasts."

Today, the holiday is observed for two days,[30] and both are days of rest with synagogue services, the sounding of commemorative shofars, special rituals and prayers, and mention of the moderate additions to the sacrifices that were offered on other new moon days (Num. 29:6).[31] As the name *Rosh Hodesh* means "head of the month," *Rosh HaShanah* means "head of the year" and is usually rendered in English as New Year's Day.[32] The themes of Rosh HaShanah can be seen in the alternate names for the holiday: the Day of Sounding (a shofar), the Day of Remembrance, and the Day of Judgment (because God is sovereign). These three aspects are highlighted in the Musaf service which is held immediately after the main service and focuses on each of Rosh HaShanah's three themes:

- God's role as Sovereign (and hence Judge),
- God's remembrance, and
- shofar blasts.[33]

The main service on the morning of each day includes elements that proclaim God's coronation as sovereign of the universe and celebrate the creation of the world in six days, culminating in the creation of humankind on the day that became Rosh HaShanah—the ultimate New Year's Day!

In the spirit of this yearly anniversary of creation, Rosh HaShanah is a day to take stock as God carries out judgment over everything that he has made. Festivity may seem inappropriate at a time of divine judgment, but confidence in God's mercy makes this a joyful occasion. A central prayer, "Avinu Malkenu" ("Our Parent, Our Sovereign"), invokes God not only as our ruler but also as our parent, and calls upon him to show us parental

Traditionally, challah bread dipped in honey is eaten on Rosh HaShanah. Challah is also eaten on Shabbat.

mercy and love alongside judgment: "Our Father, Our King! Be gracious and hear our prayer, for we have insufficient good deeds. Treat us charitably and kindly, and rescue us."

In the spirit of Isaiah 1:18, which says "If your sins are like scarlet, they shall be white as snow," a white curtain is hung before the Holy Ark (the cabinet in the front of the synagogue where the Torah scrolls are kept) and white Torah mantles replace the usual coverings. Prayer leaders, and also some in the congregation, dress in white robes. One early rabbinic teaching gives this reason for wearing white so confidently:

> It is the worldly custom that when one knows one is on trial one wears black ... for one doesn't know what will be the outcome of the trial. But the [people of] Israel wear white [on Rosh HaShanah] ... and eat and drink happily for they know that the Holy One, blessed by God, will perform a miracle for them [and judge them mercifully].[34]

The shofar is the most striking symbol of the day. The horn making the "loud blasts" in Leviticus 23:24 is understood to be a shofar because the holiday falls so close to Yom Kippur on which a shofar is blown (Lev. 25:9) and because it is described in the monthly new moon celebrations: "Sound the shofar at the [new] moon" (Ps.81:3 [Hebrew v. 4]).[35] While the shofar may be fashioned from the horn of various animals, it is generally the horn of a ram, though Yemenite Jews use the long horn of an antelope. While both animals are acceptable, preference for the ram's horn comes from one of the shofar's central aspects: not only does the loud call of the shofar startle us and call us to repentance, but it also reminds God of Abraham's willingness to sacrifice his "only son Isaac, whom you love" (Gen. 22:2). Abraham, we

read, sacrificed in Isaac's place a ram caught in a thicket by its horns (Gen. 22:13).

The shofar blower sounds one hundred blasts over the course of the morning service on Rosh HaShanah. The sound is piercing (to put it mildly), a sound that the rabbis over the centuries have explained with many symbolic ideas. For instance, Rabbi Saadia Gaon (tenth century CE, Babylonia) suggested that the shofar is a reminder of the revelation at Sinai, exhortations of the prophets to repent, the return from exile, and the coming of the Messiah, all happenings worthy of strident attention.[36]

> In that day, a great ram's horn will be sounded;
> and those lost who are in the land of Assyria
> and the expelled who are in the land of Egypt
> shall come and worship the Lord on the holy
> mount in Jerusalem. (Isa. 27:13)

The Talmud remarks that God remembered Sarah, Rachel, and Hannah on Rosh HaShanah by answering their prayers for a child.[37] Scripture readings for Rosh HaShanah highlight this. The Torah reading for the first day is about the birth of Isaac (Gen. 21). The reading from the Prophets (*haftarah*) for this day tells of the prophet Samuel's birth to Hannah (1 Sam. 1:1–2:10). On the second day of Rosh HaShanah, Abraham's binding of Isaac is read (Gen. 22),[38] along with Jeremiah 31:2–20 which depicts the formerly barren Rachel "weeping for her children" (v. 15).[39]

Rachel's prayers for the redemption of her children are answered in words that highlight the Hebrew verb *shuv*, "to return," (from the root *sh,w,b*) to indicate repentance, a major theme of the day. (Words sharing the root *sh,w,b* are shown here in bold.)[40]

> I will bring them in from the northland,
> Gather them from the ends of the earth,
> The blind and the lame among them,
> Those with child and those in labor
> In a vast throng they shall **return** here …

Eating apples dipped in honey is a way we express our wish on Rosh HaShanah for a sweet new year. Pomegranates are among the other symbolic foods. They are said to have 613 seeds, which is the number of commandments in the Torah.

> Thus said the LORD:
> A cry is heard in Ramah
> Wailing, bitter weeping
> Rachel weeping for her children.
> She refuses to be comforted for her children,
> who are gone.
> Thus said the LORD:
> Restrain your voice from weeping,
> Your eyes from shedding tears;
> For there is a reward for your labor—
> declares the LORD.
> They shall **return** from the enemy's land.
> And there is hope for your future—
> declares the LORD:
> Your children shall **return** to their country.
> I can hear Ephraim lamenting:
> You have chastised me, and I am chastised
> Like a calf that has not been broken.
> **Bring me back**, that **I may return**,[41]
> For You, O LORD, are my God.

Now that I have **turned back,**
I am filled with remorse;
Now that I am made aware,
I strike my thigh.
I am ashamed and humiliated,
For I bear the disgrace of
my youth.
Truly, Ephraim is a dear son
to Me,
A child that is dandled!
Whenever I have turned against him,
My thoughts would dwell on him still.
That is why My heart yearns for him;
I will receive him back in love
—declares the Lord. (Jer. 31:8, 15–20)

It is customary during the festive meals eaten at home on Rosh HaShanah to dip the *challah* (holiday loaf) in honey, symbolizing hope for a sweet year.[42] Indeed, apples dipped in honey are among the holiday's most prominent symbols. Some Jews conduct a brief Rosh HaShanah seder, similar to the one on Passover, which includes eating symbolic foods. This seder is accompanied by blessings and wishes for prosperity, progeny, protection, primacy, and the performance of God's commandments. Since Rosh HaShanah literally means "head of the year," the seder might include a fish or sheep's head. (Vegetarians often substitute a head of lettuce.) When eating from the head, we recite "May it be Your will that we should be like the head and not the tail," echoing the blessing of Deuteronomy 28:13. This was inspired by the rabbis who taught that Ezra ordained reading the curses in Deuteronomy 27:15–26 a few weeks before Rosh HaShanah "so that the year and its curses will end;" it was only natural that they also added the wish, "May the [New] Year and its blessing commence."[43]

TEN DAYS OF REPENTANCE

The two days of Rosh HaShanah, the day of Yom Kippur, and the seven days between them together make up the Ten Days of Repentance. These days continue the period of reflection that comes before Rosh HaShanah, but they are more intense. Prayers of penitence continue, as do the shofar blasts. Some prayers at this time replace the word *God* with *King* to acknowledge God's coronation on Rosh HaShanah. This kingship imagery is inspired by verses such as Exodus 15:18: "YHWH shall reign for eternity" (see also Matt. 5:34–5; Heb. 4:16).

A prominent image during this season is that of God inscribing the names of people in one of three books:[44]

- The Book of Life for the entirely righteous
- The Book of Death for the wicked

The scales of Libra symbolize the month of Tishri (written beneath the scales) in the mosaic floor of the fifth-century synagogue in Sepphoris in Galilee. The scales represent judgment, a theme of the High Holidays. (Photo by Paul H. Wright)

For the Ten Days of Repentance, white fabrics are used for the mantles covering the Torah scrolls and the curtain on the Holy Ark in which they are kept. (Photo by Brian Negin)

- A third book for all of those who are in between, the overwhelming majority of humanity

In our prayers, we ask that God "inscribe us in the Book of Life." We are taught to consider our good and bad deeds as equally balanced, with one addition to either side able to tip the scale. Maimonides, the leading Jewish medieval sage and philosopher, described the balance this way:

> Throughout the year all must see themselves as equally balanced between innocence and guilt. Consequently, the entire world is evenly balanced. If a person commits even one sin, the whole world will be tipped to the side of guilt and cause its destruction. But if that person observes but one commandment, the whole world will be tipped to the side of merit, bringing about one's own, and the whole world's, salvation.[45]

The prophetic reading on the Shabbat that falls during these seven days is taken mostly from Hosea 14:1–9 (Hebrew vv. 2–10), which begins:

> Return, O Israel, to YHWH your God,
> For you have fallen because of your sin.
> Take words with you and return to YHWH.
> Say to Him: "Forgive all guilt and accept what is good;
> Instead of bulls we will pay [the offering of] our lips." (vv. 1–2 [Hebrew vv. 2–3])[46]

The Hebrew word that underlies the opening word is *shuv*, "to return." In verse 9 (Hebrew v. 10) of this reading, the act of returning to the "ways of YHWH" is *teshuva*, "repentance"—the theme of the day.

Ten Days of Repentance

The Ten Days of Repentance are bookended by Rosh HaShanah and Yom Kippur in the month of Tishri, the start of the Jewish civil new year.

YOM KIPPUR

Yom Kippur is the culmination of the Ten Days of Repentance and the entire season of penitence.[47] Families gather for a pre-fast meal before sunset just before the start of Yom Kippur, as well as for a breakfast after dark, twenty-six hours later. The evening and most of the daylight hours are spent in prayer that is a blend of gravity and joy. Yom Kippur is the only day of the year on which there are five synagogue services.[48] Though Yom Kippur is a day of judgment, as is Rosh HaShanah, we are confident that God's mercy will overcome strict judgment.

The day is introduced with a ritual called *Kol Nidre,* "All Vows." This is not a prayer but rather a declaration annulling vows (see Num. 30:1–16). This was introduced because Jews were concerned that they had undertaken (or been forced to undertake) an ill-advised vow that they sought to wipe away before Yom Kippur. This ritual continues to be one of the central elements of the High Holiday season.

The severity of Yom Kippur is well represented in one of the most prominent liturgies of the Jewish year, *U'netaneh toqef*:[49]

> Let us voice the power of this day's sanctity—it is awesome, terrible.... In truth it is You: Judge and Accuser.... You open the book of memories.... Angels rush forward ... trembling, shaking; they say, "Here is the Day of Judgment, visiting all the heavenly host for judgment."... And all who have come into this world pass before You.[50]... You ... regard the soul of every living thing ... On Rosh HaShanah it is written and on Yom Kippur will be sealed: how many will pass away and how many will be born; who will live and who will die; who in his due time and who before.

While this liturgy paints a gloomy picture, its crescendo promises hope: "But repentance, prayer, and charity avert the evil of the decree!"[51] It is in our hands to influence God's judgment.

The theme of judgment—which is absent in the depiction of Yom Kippur in the Torah—is enhanced by themes found elsewhere in Leviticus. Traditional liturgies for Yom Kippur recount the scapegoat ceremony and atonement rites in great detail (Lev. 16). One popular *piyyut*, "Mareh Kohen" ("The High Priest's Appearance"), describes the joy of the people in Second Temple times at the sight of the high priest exiting the Holy of Holies in the temple after making atonement: "Truly how splendid was the High Priest, as he came out of the Holy of Holies in peace, without harm."[52]

In the afternoon service, we read the book of Jonah in its entirety. The repentance of the people of Nineveh—while frustrating for Jonah—serves as an example for us. The day's fifth and final service is called *ne'ila* ("closing"), which is infused with the image of the heavenly gates of repentance closing at the end of the season of penitence. Many people remain standing for this entire service, a highlight of the day. Some liturgies include the verse, "Go, eat your bread with rejoicing and drink your wine with a merry heart, for God has already been pleased by your deeds" (Eccl. 9:7). After dark, as Yom Kippur ends, the shofar is blown and everyone declares, or sings, "Next year in Jerusalem!" Then everyone breaks the fast with a shared meal.

PILGRIMAGE FESTIVALS

In the Bible, the three holidays of Passover, Shavuot, and Sukkot have roots in agricultural celebrations and were observed as pilgrimage festivals, first to local holy places and then to Jerusalem. In Exodus 23:14, the first passage in the Bible where these feasts appear together, they are called *regalim* (plural) and *regel* (singular) to emphasize that they are pilgrimage festivals. *Regel* means "foot," and the biblical term for pilgrimage means "ascent by foot."[53] But they are more commonly known as *haggim* (singular *hag*; Ex. 13:6; Deut. 16:10, 13), a general term for any feast in the Bible that over time came to refer to these three pilgrimage festivals in particular.

> Three times a year—on the Feast [*hag*] of Unleavened Bread [Passover], on the Feast [*hag*] of Weeks [Shavuot], and on the Feast [*hag*] of Booths [Sukkot]—all your males shall appear before the Lord your God in the place that He will choose. (Deut. 16:16)

After the destruction of the Second Temple in 70 CE, the people of Israel lost their sacrifices, their sovereignty, and, for many, a chance to live in their historic homeland. How could they continue to be observant Jews when these most important parts of their identity were gone? One way was to focus on the pilgrimage festivals, which were deeply connected to the agricultural seasons and historical

In the Middle Ages, one of the most frequently illustrated Jewish books was the Haggadah used in the Passover Seder. This is the Sassoon Spanish Haggadah dating to c. 1300–1350. Its colorful illustrations depict artistic traditions of the Sephardi Jews prior to their expulsion from Spain. It is part of the collection of the Israel Museum, Jerusalem. (Photo by Paul H. Wright)

associations of the Land of Israel. Another was to strengthen their attachment to the Torah's oral traditions, which explained and expanded its teachings on the festivals. This they did by collecting them and writing them down in texts such as the Mishnah and the Talmud. As a result, Jews have been able to celebrate these festivals throughout the centuries as if they were pilgrims to the land of their forefathers, reciting (though, to be honest, for the most part not really believing) "Next year in Jerusalem!"

Now that millions of Jews are living in Israel again, there is a renewed emphasis on the agricultural aspects of these festivals since their celebration in Israel coincides with the biblical seasons.

PESACH (PASSOVER)

Let's begin our discussion of the pilgrimage festivals with Pesach, or Passover, which occurs at the beginning of the biblical liturgical year, in the spring in the month of Nisan.

Pesach is the most historically oriented of the festivals because it is tied to a specific event in the Torah. Exodus 12 narrates the first Pesach in Egypt and how God brought the Israelites out of that land of bondage. Chapter 13 establishes what the hallmark of the holiday would be—the Seder:

> And you shall *tell* your child on that day, "It is because of what YHWH did for me when I went out from Egypt." (Ex. 13:8; emphasis added)

This "telling" is expressed with the verb *h,g,d*, from which we get the Hebrew term *Haggadah*, the name of the book containing the instructions for conducting a Passover Seder and the texts that the rabbis chose to *tell* the exodus story.

Pesach is a seven-day holiday of which the first and last days are Shabbat-like holy convocations. It begins with the full moon of Nisan (March/April) and extends from the fifteenth to the twenty-first of that month. When the temple still stood, the Passover lamb was sacrificed in the afternoon of the fourteenth day of Nisan and the meal eaten that night, which was the beginning of the fifteenth day (Num. 28:16–17). Without a temple, Jews are no longer able to make the sacrifice. But the fourteenth day is still a busy day of preparation for the Passover Seder.

A Haggadah book guides us through the steps of a Passover Seder. Matzah (unleavened bread) is pictured here at the center of the table along with other foods for the meal. (Photo by Inna Reznik/Shutterstock)

Even though most people today call the entire seven-day holiday Passover, that name actually refers only to the first day when the Passover meal is eaten. The more proper name for the entire festival is the Feast of Matzah or the Feast of Unleavened Bread: "For seven days eat bread made without leaven [*hametz*]" (Num. 28:17).

From the Lovell Haggadah, this illustration depicts family and friends gathered to retell the story of the exodus at the Passover Seder. (Art by Matthew L. Berkowitz)

On the eve of the holiday, we remove all *hametz*—fermented or leavened grain and grain products[54] —from the home in fulfillment of Exodus 13:7: "None of your hametz shall be seen ... in all your territory." This cleaning process can begin days or even weeks before the holiday and is done at home, work, and synagogue—and even in the car. Regular kitchenware is put aside and only special utensils are used for entirely *hametz*-free food. Indeed, without the temple sacrifice, the special food preparation during the seven-day festival has become the most visible aspect of the holiday.

Seder, which means "sequence," is a festive meal with symbolic food appetizers and a ritualized retelling of the story of the exodus. On the table will be a Seder plate that holds several items symbolizing the exodus story, but the star of the show is the matzah, which symbolizes both the bread of affliction and the bread of freedom, hastily prepared for the exodus from Egypt. The Seder itself is a series of rituals that includes: eating most of these symbolic foods, relating the ten plagues with which God afflicted the Egyptians (Ex. 7–12), drinking four cups of wine, reciting the *Hallel* (Hallelujah Psalms, 113–118), and eating a festive meal. The exodus story is told mostly through rabbinic texts and one biblical passage (Deut. 26:5–8). Other verses from the Bible are scattered throughout the Haggadah.

One drop of wine is removed from our cup for each of the ten plagues that afflicted the Egyptians. Our joy is incomplete, for our ancestors' freedom was gained at the cost of human life (including that of our Egyptian enemy), as we are taught "God's mercy is over *all* his creatures" (Ps. 145:9). (Photo by Ophir Yarden)

Participating in a Passover Seder is one of the most widely observed practices among American Jews.[55] I think of the Seder as akin to Thanksgiving dinner in the United States, which is often preceded by reading the Pilgrims' story. David Ben-Gurion, who was Israel's first prime minister, also compared the two holidays, though in a different way. Two years before Israel became a country, he explained to the world why the Jews deserved a state in their historic homeland:

> About 300 years ago the *Mayflower* set sail to the new world. It was a great event in the history of England and America. But I am curious to know if anyone in England knows exactly when that ship sailed. And how many Americans know? Do they know how many people were onboard? And do they know the nature of the bread they ate in their exodus? Now, over 3,300 years before the *Mayflower* sailed, the Jews left Egypt. And every Jew in the world—whether in America or Soviet Russia—knows the exact date of their exodus. It was the fifteenth of Nisan. And they all know exactly what bread the Jews ate: Matzah. And to this day, Jews all over the world eat matzah on the fifteenth of Nisan. They eat matzah in America, in Russia and in other lands as they tell the story of the Exodus from Egypt and speak of the troubles which befell the Jews from the time of their exile [from the Land of Israel]. And they conclude with two sayings: "This year we are slaves; next year may we be free! This year we are here; next year in Jerusalem! In Zion, the Land of Israel."[56]

Passover Seder Plate

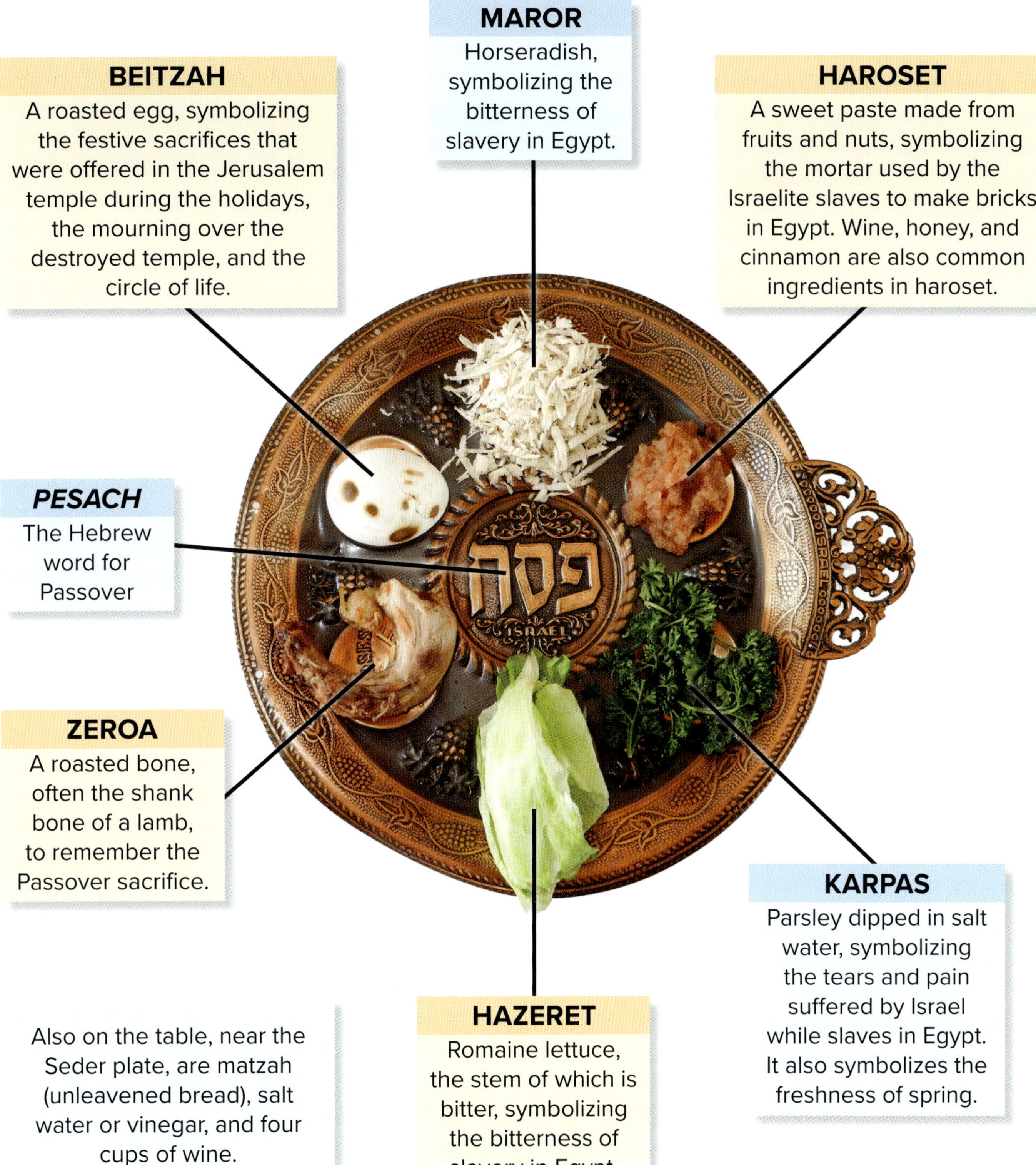

These symbolisms are some of the widespread meanings attributed to the items. Many more have been suggested.

In addition to the Seder, we observe Passover in other ways throughout the week. In commemoration of (and in symbolic commiseration with) the Egyptians whose firstborn were slain in the tenth plague, the day of Passover eve is observed as a fast by firstborn males. On the first day of Pesach, we cease our traditional winter prayers for rain, since rain is not expected in the Land of Israel in the summer months. Days two through six are semi-holidays. Their daily liturgy and scriptural readings are special, with shortened Hallel Psalms, but the days are not Shabbat-like. We continue to eat only hametz-free food the entire week.

When the Israelites crossed the Red Sea, they sang the Song of the Sea (Ex. 15:1–18). According to Jewish tradition, the Egyptians drowned in the sea on the seventh day of Pesach. Many Jews explain the reason for the shortened Hallel on the last days of Pesach with this story from the Babylonian Talmud: As the Israelites were crossing the Red Sea, "the ministering angels began to sing God's praises [Hallel]. The Holy One, blessed by God, [stopped them and] said, 'How can you sing My praises when My creatures are drowning in the sea!?'"[57]

From the Lovell Haggadah, this illustration depicts the Hallel of Miriam and other women rejoicing after the Israelites crossed the Red Sea. (Art by Matthew L. Berkowitz)

How Many Days Is Pesach?

In ancient times, the holiday was extended for practical reasons to the twenty-second day of Nisan for Jewish communities who lived outside of Israel, making it eight days rather than seven. The reason had to do with the speed of communication. The Bible commands that Passover begin on the fifteenth day of Nisan, but the exact day when Nisan began was not known until witnesses actually saw the new moon in the sky, only two weeks earlier. Since communication in the ancient world was slow, an additional, second, day was observed for the "holy convocations" which take place on the first and seventh (last) days of the holiday, so that one of the two days was sure to fall on the correct date (Lev. 23:7–8).

As a result, Passover for Jewish communities outside the Land of Israel, became an eight-day holiday with two Shabbat-like holy convocations on the first and second as well as the seventh and eighth days. These extra days are called "holidays for those in exile," and this eight-day celebration of Passover has persisted to this day for Jews living outside of Israel, even though we are no longer dependent on the visual observations of the moon. The holy convocations at the beginning and end of Sukkot are similarly doubled, as is the one day of Shavuot; but all other holidays are celebrated on the same dates whether in Israel or elsewhere.

SHAVUOT (WEEKS, PENTECOST)

The holiday Shauvot (Weeks or Pentecost) is known in the Hebrew Bible only in an agricultural context, as the pilgrimage feast of the harvest and the day of the firstfruits (Ex. 23:16; Num. 28:26).[58] In the Hebrew Bible, it is described only as falling on the fiftieth day,[59] following a "week of weeks" (Lev. 23:15–16) after Pesach, without a specific event connected to Israel's founding historical narrative.[60]

While Pesach commemorates the Israelites' departure from Egypt and Sukkot marks their journeying to the Land of Israel, it was only in the late Second Temple period that Shavuot began to be associated with a specific event from the exodus narrative: the divine manifestation to Moses at Sinai. This event took place "in the third month after the Israelites departed Egypt" (Ex. 19:1). The rabbis fixed the date of Shavuot as the sixth day of Sivan (the third month, May/June) and attributed the revelation at Sinai to that date.[61]

Today, Shavuot is celebrated with fewer rituals and commandments than either Pesach or Sukkot. The theme of the holiday is the revelation of the Torah. In the liturgy, the day is called "The Day of God's Giving the Torah." Current practice emphasizes Israel receiving the Torah—God's instructions for how his people should live with each other and in relationship to him now that they were called out of bondage and were called to be a distinct people among the nations. This is marked with all-night Torah study of both the written Torah (Bible) and the oral Torah (the Talmud and other rabbinic writings). By studying these texts, we show that we, too, and not just ancient Israel, have received these texts and they are part of our lives. Many conclude their all-night study with a service at dawn.

Exodus 19:1–20:23 is the Torah reading for Shavuot, a passage that includes the revelation of the Ten Commandments at Sinai. We also read the book of Ruth in its entirety.[62] The story of Ruth echoes the holiday's themes because it takes place at the time of the grain harvest and depicts Ruth's conversion, which is likened to accepting Torah. Some Sephardi Jews follow the mystical custom of reading a "marriage contract" (*ketubah*) describing the betrothal of God and the Jewish people in the spirit of verses from the book of Hosea:

> I will betroth you to Me forever;
> I will betroth you to Me in righteousness,
> justice, kindness and mercy.
> And I will betroth you to Me in faithfulness,
> and you shall know YHWH.
> (Hosea 2:19–20 [Hebrew vv. 21–22])[63]

Like in other festivals, the joy of Shavuot is expressed by reciting the Hallel Psalms. Worshipers convey the harvest theme of Shavuot by decorating synagogues with greenery. It is customary to eat dairy foods on Shavuot, and some people dress in white.

The Scroll of Ruth, handwritten on parchment and written without vowels (unvocalized). The story of Ruth is read on Shavuot, though usually from a book rather than a scroll. (Photo by Paul H. Wright)

SUKKOT (BOOTHS)

Sukkot begins with the full moon of the month of Tishri (September/October) and extends over seven days. It's called *the* feast in 1 Kings 8:2 and Nehemiah 8:14, as well as by the rabbis, because it is regarded as *the* holiday of special gladness: "You shall have nothing but joy" (Deut. 16:15).[64]

The primary ritual of Sukkot is dwelling in a *sukkah,* a thatch-roofed hut, fulfilling the commandment in Leviticus 23:43: "... in order that future generations may know that I made the Israelite people live in booths when I brought them out of the land of Egypt." The rabbis defined "dwelling" as eating one's meals in the sukkah, though many today sleep there as well. According to one mystical custom, biblical heroes are invited symbolically into the sukkah. These include Abraham, Isaac, Jacob, Moses, Aaron, Joseph, and David. Today, some people also add seven heroines: usually Sarah, Miriam, Deborah, Hannah, Abigail, Huldah, and Esther.[65] Others include Rebecca, Rachel, Leah, Ruth, and Tamar.

The agricultural roots of Sukkot, which is also called the "Feast of Ingathering" (Ex. 23:16; see also Deut. 16:13), are more apparent in a second commandment specific to the holiday: "On the first day you shall take the product of hadar trees, branches of palm trees, boughs of leafy trees, and willows of the brook, and you shall rejoice before YHWH your God seven days" (Lev. 23:40). According to rabbinic interpretation, these four species of plants, in order, are the etrog, a citron (a lemon-like citrus fruit); the lulav, an unopened palm branch; sprigs of myrtle; and willows. The rabbis interpreted this verse to suggest that the bouquet actually represents God:

- The fruit of a stately (hadar) tree (etrog)—this is the Holy One of Being, for it is written of God "You are clothed with grandeur and glory [hadar]" (Ps. 104:1);
- Fronds of palm (lulav)—"The Righteous blossoms like a date palm" (Ps. 92:12 [Hebrew v. 13]);
- Myrtle—"[God] was standing among the myrtles" (Zech. 1:8); and
- Willow (*aravah*)—"Pave the way for the one who rides through the deserts [*aravot*, plural form of *aravah*], for Yah is His name" (Ps. 68:4 [Hebrew v. 5]).[66]

During the synagogue service, we wave the lulav and etrog (which, by implication, means all four species) while reciting the Hallel Psalms, then again during the procession as we recite the Hosanna prayers. Each of these is a liturgical poem (*piyyut*) with the refrain "Deliver us!" (Ps. 118:25). One *piyyut* is recited during the synagogue procession each day of Sukkot. Then, on the seventh day, there are seven processions with seven *piyyutim*, giving this day the name *Hoshana Rabbah*, "The Day of Many Hosannas."

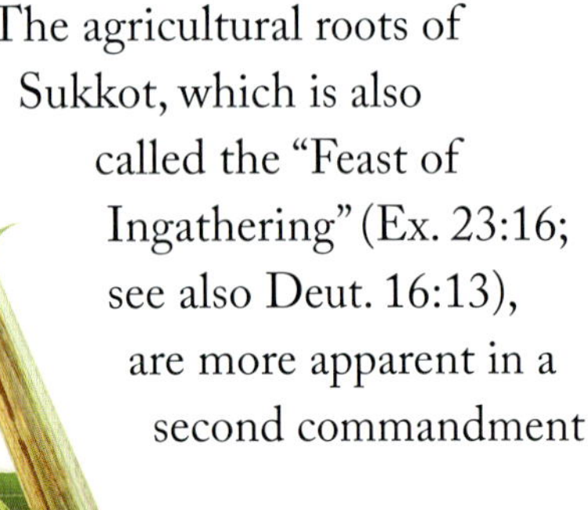

The lulav is used by holding it and waving it right, left, front, back, up, and down, symbolizing God's sovereignty over all creation.

This sukkah is decorated with a printed Hebrew blessing along its sides: "Grant peace everywhere goodness and blessing, Grace, lovingkindness and mercy to us and unto all Israel, Your people." (Photo by alefbet/Shutterstock)

Sukkot lasts seven days, of which only the first day is a sacred occasion, a Shabbat-like holy convocation. The day after Sukkot, the eighth day, is specified separately as a sacred occasion in its own right and also as a day of "solemn assembly" (*atzeret*; v. 36).[67] Because this day follows immediately after Sukkot it may feel like part of that holiday, but it isn't. To make the distinction clear, none of the Sukkot rituals are performed on this eighth day, and it is improper to sit (and eat) in the sukkah on this day.

While the three pilgrimage festivals gained a level of historic significance in the exodus cycle, this day that follows Sukkot gained a liturgical role instead. It has a double name: Shemini Atzeret, "The Eighth Day of Assembly," and Simchat Torah, "[The Day of] Rejoicing of the Torah." (Outside of Israel, this eighth day is doubled so that the eighth is observed as Shemini Atzeret and the ninth as Simchat Torah; in Israel both are observed on the same day.)

In the liturgical calendar, this is the day on which the annual cycle of Torah reading concludes; then it begins again for the following year. In the synagogue, the last verses of the last book of the Torah (Deut. 33:1–34:12) are read over and over to give everyone a chance to be called up for the reading. This is followed by reading the first verses of the first book of the Torah (Gen. 1:1–2:3). We rejoice in the Torah by walking in a procession around the sanctuary seven times, which in most synagogues become circles of ecstatic dancing with the Torah scrolls.

Those of us who may be weary after eleven days of holidays in the month of Tishri (or weary of reading about them) may be consoled by the rabbis' humorous portrayal of this feeling:

> Rabbi Levi said: God desired to give to the children of Israel a festival for each and every

Winter prayers for rain begin at the conclusion of Sukkot. The use of fruit and vegetables in the holiday ritual together with these prayers for rain help us connect the holiday to its agricultural origins.

Shemini Atzeret (Simchat Torah)

Sukkot's seventh day, Hoshana Rabbah, is a semi-holiday like days two through six and the intermediate days of Pesach. But on its heels, day eight, comes another holiday. We can see this structure in Leviticus:

> Say to the Israelite people: On the fifteenth day of this seventh month there shall be the Feast of Booths to the Lord, [to last] seven days. The first day shall be a sacred occasion: you shall not work at your occupations; seven days you shall bring offerings by fire to the Lord. On the eighth day, you shall observe a sacred occasion and bring an offering by fire to the Lord; it is a solemn assembly: you shall not work at your occupations. (Lev. 23:34–36)

month during the summer, so He gave them Pesach in Nisan, the minor Pesach [see Num. 9:10–12] in Iyar, and Shavuot in Sivan. But as He was about to give them a notable feast in Tammuz, they made themselves the golden calf, and as a result He took away the festivals He had intended for the months of Tammuz, Av, and Elul. He made up, however, for Israel's being deprived of the festivals He had intended them to celebrate during the three previous months by assigning them all to the following month, Tishri, and having the three festivals—Rosh HaShanah, Yom Kippur, and Sukkot—celebrated within Tishri's span. Then the Holy One, blessed be God, said to them: Since Tishri has been used to make up for the other months and has not been given a festival that is its own, let it be given its own day. Hence, "On the eighth day ye shall have [an additional] solemn assembly" [Num. 29:35].[68]

Shemini Atzeret concludes the autumn season of penitence and rejoicing. In biblical times, the sacrifices of this eighth day closely resembled those of Rosh HaShanah and Yom Kippur but not those of Sukkot.[69] Today, as is the custom for the High Holidays, the prayer leader dresses in white for Hoshana Rabbah, the day before (the seventh day of Sukkot), and leads prayers using melodies echoing those of Rosh HaShanah and Yom Kippur. It is a fitting conclusion for this somber yet joyous season.

Lifting up the Torah scroll during Simchat Torah, here at the Western Wall, Jerusalem. (Photo by John Theodor/Shutterstock)

PURIM

Purim, or the Feast of Esther, is our last biblical festive holiday. It occurs in the month of Adar, the twelfth month of the Jewish liturgical calendar. Purim is both the youngest of the biblical holidays and concludes the liturgical year, which ends in the spring, the month before Passover. It is a joyous festival celebrating the deliverance of the Jews as described in the Scroll of Esther. The name *Purim* is taken from the word *lots* (*purim;* singular, *pur*), which were cast to determine the date of the Jews' annihilation by Haman (Est. 9:24–26). Esther is one of the five books, or scrolls, of the Hebrew Scriptures, each of which has been read on a different feast or fast day since the Middle Ages:

- Esther on Purim
- Song of Songs on Pesach
- Ruth on Shavuot
- Lamentations on the ninth of the month of Av
- Ecclesiastes on Sukkot

The reading of Esther is the central commandment of the day of Purim. This reading must be done from a handwritten, unvocalized (written without vowels) parchment scroll, like the scroll from which we read the Torah. (The text of the other scrolls may be read ritually on their particular day from a book.) Esther is read after sunset on Purim eve as well as the following morning. Children—and in some communities adults too—dress up in costumes for the reading and other Purim events. When the name of the villain Haman is read, the congregation uses noisemakers with great delight to "blot him out." All in all, there is much merriment throughout the day in the spirit of the royal feasts and banquets described in the Scroll of Esther (see Est. 1:5–9; 5:4–5, 8; 7:1–2). (In Israeli schools, the celebration lasts for an entire week.) This line from "Al HaNissim" ("For the Miracles"), the liturgy of Purim (and Hanukkah too), captures the excitement of the holiday: "For the miracles, the redemption, the mighty acts, the deliverance and the battles which You did for our ancestors in those days, at this season."[70]

School children dressed in costume for Purim in Safed, Israel, a custom that dates back to medieval times. (Photo by David Cohen 156/Shutterstock)

The three other commandments of the day are feasting, gift-giving to friends, and gift-giving to the poor. These are based on the practice described in Esther:

> Mordecai recorded these events. And he sent dispatches to all the Jews throughout the provinces of King Ahasuerus, near and far, charging them to observe the fourteenth and fifteenth days of Adar, every year—the same days on which the Jews enjoyed relief from their foes and the same month which had been transformed for them from one of grief and mourning to one of festive joy. They were to observe them as days of feasting and merrymaking, and as an occasion for sending gifts to one another and presents to the poor. (Est. 9:20–22)

Hamantaschen, a traditional Purim treat.

The Scroll of Esther records that Purim was first marked on the fifteenth day of the month Adar in Susa (Shushan), the walled capital of Persia, and on the fourteenth day outside the city (Est. 9:18–19). As a result, today we observe Purim on the fifteenth in Jerusalem—also a walled city—but on the fourteenth elsewhere. The thirteenth day of Adar, just before Purim, is observed as a fast to commemorate Esther's three-day fast (Est. 4:16). Some Jewish communities and families observe additional Purims at different times of the year to commemorate protection from dangers that had threatened to annihilate their own family or community.[71]

The traditional food for Purim is the hamantaschen pastries. In German and Yiddish, the name means "Haman's pockets;" the Hebrew term for the dessert means "Haman's ears." Hamantaschen are triangular pastries filled with sweet ingredients like poppy seed, apricot jam, dates, or chocolate—an annual delight!

HANUKKAH

Hanukkah shares the theme of deliverance with its biblical cousin Purim but is not itself a biblical holiday. Its story of the victory of the Jews over the Seleucid Greeks in the second century BCE is told in the books of 1 and 2 Maccabees. Some Jewish literature of the late Second Temple period, including the books of Maccabees, was preserved by some churches and became part of their Bible, but for others, including the Jews, the writings became apocryphal (not considered part of Scripture). While of interest to scholars of Jewish history and thought, the two books have no religious standing in Judaism.

The liturgy for Hanukkah reflects the holiday's theme of redemption: "You effected a great redemption for your people Israel.... Your children ... purified your sanctuary and lit lamps ... establishing these eight days of Hanukkah for thanksgiving and praise of Your great name."[72]

The rabbis present Hanukkah in the Talmud by introducing the miracle story of the temple candelabrum.[73] Following the liberation of Jerusalem from the Greeks and the purification of the temple, the candelabrum, they say, burned for eight days with pure oil, even though there had only been sufficient pure oil for twenty-four hours.

The dreidel, a spinning top, is a Hanukkah toy. Shown here are the letters *gimmel* in green representing "great," and *nun* in blue representing "miracle."

Eight candles on a Hanukkah menorah are lit on the eighth (and last) night of the festival using a ninth candle.

This miracle story is the origin of the custom of lighting a Hanukkah menorah (lamp) with eight wicks. On the first night one candle is lit, on the second two, and so on for eight days. There is a place on the menorah for a ninth candle, the *shammash*, which is used to light the others. It is customary to place the lamp in the window to publicize the miracle for passers-by.

The holiday of Hanukkah is centered on the home. It is customary to eat foods cooked with oil to remember the oil miracle. In North America, this food is *latkes,* which are potato pancakes. In other parts of the Jewish world, and especially in Israel, the food of choice is *sufganiyot,* filled doughnuts. Children play with a special spinning top, a *dreidel,* which has on each of its four sides one Hebrew initial of each word of the phrase "a **G**reat **M**iracle **H**appened **T**here" (or **H**ere, when the game is played in Israel). In North America, Hanukkah has become a holiday of gift giving, as it falls so close in the calendar to Christmas. This has made it a popular holiday, although it is not one of the major Jewish festivals.

We recite the Hallel Psalms in the morning synagogue service each day of Hanukkah. The Torah readings describe the offerings of the chiefs of the twelve tribes of Israel and the first lighting of the seven branched menorah at the dedication of the tabernacle (Num. 7–8).

THE FASTS

The Jewish calendar includes a cycle of four fasts, all related to national catastrophes. They commemorate the destruction of both the First and Second Temples in Jerusalem and the loss of Israel's national independence as a result. The four are all mentioned in one verse in the Hebrew Bible, a statement of consolation in which Zechariah prophesies:

> Thus said the Lord of Hosts: The fast of the fourth month, the fast of the fifth month, the fast of the seventh month, and the fast of the tenth month shall become occasions for joy and gladness, happy festivals for the House of Judah; but you must love honesty and integrity. (Zech. 8:19)

To know which month each of these fasts are observed in, we must remember that these months are counted from Nisan (Abib) the first month of the biblical year, not the month of Tishri which begins the civil new year with Rosh HaShanah.

- **The fast of the fourth month** is the seventeenth day of Tammuz (summer), commemorating the Babylonians' breach of the walls of Jerusalem in 586 BCE (2 Kings 25:3–4).
- **The fast of the fifth month** is Tisha b'Av, the ninth of Av (late summer), which

On the eve of Tisha b'Av, people gather to read Lamentations and dirges to mourn the temple's destruction. Pictured here are mourners gathered at the women's section of the Western Wall a remnant of the temple complex (left), and overlooking Jerusalem's Old City (right). (Photos by Ophir Yarden [left] and Brian Negin [right])

commemorates the temple's destruction by both the Babylonians in 586 BCE and by the Romans in 70 CE.[74]

- **The fast of the seventh month** (autumn) is the fast of Gedaliah, which commemorates the assassination by fellow Judeans of Gedaliah, son of Ahikam, who had been appointed governor by the Babylonians after they destroyed the temple (2 Kings 25:25; Jer. 41:1–3).
- **The fast of the tenth month** is the tenth of Tevet (winter), which marks the onset of the Babylonian siege of Jerusalem in 587 BCE (2 Kings 25:1).

With the exception of the fast of the fifth month, these fasts are minor fasts and observed only from dawn to dark.[75]

The fifth-month fast, Tisha b'Av, is the saddest day of the Jewish year. The Babylonian Talmud likened mourning for the destroyed temples to the anguish felt by one in the presence of yet-unburied kin, a time without closure when the sense of loss is most acute.[76] The liturgy of Tisha b'Av calls for divine comfort for our profound loss: "Comfort, YHWH our God, the mourners of Zion and Jerusalem." We observe the customs of mourning while sitting on the floor or low stools. Lamentations is read—in subdued lighting and usually from a book rather than a scroll—followed by dirges, both in the evening as well as the morning. Other than Yom Kippur, which lasts just over twenty-four hours, this is the only fast from dusk one day till dark the next. We do not wear tefillin (phylacteries) in the morning service as they are considered inappropriate ornaments for a day of lamenting. Instead, we wear them in the afternoon service when the mourning is less intense. Washing, wearing perfume, sexual relations, and wearing leather shoes are forbidden on this day. (In ancient times, leather-soled shoes were more comfortable than the alternatives, so they were considered inappropriate for times of mourning.) Before the fast, it is customary to eat a simple meal including a hard-boiled egg dipped in ash. The egg's round shape is a sign of the lifecycle.

OTHER OBSERVANCES AND SPECIAL TIMES

Counting the Omer

As the Christian calendar has Advent and Lent, so the Jewish calendar also marks special periods of time that fall between or lead up to the holidays. The first of these is the period of Counting the Omer. The *omer* is a sheaf of barley that was brought to the temple after Pesach (Lev. 23:10). The forty-nine days of this seven-week period are counted as commanded in Leviticus:

> And from the day on which you bring the sheaf of elevation offering—the day after the Shabbat—you shall count off seven weeks. They must be complete: you must count until the day after the seventh week—fifty days; then you shall bring an offering of new grain to YHWH. (Lev. 23:15–16)

Pesach marks the barley harvest and Shavuot the wheat harvest, which made the in-between seven weeks a period fraught with agricultural uncertainty and anxiety: *Will the harvest be bountiful or poor?* So the span between Pesach and Shavuot became a semi-mourning period. It is observed by refraining from weddings and includes restrictions on grooming. The period is punctuated by a minor festival, Lag b'Omer, which falls on the thirty-third day of Counting the Omer and serves as a break from the somberness. Throughout the counting period, excitement grows, continuing to rise as we approach the anniversary of the receiving of the Torah that is commemorated on Shavuot.

The omer is counted for seven weeks from Passover to Shavuot. Special calendars are used to remind worshipers of the correct date. Pictured here is an omer calendar from Italy, produced in 1804, today in the Jewish Museum, London. (Photo by Ethan Doyle White/Wikimedia)

Date honey is often eaten on Rosh HaShanah and the seder for Tu b'Shevat.

Tu b'Shevat, Jewish Arbor Day

The fifteenth day of the eleventh month, Shevat (January/February), is Tu b'Shevat, Jewish Arbor Day. The Talmud fixed this date as one of four New Year's Days, each for a different purpose.[77] Today, just as there are "years" such as school years and fiscal years, Tu b'Shevat marks the beginning of the year for orchards. The date is not mentioned in the Bible, but it is important for observing the biblical commandment to tithe (Deut. 14:22–27). Fruit that budded before this holiday is tithed with the prior year's produce, while fruit that buds after is tithed with that of the coming year. In places outside of Israel, historically this was a day on which the Land of Israel was remembered by eating the dried fruits of its trees. In Israel today, it is also a time to plant trees and become more ecologically aware of the world in which we live. It has become popular to conduct a seder (like for Pesach) on this holiday.[78] This seder usually involves eating many types of fruit and produce, especially the seven species with which the Land of Israel was blessed: wheat, barley, grapes, figs, pomegranates, olives, and honey, often understood to be made from dates (Deut. 8:8). The day is accompanied by singing songs and reciting biblical and rabbinic passages that mention fruit and produce.

It's traditional to use the foods and other elements from one holiday in the observance of other holidays. This emphasizes the cycle of the Jewish year. For example, Jews of my ancestral community in Tzvil, Ukraine, eat etrog jam on Tu b'Shevat and pray for a beautiful etrog for next Sukkot.[79] In Turkey and Cochin, India, leftover candles from

Reform Judaism

The Reform movement in Judaism, which arose in Europe in the nineteenth century, has departed in many ways from traditional observances. With regard to the holidays, its most significant change was to eliminate the second days of the holidays for those in exile. As a result, most Reform communities follow a calendar that adheres more closely to the dates of the feasts as they appear in the Bible than those in common Jewish practice. Pesach is seven days and only the first and last days are observed as Shabbat-like holidays, rather than eight days with the first two and last two as full holidays. Shavuot is one and not two days. Sukkot, like Pesach, is seven days, with the eighth day observed as Simchat Torah. Rosh HaShanah may be observed as either one or two days in Reform synagogues. With the exception of Rosh HaShanah, which is always observed as two days in Israel, the Reform calendar matches the calendar followed in Israel.

Hanukkah and palm branches (lulav), thatch, and willows from Sukkot are used to burn the hametz and/or bake matzah for Pesach. Afghani Jews use leftover nuts and almonds from the Tu b'Shevat seder to make haroset for Pesach.[80]

Tu b'Av, a Jewish "Valentine's Day"

The fifteenth day of the month of Av (July/August) is Tu b'Av, a happy day falling just a week after the sadness of Tisha b'Av (the ninth of Av). The Talmud attributes several positive events to this date, including permission for cross-tribal marriage that had been prohibited according to the story in the Bible of the daughters of Zelophehad (Num. 36:1–12).[81] As a result, the day has acquired characteristics of matchmaking and romance, serving as a kind of Jewish "Valentine's Day."

It was also regarded as the date on which preparation of the wood for the needs of the temple in the coming year was completed (Neh. 13:31).

Holidays of Modern Israel

Jews living in Israel also celebrate holidays related to modern Jewish history and the establishment of the State of Israel. Many Jews (and some Christians) find connections between ancient Jewish history and recent events through Zionism, an ideology and national movement that advocates the return of the Jewish people to the Land of Israel.

Modern Zionism, which rests on the abiding connection of the people of Israel to the Land of Israel, was first advanced by secular Jews. While for the early adherents of Zionism, *secular* meant "distanced from traditional Jewish belief and practice," it did not mean abandonment of a Jewish identity. Quite the contrary. For these pioneers of Zionism, the return to the Land of Israel was a return to the land of the Bible and a biblical Judaism. While they diminished the theological aspects of the holidays (particularly Rosh HaShanah and Yom Kippur), they strongly reconnected with the agricultural aspects of the pilgrimage festivals. New versions of traditional ceremonies were developed to articulate the holidays' historical and agricultural features for modern Israel. Pesach, for example, was reinvested with the symbolism of the spring season (Deut. 16:1), while at Shavuot, kibbutz farmers brought their firstfruits to Jerusalem (Deut. 26:1–3).[82]

Following the Holocaust and the establishment of the State of Israel, several new dates were added to the Jewish/Israeli calendar. Foremost is **Yom HaAtzmaut, Independence Day,** which commemorates the Hebrew date of Israel's Declaration of Independence on May 14, 1948.[83] It is observed on the fifth of Iyar (April/May) on the Jewish calendar. While it is mostly a secular holiday,[84] some Israelis hold religious services and recite the Hallel Psalms during the day.[85]

Fireworks light up the night sky for Independence Day in Tel Aviv, Israel. (Photo by Orlov Sergei/Shutterstock)

Yom HaZikkaron, Memorial Day, honors fallen soldiers and victims of hostile acts and is observed the day before Independence Day.[86] Though mostly a secular day, its opening ritual held at the Western Wall in Jerusalem includes both religious and secular elements.[87]

During the previous week, on the twenty-seventh of Nisan (April, falling just after Pesach), is **Yom HaShoah, Memorial Day for the Holocaust and Heroism.** This day honors not only the six million Jews who were exterminated in the Nazi Holocaust but also the heroism of those who resisted. This sad day sits awkwardly in Nisan, the month of redemption, which is otherwise a happy time.[88]

These three days in the Israeli calendar form a unit that parallels the three pilgrimage festivals of the Bible. By observing the festivals in a yearly cycle, we retell our shared history, from exiting Egypt to receiving Torah at Mount Sinai to traveling through the desert on the way to the Land of Israel. These modern Israeli days involve a similar retelling, taking us from the Holocaust, through Israel's War of Independence, and on to the establishment of the State of Israel. It is fitting to call this springtime period the Ten Days of Deliverance to parallel the Ten Days of Repentance observed in the autumn.

A CLOSING WORD

The Jewish calendar is a synopsis of Judaism. The festivals, fasts, and other holidays together form a tapestry, woven of the joyous and the somber. Special days are marked with ceremonies and rituals in the home and in the synagogue (and beyond). Our calendar is comprised of elements from the biblical, rabbinic, medieval, and modern eras and has evolved in both the Land of Israel and for Jews in all parts of the globe. To follow the Jewish year is to take the pulse of the Jewish people.

Notes for Chapter 3

1 Mizrahi Jews are sometimes also called Oriental Jews.

2 In the Jewish tradition, weeks have names, each called by the name of the portion of the Torah that is read in the synagogue that week.

3 *b. Berakhot* 26a.

4 A leap month is added in seven out of nineteen years.

5 In ancient times, before the calculated calendar, the extra month was added according to the seasons and the state of the crops. The holidays of Pesach, Shavuot, and Sukkot are harvest holidays and also must fall at the appropriate times.

6 Because the holidays are celebrated in Adar II, the month that is added is technically Adar I.

7 Some have rendered the name "Jehovah," but the initial consonant would have had a *Y* rather than a *J* sound. The letters of God's name seem to be closely connected to the verb "to be," which seems quite appropriate and reminds us of God's own description of his name given at Moses's request. "Moses said to God, 'When I come to the Israelites and say to them, "The God of your fathers has sent me to you," and they ask me, "What is His name?" what shall I say to them?' And God said to Moses, 'Ehyeh-Asher-Ehyeh,'" which is variously translated "I Am That I Am;" "I Am Who I Am;" "I Will Be What I Will Be;" etc. (Ex. 3:13–14).

8 Some communities recite Isaiah 58:13 and the next verse in the sanctification of the Shabbat that is recited at lunchtime.

9 Indeed, the reference to "the third day" in John 2:1 most probably means that the wedding in Cana happened on a Tuesday. This is a day that is especially popular for Jewish weddings because on the third day of creation, God "saw that it was good" twice (Gen. 1:10, 12).

10 All translations of classical Jewish sources in this chapter are at the author's discretion. For biblical quotations, the author draws heavily from *TANAKH: The Holy Scriptures, Jewish Publication Society of America* (NJPS, 1985) and Robert Alter, *The Hebrew Bible: A Translation with Commentary*. 3 vols. (New York: W. W. Norton, 2018).

11 The Hebrew word *melakhah* is usually translated "work," but this is inadequate because it tends to make the reader think of things primarily performed with physical exertion and/or vocationally, related to one's job. It is better to think of *melakhah* as tasks related to the normal pace of life throughout the week. The word is also used in the Torah in connection with the creative activities done to construct the tabernacle (Ex. 35). As God ceased creating on Shabbat, so do we.

12 *b. Avodah Zarah* 3a.

13 In many Christian liturgies, the "Priestly Blessing" concludes an element of the service. Outside the Land of Israel, the words are recited by *kohanim*, descendants of Aaron, on the five biblical holidays: Rosh HaShanah, Yom Kippur, and three festivals. In Israel, *kohanim* recite the blessing on Shabbat as well, and in Jerusalem they recite it daily.

14 There is a less widely observed custom to recite Psalm 137 before grace on weekdays.

15 This reunion imagery originates in the Talmud (*b. Shabbat* 119a) and was developed by the Jewish mystics in the Galilean city of Safed in the sixteenth century CE.

16 Psalms 95–99, 29, 92, and 93.

17 *Midrash Genesis Rabbah* 11:8; Ex. 20:8. The Hebrew word rendered here as sanctify/betroth is *leqadsho* which means sanctify, similar to *qiddush*. This rabbinic wordplay is based on the Jewish marriage ceremony in which the bride is sanctified to the groom.

18 Psalms 19, 34, 90, 91, 135, 136, 33, 92, and 93 are added in their entirety. Psalms are ubiquitous in Jewish liturgy. These are the Shabbat additions to the six daily psalms in one segment of the liturgy.

19 The Jewish Bible (Tanakh) regards more books as prophetic than the Christian Bible, and the *haftarah* is often taken from them. The following story illustrates the difference. Some good Anglican friends were once guests at my Shabbat dinner table. Conversation turned to the weekly Torah portion, which related the story of Moses sending the spies into Canaan (Num. 13). My guest, a Canon in the Church of England, inquired, "Ophir, what is read as the *haftarah* tomorrow?" I grinned and suggested that he might guess, as it seemed to me an obvious choice. After a few uncomfortable moments, he gave up and asked for the answer. Embarrassed at the situation, I replied, "It's the story of Joshua sending the spies!" (Josh. 2), to

which he responded, "But Ophir, the book of Joshua isn't among the prophets." And so I sheepishly explained that Jews consider the historical books Joshua, Judges, Samuel, and Kings to be the "Former Prophets," from which the *haftarah* can be taken.

20 Although the word *musaf* comes from the same root as the name Joseph (*Yosef*, Gen. 30:24), it itself is not found in the Bible. It first appears in the Mishnah (for example, *m. Ta'anit* 4:4 and *m. Zevahim* 10:1).

21 Additions include a Musaf service, Hallelujah Psalms, and an additional person called up to read the Torah.

22 The origin of this name is found in the midrash *Pesikta Hadata* section 46 on Joel 2:11: "For great is the day of YHWH—this is Rosh HaShanah, 'and very awesome (*nora*)—who can take it in?'—this is Yom Kippur."

23 The Hebrew word for these prayers of penitence is *slichot*.

24 *Zohar,* Gen. 1:132b. Nathan Wolski, "Time and Exegesis in the Zohar," *Prooftexts* 28/2 (2008): 101–128. The *Zohar*, or "Book of Splendor," likely authored in thirteenth century Spain, is the central work of Jewish mysticism. Passages from the *Zohar* are included in the *siddur* (prayerbook).

25 Each word or phrase in these verses (counting God's name twice) is reckoned as a divine attribute. In rabbinic thought, this name, the Tetragrammaton or four-lettered name of God (YHWH), represents God's attribute of mercy (*Midrash Sifrei,* Deuteronomy 26).

26 *Israel* has been the term most widely used by the Jews to refer to themselves from Second Temple times until the beginning of modernity.

27 "Our mothers" refers to Sara, Rebecca, Rachel, and Leah.

28 This *piyyut*, "Anenu," is based on *m. Ta'anit* 2:4. The reader should not confuse this with another prayer of the same name recited on fast days.

29 The shofar is blown by Mizrahi and Sephardi Jews during slihot and by Ashkenazi Jews during the morning service.

30 Rosh HaShanah is observed for two days, both the first and second of the month. This has its origin in the period before the calculated calendar, when there was uncertainty about which night the first sliver of the new moon could be seen.

31 Hayim Lapin, "Temple: Cult, and Consumption in Second-Temple Jerusalem," in *Expressions of Cult in the Southern Levant in the Greco-Roman Period: Manifestations in Text and Material Culture*, eds. Oren Tal and Zeev Weiss (Brepols: Turnhout 2017), 242.

32 The practice of considering January 1 as New Year's Day is so prominent worldwide that it tends to overshadow Rosh HaShanah as the start of the year for most Jews. The exception is in Israel, where Rosh HaShanah is prominent and the Hebrew calendar is in official use. Nevertheless, most Israelis are more familiar with the Gregorian calendar than the Jewish, though in some religious communities and schools the Hebrew calendar is dominant. See Charles S. Liebman and Eliezer Don-Yihiya, *Civil Religion in Israe*l (Berkeley: University of California Press, 1983), 50–51.

33 Each theme is illustrated by ten biblical verses. Three are taken from Torah, three from the Prophets, and three from the Writings. The tenth verse is again from the Torah.

34 *y. Rosh HaShanah*, 1:3/7b.

35 *b. Rosh HaShanah* 8a–b, 34a

36 David Ben Joseph Abudarham, *The Complete Book of Abudarham: Commentary on the Blessings and Prayers*. (Warsaw: Shriftgissen, 1877), 73r, column 145. This is an edition of a book that was first written in the fourteenth century and its author, Abudarham, seems to be the last person to have read Saadia Gaon's original text. It has since been lost.

37 *b. Rosh HaShanah* 29a.

38 In Jewish tradition, this narrative is referred to as the *akeda*, or "binding," of Isaac, rather than his sacrifice.

39 Rachel gave birth to her first son, Joseph, in Genesis 30:22–24 and to Benjamin in Genesis 35:16–18.

40 Martin Buber observed that such a multiple refrain of the root word shows it to be a guideword that "convey[s] meaning without expressing it [explicitly]" so that "the meaning will be revealed more strikingly." Robert Alter, *The Art of Biblical Narrative* (New York: Basic Books, 1981), 93.

41 NJPS reads, "Receive me back, let me return."

42 During most of the year, the custom is to use salt. In the Land of Israel, in ancient times, the honey was likely date honey (Deut. 8:8).

43 The first phrase is from the Babylonian Talmud (*b. Megilla* 31b) and the second was added to it in a *piyyut* composed by Rabbi Abraham Hazzan of Gerona in the thirteenth century.

44 *b. Rosh HaShanah* 16b.

45 Maimonides, *Laws of Repentance* 3:4.

46 Hosea's injunction to take words and replace sacrificial bulls (and other animals) with the [fruit of] the lips is the Sages' proof text that prayer replaces sacrifice (*Midrash Pesiqta deRav Kahana* 24; *Midrash Numbers Rabba* 18:21).

47 Of course, the need for repentance is a permanent condition. As the Mishnah teaches, "Repent one day before your death" (*m. Avot* 2:4), upon which the Talmud comments, "One should repent today [in other words, every day] lest one die tomorrow. As a result, one will repent each and every day" (*b. Shabbat* 153a). In their daily prayers, Jews seek God's support in repenting.

48 There are three services on weekdays. On Torah holidays, a fourth (Musaf) is added immediately following the morning Torah reading.

49 Difficult to translate, this *piyyut's* full opening phrase (*U'netaneh toqef qedushat hayom*) might be rendered "Let us validate the holiness of this day." The translation given here is from *The Koren Rosh HaShana Mahzor*, trans. Jonathan Sacks (Jerusalem: Koren, 2011), 564–568.

50 This phrase is from *m. Rosh HaShanah* 1:2. The rest of the composition is of uncertain medieval origin.

51 *The Koren Rosh HaShana Mahzor*, trans. Jonathan Sacks, 568.

52 Several lines of the *piyyut* are based on Ecclesiastes (Ben Sira) 50:5, part of a lengthy passage comparing the high priest's appearance to delightful elements of nature (vv. 6–10).

53 *Regalim* can also mean "times," as in Numbers 22:32. For this reason, Exodus 23:14 is translated "Three *times* in the year you shall hold a festival for me" (emphasis added). The English word *times* in Deuteronomy 16:16 is a different Hebrew word, *pe'amim*.

54 Grain refers to wheat, barley, rye, oats, and spelt. Grain products include bread, crackers, pasta, cookies, cakes, and fermented grains such as whiskey or beer.

55 Pew Research Center, "Jewish Americans in 2020," May 11, 2021. https://www.pewforum.org/2021/05/11/jewish-practices-and-customs (accessed June 8, 2021).

56 *Davar*, Tel Aviv, March 12, 1946.

57 *b. Sanhedrin* 39b.

58 In the rabbinic tradition, Shavuot is also known as *Atzeret*, "assembly," see Lev. 23:36; *m. Rosh Hashanah* 1:2, *b. Pesahim* 68b, and the Targum *ad* Numbers 28:26.

59 Hence the Greek name Pentecost, meaning "fiftieth."

60 The exact date was disputed amongst the Pharisees, Sadducees, and Qumran community, and to this day by the Karaites as well. See Marvin A. Sweeney and Zev Farber, "When Does Counting the Omer Begin?" www.thetorah.com/article/when-does-counting-the-omer-begin (accessed June 24, 2021).

61 Shavuot is also observed on the seventh day of Sivan in the Diaspora.

62 Ruth is one of the "five scrolls" (five short books of the Hebrew Scriptures) grouped together in Jewish liturgy since each is read on a particular holy day. For the others, see the Purim discussion in this chapter.

63 These verses from Hosea are recited daily while wrapping the straps of the tefillin (phylacteries).

64 *m. Rosh HaShanah* 1:2.

65 This list is based on a Talmudic pericope, *b. Megillah* 14a–b, which enumerates seven prophetesses and cites the following passages as support: Sarah (Gen. 21:12), Miriam (Ex. 15:20), Deborah (Judg. 4:4), Hannah (1 Sam. 2:1), Abigail (1 Sam. 25:20), Huldah (2 Kings 22:14), and Esther (Est. 5:1).

66 *Midrash Leviticus Rabbah* 30:9.

67 *b. Hagigah* 17a.

68 Translation adapted from William G. Braude and Israel J. Kapstein, *Pesikta de-Rab Kahana* (Philadelphia: Jewish Publication Society of America, 2002), 572.

69 Lapin, "Temple: Cult, and Consumption in Second-Temple Jerusalem," 242.

70 *The Koren Siddur*, trans. by Jonathan Sacks (Jerusalem: Koren, 2009), 130.

71 A long and interesting list can be found in "Purims, Special," *Encyclopaedia Judaica*, eds. Michael Berenbaum and Fred Skolnik, 2nd ed., vol. 16 (New York: Macmillan, 2007), 742–744.

72 *The Koren Siddur,* 130.

73 *b. Shabbat* 21b.

74 Second Kings 25:8 states that the Babylonian official Nebuzaradan came to Jerusalem on the seventh of the month and burned the temple and other prominent buildings in the city. Jeremiah 52:12 mentions that this happened on the tenth of the month. The Talmud reconciles the dates by saying that the actual burning began on the ninth (Tisha b'Av) and continued into the next day.

75 The fast of Esther before Purim and the fast of the firstborn before Pesach are also observed only from dawn to dark.

76 *b. Ta'anit* 30b.

77 There are four [different] New Year's Days. On the first of Nisan [March/April] is the New Year's Day for (counting the reigns of) kings and for the holidays. The first of Elul [August/September] is the New Year's Day for animal tithes. The first of Tishri [September/October] is the New Year's Day for [counting] years, [including] sabbatical years and jubilee years. The fifteenth of Shevat is the New Year's Day for [tithing the fruit of] tree[s] (*m. Rosh HaShanah* 1:1).

78 This is based on the practices of Galilean mystics of the sixteenth century.

79 Now Novograd-Volynsky. The custom is described in the story *Esrog Jam on Tu B'shvat*, http://www.myascent.org/esrog-jam-on-tu-bshvat (accessed July 8, 2021), which spells Tzvil, Zevhil.

80 Esther Shkalim, *A Mosaic of Israel's Traditions* (Jerusalem: Devorah, 2006), 191, 195, 207.

81 *b. Ta'anit* 30b–31a.

82 Charles S. Liebman and Eliezer Don-Yihiya, *Civil Religion in Israe*l (Berkeley: University of California Press, 1983), 50–51.

83 Prime Minister David Ben-Gurion had preferred the name "Day of Walking Upright" (*Yom Qomemiut*) based on Leviticus 26:13.

84 Ophir Yarden, "The Sanctity of Mt. Herzl and Independence Day in Israel's Civil Religion," in *Sanctity of Time and Space in Tradition and Modernity, eds.* A. Houtman, J. Schwartz, and M. Poorthuis (Leiden: Brill, 1998), 317–348.

85 The fact that this happy day falls during the counting of the omer, which is a mourning period, has been a conundrum for some traditional Jews.

86 *Yom HaZikkaron* is also a rabbinic term for Rosh HaShanah and the phrase used for it in Jewish liturgy (see Lev. 23:24).

87 Don Handelman, *Models and Mirrors: Towards an Anthropology of Public Events* (Cambridge: Cambridge University Press, 1990), 204.

88 Liturgically, the month of Nisan is marked as a happy time. Some who feel that commemorating the Holocaust in Nisan is inappropriate instead commemorate it on the fast day on the tenth of Tevet.

The Biblical Feasts and the Messianic Movement

Steven P. Lancaster

In the days of Yeshua[1] (Jesus) and his disciples, a rabbi's students memorized their teacher's words, learned to pray, celebrated Sabbath, discussed the Torah, observed the feasts, and so on, in the manner of their master. In fact, Yeshua himself taught, "A disciple is not above his teacher, but everyone when he is fully trained will be like his teacher" (Luke 6:40). Matthew records a parallel saying: "A disciple is not above his teacher, nor a servant above his master. It is enough for the disciple to be like his teacher, and the servant like his master" (Matt. 10:24–25; see also John 13:16–17).

Do we know that Master Yeshua kept the Jewish feasts? Yes. Because his parents modeled the practice of pilgrimage "according to custom" (Luke 2:42), we must believe that he too would have journeyed to Jerusalem at least three times a year following their example. Indeed, the Gospels record six times that Yeshua was in Jerusalem during a feast, plus a time when he was in Galilee during a feast:

1. Passover with his parents as a child (Luke 2:41–42)
2. Passover at the beginning of his ministry (John 2:13)
3. An unnamed feast, perhaps the Feast of Weeks, in the first year of his ministry (John 5:1)
4. In Galilee, he fed five thousand people as another Passover approached; he and they may have been on procession to Jerusalem (John 6:1–14).
5. Feast of Booths (Tabernacles) (John 7:2–38)
6. Feast of Dedication (Hanukkah) (John 10:22–23)
7. His last Passover (Matt. 26:17–30; Mark 14:12–26; Luke. 22:7–20; John 13:1–5)

Then, following his example, Yeshua's disciples remained in Jerusalem for the Feast of Weeks (Pentecost) after Yeshua had ascended to heaven just ten days earlier (Acts 1:4; 2:1).

What is our task as disciples of Yeshua today? As messianic believers, we strive to learn to be like our master and to walk in his paths as he walked. Our master Yeshua kept the feasts, and as his disciples, so should we. Keeping the biblical feasts is a matter of true discipleship.

With five barley loaves and two fish, Yeshua fed a multitude five thousand strong. John's gospel tells us that this happened when "the Passover, the feast of the Jews, was at hand," adding the accurate springtime detail that "there was much grass in the place" (John 6:4, 10). This depiction of the meal is in the Greek Orthodox Church of the Holy Apostles, Capernaum. (Photo by Paul H. Wright)

WHAT IS THE MESSIANIC MOVEMENT?

The messianic movement is a broad tent over both Jews and gentiles who believe that:

- the New Testament and its message is essentially a Jewish work written by Jewish authors;
- the New Testament is heavily dependent on the Jewish Scriptures (the Hebrew Bible); and
- the New Testament continues the theme of God's great redemptive work from those Jewish Scriptures.

The New Testament's message is that Yeshua of Nazareth is the long-awaited Messiah who was sent by God and "bore the sin of many" (Isa. 53:12).[2] Beyond this broad general statement, many distinctive beliefs begin to emerge within the movement.

The movement divides into two main groups. The first encompasses messianic Jewish believers, while the second embraces gentile believers discovering the Jewish—or some say "the Hebrew"—roots of their faith. Both tracks seek to uncover the confession and practice of the early believers in Yeshua in the first century and, to varying degrees, recover that confession and practice for today.

Modern messianic Judaism began in the late nineteenth and early twentieth centuries. It blossomed more fully into a congregational movement in the late twentieth century when several umbrella organizations emerged in an attempt to bring unity to the movement.[3] The basic statement of one such organization defines messianic Judaism as "a movement of Jewish congregations and groups committed to Yeshua the Messiah that embrace the covenantal responsibility of Jewish life and identity rooted in Torah, expressed in tradition, and renewed and applied in the context of the New Covenant."[4]

For most messianic Jews, the phrase "embrace the covenantal responsibility of Jewish life" implies observance of Sabbath, the biblical festivals, and God's instructions for life in a manner that is practiced by greater Judaism.

Rabbi David Rudolph, who has written extensively on the messianic movement, acknowledges that "thousands of Yeshua-believing Gentiles with love for the Jewish people are finding a home in the Messianic Jewish community."[5] Boaz Michael uses the term "messianic gentile" for such a believer, defining the messianic gentile as "a non-Jewish Christian who appreciates the Torah, his or her relationship with Israel, and the Jewish roots of his or her faith."[6]

These gentile believers (of whom I am a part) often face an identity crisis. *Who are we? Where do we fit in the body of Messiah and in the plan of God? What should be our practice regarding food, Sabbath, and the festivals?*[7] Many Yeshua-believing gentiles do not live near messianic synagogues or communities, yet in their desire to follow their master Yeshua in close discipleship, they seek to begin walking the path of Torah beyond what are usually called its ethical commands ("You shall not kill," etc.). One important way that messianic believers do this is by keeping the Sabbath and the biblical feasts.

This discussion of terms and identities is important for my disclosure. As a God-fearer, or messianic gentile, I cannot claim to represent all of messianic Judaism's observances of the

This messianic symbol, especially popular in North America, combines a seven-branched menorah with the Star of David and the *ichthyus*, an early Christian fish symbol still common today.

feasts.[8] How believers participate in the feasts can vary widely among messianic congregations. I am the pastor of a messianic gentile assembly in the United States.[9] At first glance, our assembly probably looks to many like a typical American church: no *kippot* (Jewish male head coverings), no Jewish prayer shawls, and no visible *tzitzit* (tassles). But at our heart, we desire a first-century practice of the faith, and this includes celebrating the biblical feasts in ways that are consistent with New Testament teaching.

THE SABBATH

Most messianic gentiles begin their journey in keeping Torah regulations by learning about the Sabbath and observing it in some formal manner. From Sabbath observance, interest in God's calendar grows and the biblical feasts become a matter of practice as well.

As we see in Isaiah, the Lord welcomes gentiles to observe his Sabbaths:

> And the foreigners who join themselves
> to the Lord,
> to minister to him, to love the name
> of the Lord,
> and to be his servants,
> everyone who keeps the Sabbath and does not
> profane it,
> and holds fast my covenant—
> these I will bring to my holy mountain,
> and make them joyful in my house of prayer;
> their burnt offerings and their sacrifices
> will be accepted on my altar;
> for my house shall be called a house of prayer
> for all peoples.
> (Isa. 56:6–7)

Sabbath rightly heads up the list of "appointed times" with the Lord:

> Six days shall work be done, but on the seventh day is a Sabbath of solemn rest, a holy convocation. You shall do no work. It is a Sabbath to the Lord in all your dwelling places. (Lev. 23:3)

From the perspective of messianic Sabbath-keepers, the Sabbath is more than a festival. It is a weekly engagement with the Lord, a weekly check on our walk with Master Yeshua. Sabbath teaches us the regularity of a biblical walk. It follows the example of God himself, who after the six days of creative activity "blessed the seventh day and made it holy, because on it God rested from all his work that he had done in creation" (Gen. 2:3). How did he make it holy? He set the day apart from the preceding six days of creation. He stopped creating. So with a cycle of regularity, messianic Sabbath-keepers—week after week, month after month, year after year—fill the first six days of each week with the creative labor of our required responsibilities, but the seventh day we set apart as twenty-four hours in which to enjoy God, family, friends, and to enter into God's promise of rest, a weekly taste of our rest in his kingdom.

The first blessing of Sabbath begins with lighting two candles.

The day begins just before sunset on Friday evening, following the pattern of creation: "There was evening and there was morning" (Gen. 1:5). The messianic family gathers to bless (that is, to thank) God four times with accompanying acts of sanctification.

- We bless God for the Sabbath lights while lighting candles, an act acknowledging that our household observes the Sabbath.
- We bless God for the fruit of the vine, an act acknowledging that this is the Sabbath day.
- We bless God while washing our hands, an act that sets ourselves apart to keep the Sabbath.
- We bless God for the bread, an act that sets the meal apart as a special meal in recognition of the Sabbath.

The messianic family sings together, eats together, laughs together, and relaxes together. What else is there to do? This is Sabbath. This is God's rest given to us. When Sabbath morning dawns, the messianic family attends an assembly with other believers to pray, sing, study, and fellowship. We fill Sabbath afternoons with reading, visits, naps, lounging, or walks in the beauty of the day—all things for which the six days of labor offer no time.

After the sun sets and darkness settles and stars appear, the family again gathers to mark a division in time. This short, family service is called *Havdalah,* meaning division or separation. God himself "separated the light from the darkness" (Gen. 1:4) and makes other divisions or distinctions within his created world. The service ends with everyone singing a folk song called *Eliyahu HaNavi,* "Elijah the Prophet," as the prophet Elijah is expected to introduce the advent of Messiah, who will introduce rest in God's kingdom.

Greetings of *shavu'a tov,* "a good week," begin after Havdalah, and in Hebrew thought so does the countdown to the next Sabbath. The names of the day follow the pattern in creation: First day, second day, third day, fourth day, fifth day, "and there was evening and there was morning, the sixth day.… So God blessed the seventh day and made it holy, because on it God rested from all his work that he had done in creation." (Gen 1:31; 2:3). *Shabbat shalom,* "Sabbath peace."

THREE CALENDARS

The Hebrew Scriptures contain three calendars that mention the biblical feasts:

- The first we can call the **pilgrim calendar** because it includes a command about pilgrimage: "Three times a year all your males shall appear before the Lord" (Ex. 23:14–17; 34:22–24; Deut. 16:1–16).
- A second calendar, in Leviticus 23, focuses on "holy conventions" and "rest days." Its purpose was to inform the people of Israel about the days of the year that required special Sabbaths and assemblies.[10] For this reason, we will refer to Leviticus 23 as the **laity calendar**, a calendar for all people in ancient Israel.
- The third calendar is the **priestly calendar** found in Numbers 28–29. This calendar lists the sacrifices for each feast day which the priests performed on behalf of the people. The priestly calendar begins with the daily offerings of the tabernacle (Num. 28:3–8); then follows with the Sabbath offerings (Num. 28:9–10); and then the new moon offerings (Num. 28:11–15); and finally, the annual festival offerings (Num. 28:16–29:40).

In addition to the pilgrimage feasts, the laity and priestly calendars include the Sabbath. The priestly calendar also includes the new moon festival, and although it is not mentioned in the laity calendar, it is implied since recognizing when each new moon appears is necessary to keep the feasts in their correct months and on their correct days (for

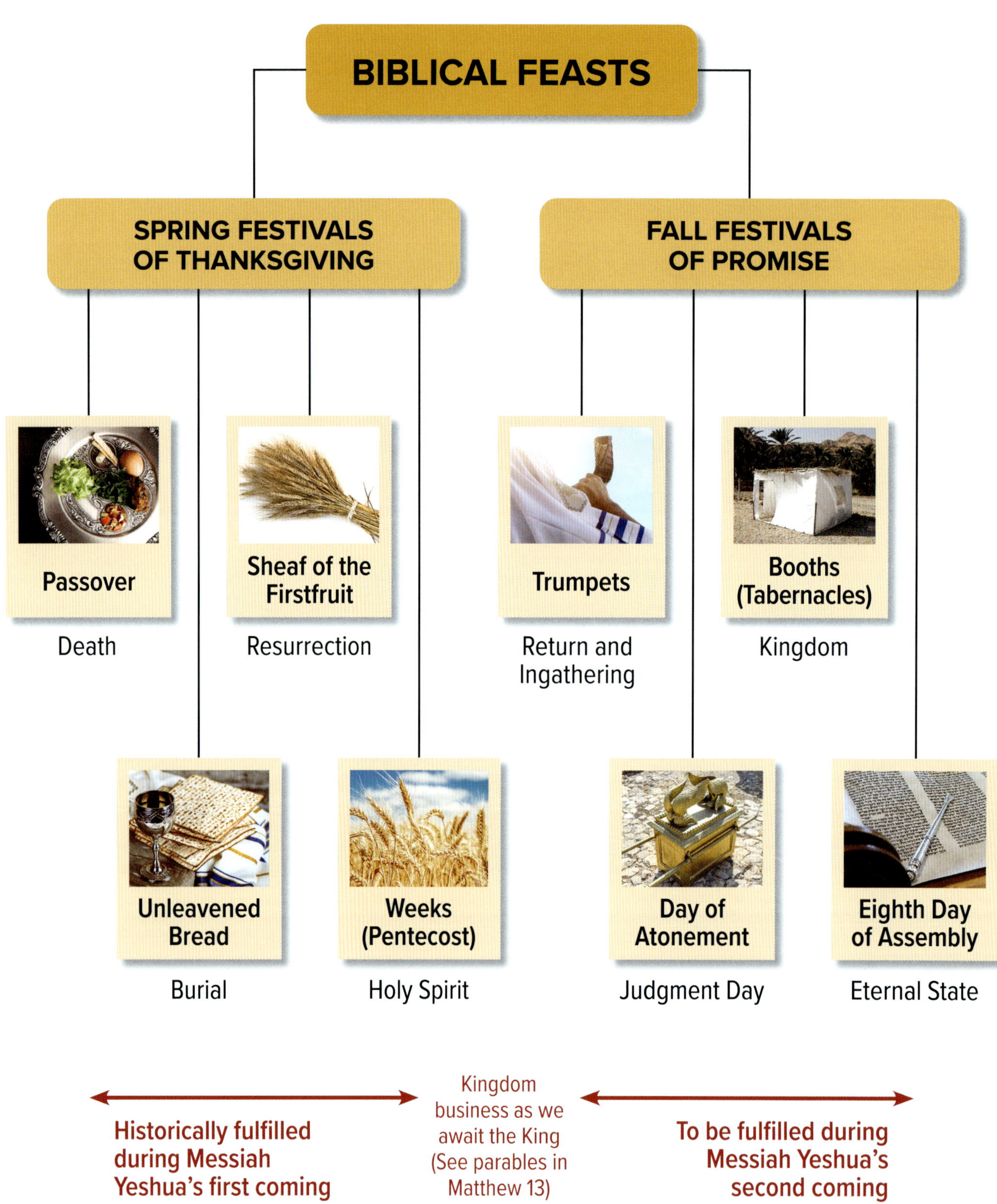
BIBLICAL FEASTS
SPRING FESTIVALS OF THANKSGIVING
FALL FESTIVALS OF PROMISE
Passover
Death
Sheaf of the Firstfruit
Resurrection
Trumpets
Return and Ingathering
Booths (Tabernacles)
Kingdom
Unleavened Bread
Burial
Weeks (Pentecost)
Holy Spirit
Day of Atonement
Judgment Day
Eighth Day of Assembly
Eternal State
Historically fulfilled during Messiah Yeshua's first coming
Kingdom business as we await the King (See parables in Matthew 13)
To be fulfilled during Messiah Yeshua's second coming

example, Lev. 23:1–5, 23–24). The Sabbath and new moons are days of the year that God has set apart to remember and celebrate. New moons are important to the Lord, for in the new heavens and the new earth, all people will observe them: "From new moon to new moon, and from Sabbath to Sabbath, all flesh shall come to worship before me, declares the LORD" (Isa. 66:23).

A MESSIANIC INTERPRETATION

The biblical feasts occur at two distinct times of the year:

- **The spring holidays** encompass the period from the end of the wet season in the Land of Israel through the barley and wheat harvests, occurring in the first through third months of the Jewish year—the months of Nisan, Iyar, and Sivan.
- **The fall holidays**, six months later, are all celebrated within the seventh month, Tishri, which falls between the harvest of summer fruit and the olive harvest, the end of Israel's dry season.

Tying the feasts to Israel's agricultural year emphasizes the need of humanity—fragile as we are—to depend on God. The feasts are set in the context of the harsh environment of the Land of Israel, a place caught between the forces of desert and sea on one hand, and the wet north and the dry south on the other.[11] Moses challenged the Israelites as they stood poised on the plains of Moab to cross the Jordan River and enter their land of promise:

> If you will indeed … serve him with all your heart and with all your soul, he will give the rain for your land in its season, the early rain and the later rain, that you may gather in your grain and your wine and your oil. And he will give grass in your fields for your livestock, and you shall eat and be full. (Deut. 11:13–15)

These three—grain, wine, and oil—encompass the agricultural year in Israel. These are tangible reminders that the biblical feasts are harvest feasts; they are feasts of dependence and trust: we need God.

The messianic movement understands God's appointed times through the lens of Yeshua the Messiah. This does not diminish the significance of the feasts for the saints of old or for Jews today as they celebrate their deliverance from Egypt, the giving of Torah on Mount Sinai, God's kingship in creation, his forgiveness as people repent, and the anticipation of an eternal kingdom. Messianic believers interpret all of these truths as reflecting the ultimate work accomplished and foreshadowing the yet-to-be-accomplished work by Yeshua. Just as the two festival periods balance the year's harvests, so they also hold two different points of significance for messianic believers: thanksgiving for the completed work of Yeshua the Messiah (the spring feasts) and anticipation of the promise of his future work (the fall feasts).

The Land of Israel in the Time of Yeshua

PASSOVER (PESACH)

For messianic believers, the spring feasts are festivals of thanksgiving, looking back at the completed work of Yeshua. He came as the Suffering Servant. He accomplished spiritual redemption as our Passover Lamb through his affliction and death on the cross, a death that sets believers free from the affliction of sin and the kingdom of darkness. He ascended to the right hand of God, and as promised, he sent the Holy Spirit to convict the world of sin and set believers apart unto righteousness and obedience to the instruction of God. For this past work as Messiah, believers in Yeshua celebrate with thanksgiving.

Mud bricks with only a bit of straw, freshly made from a muddy Nile embankment. For the Israelites, it was the lack of readily available straw that prompted the cries that led to the Passover and exodus (Ex. 5:1–22). (Photo by Paul H. Wright)

Passover, the first of the spring feasts, celebrates the deliverance of the people of Israel from their enslavement in Egypt to Pharaoh, a hard taskmaster. Their deliverance came after the tenth plague, the death of the firstborn. It came at a great cost, affecting every family in Egypt. To receive God's deliverance, the Israelites had to respond with trust, obeying the instructions God had given Moses. On the tenth day of the first month, each home was to select an unblemished one-year-old male sheep or goat. At twilight on the fourteenth day, they were to kill their lamb and mark the doorposts and lintel of their home with its blood. Then they were to roast the lamb and eat it with unleavened bread and bitter herbs, their loins girded, sandals on their feet, and staff in their hands (Ex. 12:3–13). They were ready for action! What would happen? Moses reported:

> For the Lord will pass through to strike the Egyptians, and when he sees the blood on the lintel and on the two doorposts, the Lord will pass over the door and will not allow the destroyer to enter your houses to strike you. (Ex. 12:23)

Moses, following the instructions of God, instituted the rite of Passover as an ordinance not only for that moment but for Israel and their children forever. In future generations when children would ask, "What do you mean by this service?" the parent should answer, "It is the sacrifice of the Lord's Passover, for he *passed over* the houses of the people of Israel in Egypt, when he struck the Egyptians but spared our houses" (Ex. 12:26–27, emphasis added). (The Hebrew verb for "passed over" is *pasach,* which yields the noun *pesach*, "Passover.")

The Seder

Messianic believers continue to celebrate Passover, as do all Jews. It is the story of Israel's national deliverance from the greatest human power in the world at the time. Today, the Passover Seder is conducted with a *Haggadah,* a book that guides participants through the story of God's deliverance with proper blessings and prayers, instilling Passover's ongoing significance within the Jewish family. (The word *haggadah* comes from the Hebrew verb "to tell." *Seder* means "order" and refers to the series of steps required to complete the Passover meal.)

Messianic gentiles readily observe the celebration of Passover as a matter of discipleship. Yeshua of Nazareth kept the festival, and as disciples who strive to walk in his path, so should we. When Israel left Egypt, "a mixed multitude also went up with them" (Ex. 12:38). These were gentiles, joining themselves to Israel in their moment of deliverance.[12] Messianic gentiles also celebrate Passover because this was a great step forward in God's plan of redemption for the world. God had promised that Abraham, Isaac, and Jacob would have numerous descendants, among them even kings, and that they would inherit a homeland.[13] He had also promised that in Abraham and his descendants "all the families of the earth shall be blessed" (Gen. 12:3). Jacob and his descendants had gone into Egypt as a total of seventy persons (Gen. 46:26–27). God brought them out of Egypt centuries later as a vast number who would stand at Mount Sinai and become a unified people through a covenant that God enacted with them. From this people came David; from David the Son of David, Yeshua; and through this Son of David came God's redemption for all who believe.

Passover for messianic believers is a double remembrance. At the time of the first Passover in Egypt, the Lord said, "This day shall be for you a memorial day, and you shall keep it as a feast to the LORD; throughout your generations, as a statute forever, you shall keep it as a feast" (Ex. 12:14; see also Ex. 13:9). Then, as our master Yeshua celebrated his last Passover remembering that deliverance, he introduced a new remembrance by breaking bread, giving it to his disciples, and saying,

Matzah on a table set for the Passover Seder.

"This is my body, which is given for you. Do this in remembrance of me" (Luke 22:19; see also 1 Cor. 11:24–25).

Many Christians practice Yeshua's remembrance weekly, monthly, or quarterly, and call it Communion, the Lord's Supper, or the Eucharist. Most messianic believers, however, desire to keep their master's command within its setting of the Passover meal. We observe the institution only during the yearly celebration of the first remembrance, the time when Yeshua introduced the second. Both remembrances—the Passover and Yeshua's death on the cross—point to great deliverances within God's drama of redemption.[14]

First Redemption: The Exodus	Second Redemption: The Cross
Israel enslaved	Humanity enslaved
in the kingdom of Egypt	in the kingdom of darkness and sin
under Pharaoh, the harsh taskmaster,	under Satan, the harsh taskmaster,
but spared the death of the firstborn	but spared spiritual death
by the blood of the Passover lambs	by the blood of the Lamb of God
and redeemed from slavery by God	and redeemed from slavery by God
to become God's people, Israel.	to be grafted into the people of God.

In celebrating these remembrances, messianic families use a variety of guidebooks in their Passover Seders to tell of God's deliverance. These books differ in detail depending on group or family tradition. Some families use a traditional Jewish Haggadah, often emphasizing portions of it that intersect with Yeshua's last Seder. Others use adaptations of a traditional Haggadah that are more appropriate for gentile participants.

No matter what book is used, it is possible to arrange the events of Yeshua's Seder as it is described in the Gospels with a traditional Passover Seder. The order of a Seder follows fifteen steps laid out in a way that uses rhymes to guide the participants through the service.[15] The most common is this Hebrew rhyme:

Kaddesh u-rehatz, karpas yahatz,
maggid rahatz, motzi matzah,
maror korech, shulchan orech,
tzafun barech, hallel nirtzah.[16]

In the following chart, there are the fifteen steps of the Seder by these traditional names alongside parallel events found in the Gospels. We should not expect all fifteen steps to appear in the Gospel accounts since the Passover Seder is the backdrop to the story rather than the main emphasis. Still, enough appears that it is not difficult to assume the rest.

Passover Seder Steps[17]	Steps Found in the Gospel Accounts
Kaddesh: Say blessing over wine.	"And he took a cup, and when he had given thanks …" (Luke 22:17–18).
U-rehatz: Wash hands.	Handwashing is traditional. Did it happen? Probably, but the gospel writers did not believe it needed attention and so it is not mentioned.
Karpas: Dip greens in salt water.	"He who has dipped ... will betray me" (Matt. 26:23).[18]
Yahatz: Divide middle matzah (unleavened bread).	Not mentioned
Maggid: Tell the exodus story.	It was the responsibility of the host to tell the exodus story. Imagine the joy of hearing the Master tell the narrative!
Rahatz: Wash hands before meal.	Handwashing is traditional. It probably happened.
Motzi: Say blessing over bread.	"And he took bread, and when he had given thanks, he broke it" (Luke 22:19).[19]
Matzah: Say blessing over matzah.	The motzi and matzah steps are part of the same act of eating. We do not know if both blessings were used in Yeshua's day.
Maror: Eat the bitter herbs.	Not mentioned
Korech: Combine matzah and bitter herbs.	Not mentioned
Shulchan Orech: Serve the meal.	He "rose from supper … and resumed his place" implies the time of the meal (John 13:3–5).[20]
Tzafun: Eat the hidden matzah.	Not mentioned
Barech: Say "Grace After Meals."	"Grace After Meals" at Passover is preceded by a cup of wine: "This cup … is the new covenant in my blood" (Luke 22:20).[21]
Hallel: Recite the Hallel (praise) psalms.	"And when they had sung a hymn, they went out" (Matt. 26:30).[22]
Nirtzah: May the Seder be accepted.	Not mentioned

The Passover Lamb

For messianic believers, the redemption of Israel from Egypt foreshadows the ultimate redemption from sin that is available to all humankind. The blood of the Passover lambs spared Israel the death of their firstborn sons, resulting in God's deliverance from slavery to Pharaoh. Likewise, the blood of the Lamb of God spares believers from spiritual death and results in God's deliverance from slavery to sin.

The first Passover was by Israelites living among the fields of Egypt. "Take a lamb according to their fathers' houses, a lamb for a household.... Your lamb shall be without blemish, a male a year old" (Ex. 12:3, 5). Shown here are sheep and shepherd not far from the west bank of the Nile River, near Luxor, Egypt. (Photo by Paul H. Wright)

The New Testament writers introduced Yeshua of Nazareth as the perfect Lamb of God:

- When John the Baptizer saw Yeshua, he called out, "Behold, the Lamb of God, who takes away the sin of the world!" (John 1:29; see also v. 36).
- The apostle Peter urged proper conduct because "you were ransomed from the futile ways inherited from your forefathers … with the precious blood of Christ, like that of a lamb without blemish or spot" (1 Peter 1:18–19).[23]
- Upon reading "Like a sheep he was led to the slaughter and like a lamb before its shearer is silent, so he opens not his mouth," the Ethiopian eunuch asked Philip, "About whom, I ask you, does the prophet say this?" Replying, "Philip opened his mouth, and beginning with this Scripture he told him the good news about Jesus" (Acts 8:32–35; see also Isa. 53:7).[24]
- Paul the apostle—perhaps writing to the Corinthian assembly as the feasts of Passover and Unleavened Bread approached—called for cleansing in their midst: "Cleanse out the old leaven that you may be a new lump, as you really are unleavened. For Christ, our Passover lamb, has been sacrificed" (1 Cor. 5:7).[25]
- John refers to Messiah as the Lamb twenty-eight times in the book of Revelation. Here the Lamb appears "as though it had been slain" and is declared worthy "to receive power and wealth and wisdom and might and honor and glory and blessing!" (Rev. 5:6, 11–13).

The Lamb in Revelation is a fitting culmination of Messiah's work as our Passover sacrifice and is central to the salvation and shepherding of the people of God.

FEAST OF UNLEAVENED BREAD (HAG HAMATZOT)

The Feast of Unleavened Bread begins at the same time as Passover and lasts for seven days. The laity calendar states the Lord's Passover begins "on the fourteenth day of the month at twilight" and "on the fifteenth day of the same month is the Feast of Unleavened Bread to the Lord" (Lev. 23:5–6). Since the biblical day begins at sunset, both references are to the fifteenth day. The priestly calendar lists the two feasts as if they occur on two consecutive days: "On the fourteenth day of the first month is the Lord's Passover, and on the fifteenth day of this month is a feast" (Num. 28:16–17). This is because, as far as the priesthood was concerned, preparation for Passover began on the fourteenth day of the month since they had to oversee the slaughtering of the many Passover sacrifices brought to the tabernacle after midday and before twilight.[26]

Traditional Hebrew Haggadah with matzah and wine for Passover.

The first time that unleavened bread, or matzah, is mentioned in the book of Exodus is within the context of the Passover meal. Moses commanded the Israelites to eat the Passover lamb "with unleavened bread and bitter herbs" (Ex. 12:8). How and when it is eaten dominates the next few verses: it is to be "a feast to the Lord" and "a statute forever" (v. 14); "in the first month, from the fourteenth day of the month at evening, you shall eat unleavened bread until the twenty-first day of the month at evening" (v. 18) for "seven days" (v. 15). The reason? Because "on this very day I brought your hosts out of the land of Egypt" (v. 17)—an event worth celebrating!

The Feast of Unleavened Bread appears again in Exodus 13:3–10 with an even greater stress on why the day should be remembered. This was the day the Lord brought Israel "out of the house of slavery.... For with a strong hand the Lord has brought you out of Egypt" (vv. 3, 9). Israel was not just living in Egypt but under slavery, and their freedom came through the power of God.

The Meaning of the Feast

But why unleavened bread? Recall Israel's hasty departure from Egypt. Israel fled from their slavery with unleavened dough still in their kneading bowls, bound to their shoulders by their garments; indeed, the people "were thrust out of Egypt and could not wait;" they had no time to prepare proper provisions for the way (Ex. 12:39).

Deuteronomy's pilgrim calendar also recalls this hasty departure, but it shifts the focus to the affliction Israel experienced as slaves in Egypt: "Seven days you shall eat it with unleavened bread, *the bread of affliction*—for you came out of the land of Egypt in haste—that all the days of your life you may remember the day when you came out of the land of Egypt" (Deut. 16:3, emphasis added).

Depiction of slaves in ancient Egypt. This relief at Abu Simbel, Egypt, dates to the thirteenth century BC, a time when some scholars believe the exodus may have taken place. (Photo by Niall O'Donoghue/Shutterstock)

What then is the biblical meaning of this feast? God delivered his people from their bitter experience of a long enslavement. One day they were slaves to Pharaoh in Egypt; the next they were free. In like manner, the apostle Paul discusses humanity's predicament of spiritual enslavement:

> Do you not know that if you present yourselves to anyone as obedient slaves, you are slaves of the one whom you obey, either of sin, which leads to death, or of obedience, which leads to righteousness? … For just as you once presented your members as slaves to impurity and to lawlessness leading to more lawlessness, so now present your members as slaves to righteousness leading to sanctification. (Rom. 6:16, 19)

As messianic believers eat unleavened bread, we remember not only Israel's exodus from Egypt into freedom but also our own deliverance from sin and death into the freedom to obey God and serve righteousness.

What is the significance of leaven? With rare exception, the laws of sacrifice in the Torah forbid the use of leaven (Lev. 2:11).[27] Food historians believe that leavened bread originated with the Egyptians, perhaps as early as the third millennium BC.[28] It has been suggested that the Torah command to eat unleavened bread represents a separation from Egyptian culture, under the belief that leavening introduces decay into food, and decay represents death:

> Fermentation is a form of decomposition, and therefore represents decay and death. Egypt was known for its obsession with death: The greatest symbols of ancient Egypt are the pyramids, which are tombs. The Torah, in contrast, is rooted in the affirmation of life.… The avoidance of leaven on Passover may be seen as a symbolic rejection of the Egyptian preoccupation with death.[29]

In the New Testament, the apostle Paul mentions leaven when admonishing the Corinthian assembly about sin:

> Your boasting is not good. Do you not know that a little leaven leavens the whole lump? Cleanse out the old leaven that you may be a new lump, as you really are unleavened. For Christ, our Passover lamb, has been sacrificed. Let us therefore celebrate the festival, not with the old leaven, the leaven of malice and evil, but with the unleavened bread of sincerity and truth. (1 Cor. 5:6–8)

Messianic believers understand Paul's instruction as an important addition to the Torah teaching that unleavened bread represents the bitterness of slavery. Leaven also represents the bitterness of sin. For us, the Feast of Unleavened Bread is a time not only to remove all physical leaven from our homes but also to search our lives for the figurative leaven of sin.

The Seventh Day of the Feast

Both times that the Feast of Unleavened Bread is described in the book of Exodus, it is a seven-day observance with the final day as "a feast to the Lord" (Ex. 12:14–20; 13:3–10). The laity and priestly calendars both state that this seventh day is a "holy convocation" on which "you shall not do any ordinary work" (Lev. 23:8; Num. 28:25). Traditionally, the seventh day of the feast is viewed as the anniversary of the crossing of the Red Sea, which, like Passover, is worth celebrating.[30] Yet the command to rest and cease from work on the seventh day of the feast directs our thoughts to another significance of the feast: the weekly Sabbath and the celebration of the seventh day of creation.

Sabbath-keepers see the Sabbath as a foretaste of their rest in the kingdom of God. When observant Jews recite the prayer "Grace After Meals" on the Sabbath (it is otherwise recited after eating meals throughout the week), they add these words about the Sabbath to the prayer: "The compassionate One! May He cause us to inherit the day which will be completely a Sabbath and rest day for eternal life."[31] Some Hasidic Jewish groups expand it by concluding their celebration of the seventh day of the Feast of Unleavened Bread with a seder called *Seudat Mashiach*, "Meal of Messiah." In eating the Meal of Messiah, Hasidic Jews celebrate the coming of Messiah by rehearsing for the great banquet of the messianic age.[32]

Recently, messianic groups have also begun to celebrate the Meal of Messiah to conclude the final day of the Feast of Unleavened Bread. We find that this is a fitting expression of our longing for the return of the Messiah. Many believers feel this longing daily as they pray the prayer Yeshua taught his disciples: "Our Father in heaven, hallowed be your name. Your kingdom come …" (Matt. 6:9–10).

A Teaching Opportunity

Just as the Feasts of Passover and Unleavened Bread reminded Israel of the day they came out of Egypt, so they also provide opportunities to teach our children about God's redemptive work, including how he has redeemed us: "You shall tell your son on that day, 'It is because of what the Lord did for *me* when I came out of Egypt'" (Ex. 13:8, emphasis added). The Bible becomes more personal whenever we can see ourselves in its stories. Indeed, the Passover Haggadah declares, "In every generation let each man look on himself as if he came forth from Egypt."[33] It also uses Exodus 13:8 as a prompt to parents whose children do not know how to ask about the feasts.[34] We should tell them anyway! The feasts provide excellent opportunities for us in the messianic movement to insert these annual reminders of God's great redemptive acts into our lives and use them to teach our children about the Bible and our faith.

SHEAF OF THE FIRSTFRUIT (OMER HAREISHIT)

On the day following the Passover meal, the priesthood oversaw the first cutting of barley and the process by which people brought the first sheaves to the temple. The Hebrew word for sheaf is *omer* and the word for firstfruit is *reishit*. So this festival, which coincides with the beginning of the barley harvest, is known as Omer HaReishit, the Sheaf of the Firstfruit, or as it is called in Leviticus, "the sheaf of the firstfruits of your harvest" (Lev. 23:10). Only after Omer HaReishit could the Israelites eat any of the new harvest: "You shall eat neither bread nor grain parched or fresh until this same day, until you have brought the offering of your God" (Lev. 23:14).

The laity calendar includes detailed instructions for celebrating, or counting, the omer (Lev. 23:9–16).

The pilgrim calendar alludes to the event: "You shall count seven weeks. Begin to count the seven weeks from the time the sickle is first put to the standing grain" (Deut. 16:9). At first, the omer may seem of little significance, but it sets in motion the countdown to the next pilgrim festival, the Feast of Weeks (Shavuot), "the firstfruits of the wheat harvest" (Ex. 34:22; see also Lev. 23:15–16). Indeed, the act of counting fills the seven-week period that is framed by the celebrations of the barley (Passover) and wheat (Weeks) harvests.

For messianic believers, the offering of the firstfruit symbolizes Yeshua's resurrection from the dead, the firstfruit of the resurrection of all believers. In Paul's first letter to the Corinthians, he compares Yeshua to the first barley sheaf, the first of a great harvest to come:

> In fact Christ has been raised from the dead, the firstfruits of those who have fallen asleep. For as by a man came death, by a man has come also the resurrection of the dead. For as in Adam all die, so also in Christ shall all be made alive. But each in his own order: Christ the firstfruits, then at his coming those who belong to Christ. (1 Cor. 15:20–23)[35]

Some scholars suggest that, based on the gospel of John, Yeshua was crucified on the eve of Passover (John 19:31, 42).[36] This means that his resurrection would have taken place on the day the firstfruit was offered in the temple. For this reason, messianic believers celebrate our Master's resurrection on this day of firstfruits according to the Jewish calendar, rather than on Easter Sunday according to later, Christian calculation.

Counting the Omer

For thousands of years, faithful Jews have counted these forty-nine days—from the Sheaf of the Firstfruit to the Feast of Weeks—while entreating God's faithfulness and mercy for a bountiful harvest. In Israel, Counting the Omer is a time of trepidation and prayer for the grain farmer as he watches his wheat ripen and then harvests, threshes, winnows, and stores his crop. It is also a time when the fruit trees are pollinated. Farmers in Israel depend on God for the proper winds and temperatures to accomplish both tasks.[37]

Many Jews read Psalm 67 on each of the forty-nine days of counting. The traditional explanation for this is that the psalm in Hebrew has forty-nine words, one for each day of the count. But Psalm 67 is also appropriate for the season of grain harvest because it begins with the phrase "May God be gracious to us and bless us and make his face shine upon us" (v. 1), and ends with the blessing "The earth has yielded its increase; God, our God, shall bless us" (vv. 6–7). The psalm also captures God's mission for the Jewish people—his "kingdom of priests and a holy nation" (Ex. 19:6)—as they pray, "Bless us … that your way may be known on earth, your saving power among all the nations" (vv. 1–2), concluding, "God shall bless us; let all the ends of the earth fear him!" (v. 7). Between these

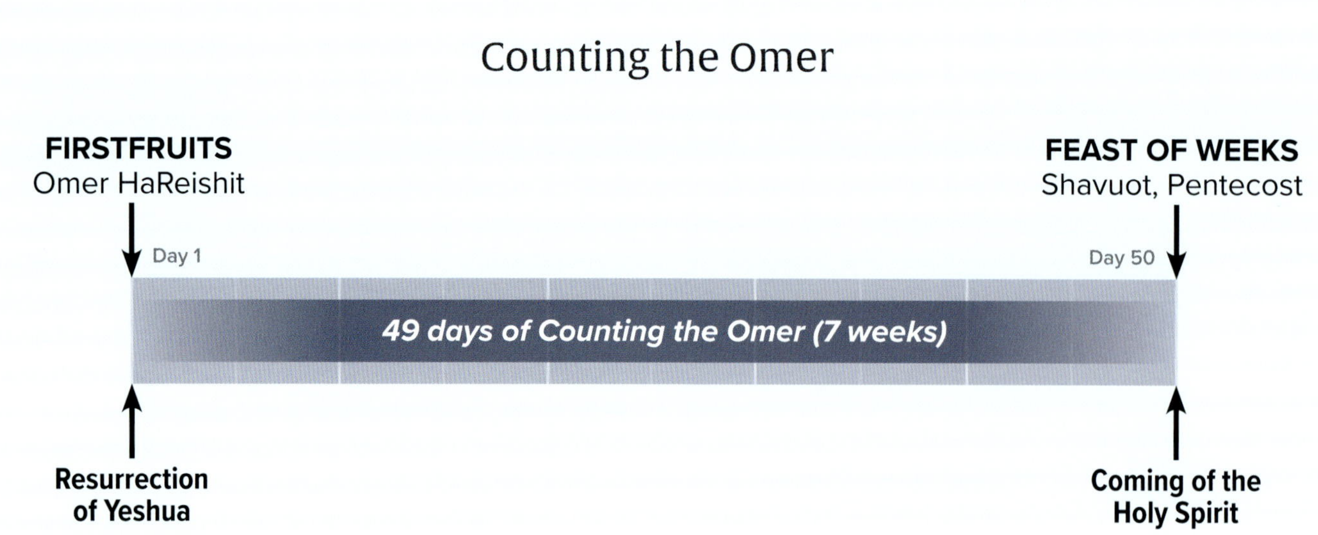

two prayers for blessing, the psalm focuses on the response of the gentiles to the work of God:

> Let the peoples praise you, O God;
> let all the peoples praise you!
>
> Let the nations be glad and sing for joy,
> for you judge the peoples with equity
> and guide the nations upon earth.
>
> Let the peoples praise you, O God;
> let all the peoples praise you!
> (Ps. 67:3–5)

Messianic believers delight in reciting this psalm, which we consider prophetic. Day one of the Counting the Omer coincides with the day of Yeshua's resurrection. As we recite the psalm for the next forty days, we emphasize its ending: "all the ends of the earth shall fear him," remembering that on the fortieth day after his resurrection, just before his ascension, Yeshua said to his disciples, "You will receive power when the Holy Spirit has come upon you, and you will be my witnesses in Jerusalem and in all Judea and Samaria, and to *the end of the earth*" (Acts 1:8, emphasis added). Messianic believers then count nine more days and celebrate the coming of the Holy Spirit in power on Yeshua's disciples on the fiftieth day—Pentecost, the Feast of Weeks.

FEAST OF WEEKS (SHAVUOT, PENTECOST)

The Mishnah provides a detailed description of the excitement that accompanied the Feast of Weeks, the fiftieth day after Passover.[38] We're told how caravans of pilgrims who had gathered in their regional centers to travel to Jerusalem arrived in the city with baskets of firstfruits filled with items from the "seven species" of the Land of Israel: barley, wheat, grapes, figs, pomegranates, olives, and dates or date honey (Deut. 8:8).[39] The pilgrims also brought pigeons for sacrifice. An ox preceded them with its horns overlaid with gold and a crown of olive leaves on its head. A flute player played the melodies of the Psalms of Ascent, which the pilgrims sang as they ascended to Jerusalem. Drawing near the city, they arranged their baskets not only with firstfruits but also with choice fruit they desired to bring to the temple. Representatives of the priests met them, asking, "Our brothers, have you come in good health?" The flute played until the procession ascended into the temple courts. Carrying the baskets on their shoulders, everyone stood before the priest and recited, "I declare today to the LORD your God that I have come into the land that the LORD swore to our fathers to give us" (Deut. 26:3). Lowering their baskets, the priest would wave each to and fro, up and down. Each pilgrim bowed and left his basket at the temple altar, after declaring:

> A wandering Aramean was my father. And he went down into Egypt and sojourned there, few in number, and there he became a nation, great, mighty, and populous.... And behold, now I bring the first of the fruit of the ground, which you, O LORD, have given me. (Deut. 26:5–10)

"When the day of Pentecost arrived, they were all together in one place. And suddenly there came from heaven a sound like a mighty rushing wind, and it filled the entire house where they were sitting. And divided tongues as of fire appeared to them and rested on each one of them. And they were all filled with the Holy Spirit and began to speak in other tongues as the Spirit gave them utterance." (Acts 2:1–4)

With no temple today, believers cannot ascend to Jerusalem with a basket of firstfruits, but they can still share in that joy. We can also mark the firstfruits of our labor by offering to the Lord whatever it is that we do have as gifts for those in need. As if to emphasize this aspect of the feast, the laity calendar adds an instruction about charity:

> When you reap the harvest of your land, you shall not reap your field right up to its edge, nor shall you gather the gleanings after your harvest. You shall leave them for the poor and for the sojourner: I am the LORD your God. (Lev. 23:22)

The Holy Spirit and Torah

It was on this fiftieth day (*Pentecost* in Greek) after the Counting the Omer the apostles and other followers of Yeshua "were all together in one place" (Acts 2:1). This "one place," and "the entire house

The model of Jerusalem on the grounds of the Israel Museum shows the city as it is believed to have been prior to its destruction in AD 70. The temple complex dominates the site. The temple itself was surrounded—and protected—by wide open courtyards, together bounded by columned porticoes. By all contemporary accounts, these were crowded on Jewish holidays such as Shavuot (Pentecost). (Photo by Paul H. Wright)

where they were sitting" (Acts 2:2) most probably refers to the temple complex in Jerusalem.[40] As observant Jews and followers of their rabbi Yeshua, one who had observed the feasts, we should expect that they would be in Jerusalem and in the temple courts for the Feast of Weeks.[41] Perhaps they were gathering with the one hundred and twenty believers for prayer in the eastern colonnade of the temple courts, bordering the Court of the Gentiles (Acts 1:15). Our master Yeshua had walked and taught in this same colonnade (John 10:22–30) and the early believers are found there on two other occasions (Acts 3:11; 5:12). While there, the "sound like a mighty rushing wind" swept through the outer temple courts and into the colonnade (Acts 2:2). Tongues of fire appeared to rest on them and they began miraculously to speak in all the languages represented by the pilgrims in the temple. Scripture says that there were Jews and converts to Judaism from Parthia, Media, Elam, Mesopotamia, Judea, Cappadocia, Pontus, Asia, Phrygia, Pamphylia, Egypt, Libya, Cyrene, Rome, Crete, and Arabia.[42] This was a temple event, as only here would Jewish pilgrims gather from all parts of the eastern and western worlds.

Immediately after was the spiritual harvest of three thousand souls, the firstfruits of the apostolic ministry in the world: "Those who received his [Peter's] word were baptized, and there were added that day about three thousand souls" (Acts 2:41).

Rabbinic tradition states that on the fiftieth day after Passover, Torah was given to Israel on Mount Sinai.[43] We read in Exodus of remarkable phenomena happening when Torah was given:

> There were voices and lightnings and a heavy cloud on the mountain and a very strong voice of a shofar, so that all the people trembled … all of Mount Sinai was smoking … its smoke went up like the smoke of a furnace … the voice of the shofar was going and strengthening.… All the people were seeing the voices and the torches and the voice of the shofar and the mountain smoking. (Ex. 19:16–19; 20:18)[44]

The sight was terrifying, but what does it mean to "see" voices? What are these voices? One early Jewish interpretation explains: "Note that it does not say 'the voice' [singular] but 'the voices' [plural].… God's voice, as it was uttered, split up into seventy voices, in seventy languages, so that all the nations should understand."[45] This description may have been a poetic way of saying that God's words of revelation at Sinai were intended for all mankind. The same explanation appears in the Babylonian Talmud: "Every single word that went forth from the Holy One, blessed be He, split into seventy languages."[46] Because seventy is the traditional number of human languages in rabbinic interpretation, the implication is that God gave the Torah to everyone.[47]

"On the morning of the third day there [was] … a thick cloud on the mountain" (Ex. 19:16)—a cloud like this one, viewed from the summit of Jebel Musa, the traditional location of Mount Sinai. (Photo by Paul H. Wright)

Pentecost by Titian (c. 1545) in the Church of Santa Maria della Salute, Venice. (Renata Sedmakova/Shutterstock)

What then were the "torches" that "all the people were seeing" (Ex. 20:18)? The Jewish sages also preserved an explanation linking the voice of God at Sinai to flames of fire. God's voice went out to Israel, circled around the large camp and returned to him: "He received it from His right hand and engraved it on the tablet, and the sound of it went from one end of the world to the other, as it says, 'The voice of the Lord hews out flames of fire' [Ps. 29:7]."[48]

The presence of fire at Sinai is also linked in the Talmud to the seventy languages by means of Jeremiah 23:29: "'Is it not so? My word is like fire,' utters the Lord, 'and like a hammer shattering rock.'"[49] The Talmud gives this interpretation: "Just as a hammer [blow] is divided [into] many sparks [as it strikes a rock], so every single word that went forth from the Holy One, blessed be He, split up into seventy languages."[50]

The Jews in the first century, including Yeshua's disciples, probably knew these rabbinic legends about God's fiery words splitting into seventy languages. For this reason, these images provide an intriguing background for Luke's description in Acts 2:3–4 of the "divided tongues of fire" that fell on everyone and allowed them to speak "in other tongues." Luke's use of the word *divided* (*diamerizomenai* in Greek) implies that the tongues of fire were "parting themselves asunder" or "distributing themselves." Biblical scholar H. B. Hackett captures the idea well:

> The fire-like appearance presented itself at first, as it were, in a single body, and then suddenly parted in this direction and that; so that a portion of it rested on each of those present.[51]

Without mentioning the rabbinic legends, Hackett's explanation nevertheless reflects the same idea. The legends of Sinai, like the Acts 2 experience in the temple, are both associated with the Feast of Weeks (Pentecost), though separated by over a millennium in time. Occurring at the same time of the year and with similar intent, God gave the instruction of Torah and then the power of the Holy Spirit to help us keep his words.

As messianic believers embrace these two gifts, we often point to a relationship drawn between them by two prophets, Jeremiah and Ezekiel, who lived at a critical time in Israel's history. As Babylon laid siege to Jerusalem in the sixth century BC, the prophet Jeremiah foresaw the restoration of Israel and Judah:

> "I will make a new covenant with the house of Israel and the house of Judah. This is the covenant that I will make with the house of Israel after those days," declares the Lord: "I will put my law within them, and I will write it on their hearts." (Jer. 31:31, 33)

The prophet Ezekiel, already a captive in Babylon during that time, saw the same: "I will put my Spirit within you, and cause you to walk in my statutes and be careful to obey my rules" (Ezek. 36:27).

Both gifts—God's Torah and God's Spirit—work together within the life of the believer.

DAY OF TRUMPETS (YOM TERUAH)

From the spring festivals of thanksgiving, we now turn our attention to the fall festivals of promise. These feasts differ from the spring feasts in that we are no longer looking back to see our master Yeshua's work fulfilling God's appointed times of redemption, but rather looking forward with the expectation that he will act at God's appointed times in the future as well. These feasts anticipate Yeshua's work as the victorious King who will return on the clouds with a great blast of the shofar to "raise David's fallen sukkah" (Amos 9:11).[52] For this reason, they are festivals of promise. The three autumn festivals foreshadow:

- the ingathering of God's people (the Day of Trumpets);
- his day of judgment (the Day of Atonement); and
- the establishment of the messianic kingdom (the Feast of Booths with the Eighth Day of Assembly).

The first of these festivals is the Day of Trumpets, the name preferred for this feast by some messianic gentiles. This is a loose translation of the biblical phrase *yom teru'ah* which appears in the priestly calendar (Num. 29:1). A more literal translation is "day of blasts," often rendered as "day of shofar blasts."[53] The laity calendar refers to the day as *zichron teru'ah,* "remembrance of blasts" (Lev. 23:24). Jews today generally call the festival Rosh HaShanah, "Beginning of the Year" or "New Year," following the tradition in the Talmud that God created the world on this day.[54] Another name for the day is Yom HaDin, "Day of Judgment,"[55] when, as the Mishnah states, "all inhabitants of the world will pass before [God], like a flock of sheep."[56] For this reason, the Day of Trumpets begins a ten-day period of serious reflection and repentance in which Jews set their accounts right with one another to prepare for the Day of Atonement (Yom Kippur), when each person's fate is decided, for life or death, for another year.

This broken stone was once part of the parapet enclosing the top of the southwestern corner of the wall of the temple compound in first-century Jerusalem. The inscription in Hebrew reads "To the Trumpeting Place" and likely marked the spot where the priest would sound the shofar on Jewish festal days. The drawing behind, part of the display at the Israel Museum, depicts the southwestern corner of the temple compound's wall. (Photo by Paul H. Wright)

The Day of Trumpets celebrates the enthronement of God as King and his faithfulness to his covenantal promises with Israel by blasting the shofar (ram's horn) one hundred times throughout the day.[57] Messianic believers combine these aspects of the celebration with Yeshua's promise to return to earth. Toward the end of his earthly ministry, Yeshua spoke of war, tribulation, and flight from Jerusalem, describing that day of darkness like the prophetic Day of the Lord:

> They will see the Son of Man coming on the clouds of heaven with power and great glory. And he will send out his angels with a loud trumpet call, and they will gather his elect from the four winds, from one end of heaven to the other. (Matt. 24:30–31; see also vv. 1–29; Mark 13:26–27; Luke 21:27–28)

With these words, our master Yeshua alluded to the end times vision of the prophet Daniel, who saw that "with the clouds of heaven there came one like a son of man.... And to him was given dominion and glory and a kingdom, that all peoples, nations, and languages should serve him" (Dan. 7:13–14).

Yeshua's words also reflect two prophecies of Isaiah:

> In that day a great trumpet will be blown, and those who were lost in the land of Assyria and those who were driven out to the land of Egypt will come and worship the Lord on the holy mountain at Jerusalem. (Isa. 27:13)

> He will raise a signal for the nations and will assemble the banished of Israel, and gather the dispersed of Judah from the four corners of the earth. (Isa. 11:12)

The appearance of King Messiah, the trumpet blast, and the ingathering of the elect also find echoes in the New Testament writings of the apostles:

> The Lord himself will descend from heaven with a cry of command, with the voice of an archangel, and with the sound of the trumpet of God. And the dead in Christ will rise first. Then we who are alive, who are left, will be caught up together with them in the clouds to meet the Lord in the air, and so we will always be with the Lord. (1 Thess. 4:16–17; see also 1 Cor. 15:51–52)

The place of trumpeting on the southwest corner of the temple in first-century Jerusalem. (Art by Balage Balogh)

Anticipating these events must awaken believers and urge them to prepare for the kingdom:

> The hour has come for you to wake from sleep. For salvation is nearer to us now than when we first believed. The night is almost gone; the day is at hand. So then let us cast off the works of darkness and put on the armor of light. (Rom. 13:11–12; see also Eph. 5:14–17)

On the Day of Trumpets, messianic believers gather in a holy convocation for prayer, confession, and instruction from Scripture and to hear the shofar blasts. The liturgies for this day lead worshipers into active repentance, which culminates on the Day of Atonement ten days later.

The gospel writer Matthew placed six of Yeshua's teachings on preparedness right after his declaration that the Son of Man will come with power and glory on the clouds:

- The lesson of the fig tree (Matt. 24:32–35)
- No one knows the day and hour (Matt. 24:36–44)
- The faithful and wicked servants (Matt. 24:45–51)
- The parable of the ten virgins (Matt. 25:1–13)
- The parable of the talents (Matt. 25:14–30)
- The nature of the final judgment (Matt. 25:31–46)

In this way, the gospel calls believers to be ready for the trumpet blast, the ingathering of God's people, and the appearance of the King.

DAY OF ATONEMENT (YOM KIPPUR)

The Day of Atonement is the final day of this ten-day period. Though grouped with the fall feasts of promise, it is neither a festival nor a feast but a solemn day of fasting. The laity calendar instructs the congregation about what to do on this most holy of days:

> Now on the tenth day of this seventh month is the Day of Atonement. It shall be for you a time of holy convocation, and you shall afflict yourselves and present a food offering to the Lord. And you shall not do any work on that very day, for it is a Day of Atonement, to make atonement for you before the Lord your God. ... It shall be to you a Sabbath of solemn rest, and you shall afflict yourselves. On the ninth day of the month beginning at evening, from evening to evening shall you keep your Sabbath. (Lev. 23:26–28, 32)

These instructions also include a severe warning for anyone who will not afflict themselves or who decides to work on that day (Lev. 23:29–31). To this, the priestly calendar adds the requirement of sacrifice (Num. 29:7–11). It is the instructions of Leviticus 16, however, that give the purpose for the sacrifices: "On this day shall atonement be made for you to cleanse you. You shall be clean before the Lord from all your sins" (Lev. 16:30).

The Day of Atonement is mentioned by name only three times in Scripture and always in the Bible as Yom HaKippurim, "Day of Atonements," plural (Lev. 23:27–28; 25:9). This plural usage probably reflects the instructions given to the priest in Leviticus 16 for making multiple atonements:

- for himself and his house (vv. 6, 11, 17),
- for the Holy Place of the tabernacle (vv. 16, 33),
- for the golden altar at the tabernacle (vv. 18, 33),
- for the tent of meeting, the tabernacle (vv. 16, 33), and
- for all the assembly of Israel (vv. 17, 24, 33–34).

On Yom Kippur, two goats were selected for making atonement. One was sacrificed at the temple and the other was released into the wilderness. This second goat, the scapegoat, symbolically carried away the sins of the people, never to return (Lev. 16:7–10).The Wadi Qilt wilderness (shown here) is typical of the wilderness east of Jerusalem into which the scapegoat would have been released. (Photo by Paul H. Wright)

Atonement for the Holy Place, the golden altar, and the tent of meeting was necessary because of human uncleanness (Lev. 23:16). The Day of Atonement, then, was an annual cleansing not only of people but also of the tabernacle itself.

The details of Leviticus 16 specify the order of the sacrifices, the necessary immersions, and changes of clothing needed for the day. The Mishnah elaborates on these instructions, giving us fascinating details about how the Day of Atonement may have been observed in the time of the New Testament.[58] The high priest secluded himself for seven days prior and then performed elaborate and carefully ordered rituals and liturgies throughout the day. These included immersions; prayers for sanctification; confessions for himself, his house, and the people; slaughtering sacrifices; entering the Holy of Holies in the temple; sprinkling blood of the sacrificed animal; sending the scapegoat into the wilderness; and reading portions of the Torah before the congregation.

With this backdrop in mind, the writer of the book of Hebrews presents the activities of the earthly temple as a reflection of the greater function of the heavenly temple (Heb. 7:1–10:18). While not all messianic believers today focus on the many details of this connection, all embrace Yeshua as their high priest in the heavenly temple, the righteous One who offered his blood as a sacrifice for sins, making a one-time atonement for them.

Parallels[59]	Significance
Two Priesthoods (Heb. 7:1–28)	Aaron's priesthood and the priesthood of Messiah who is an eternal priest after the order of Melchizedek.
Two Temples (Heb. 8:1–5)	The earthly temple as a copy of the heavenly temple.
Two covenants (Heb. 8:6–13)	The first covenant in which Israel agrees to obey the Torah; Messiah introduces the second covenant in which God writes the Torah on the heart so that Israel can obey.
Two temple-chambers (Heb. 9:1–10)	The Holy Place with daily rituals and the Most Holy Place (Holy of Holies) with an annual ritual representing this present world and the world to come.
Two eras (Heb. 9:11–14)	In this world, the high priest purifies defiled people; in the world to come, Messiah purifies people's consciences to serve the living God.

Jews and most members of the messianic movement observe Yom Kippur as a day of fasting and repentance. In Jewish tradition, it is considered a judgment day because of its associations in the Hebrew Scriptures with sin, atonement, and forgiveness.[60] It is on this day that God decides the fate of those who are neither wholly wicked nor wholly righteous: *Will they be given life or death in the coming year?*[61]

For messianic believers, the association of Yom Kippur with judgment marks another appointment on God's calendar of redemption. Messianic believers recognize that salvation does not cancel out the need for ongoing repentance. Like the Day of the Lord, the Day of Atonement is a time for God's people to mourn, plead for mercy, and seek cleansing.[62]

> I will pour out on the house of David and the inhabitants of Jerusalem a spirit of grace and pleas for mercy so that … they shall mourn for him, as one mourns for an only child. On that day there shall be a fountain opened for the house of David and the inhabitants of Jerusalem, to cleanse them from sin and uncleanness. (Zech. 12:10; 13:1)

But this day also anticipates the final judgment:

> When the Son of Man comes in his glory … he will sit on his glorious throne. Before him will be gathered all the nations, and he will separate people one from another as a shepherd separates the sheep from the goats. (Matt. 25:31–32)

So how do God's people "afflict themselves" on this day as Leviticus 16 instructs? From earliest times, affliction has been understood as a total fast from food and drink from the evening of the ninth day of Tishri until the evening of the tenth. From at least the time of the New Testament, prayer services and biblical readings have turned our attention to repentance as we stand before the judge of the universe. The day brings renewal and spiritual cleansing, as each worshiper reflects on the sins of the past year and lays open his or her secret thoughts and intentions before God.

Regular times of repentance are an important component of biblical faith that is too often overlooked in favor of the saving work of Yeshua. Repentance calls us to turn from wrong and walk in the ways of God.[63] The messianic movement embraces the grace of God, and it also believes that experiencing God's forgiveness through true repentance demands that we consciously turn from wrong and do what is right. Yom Kippur, above all, points to God's grace.

Multiple times on Yom Kippur, Jews recite a confession called the "Thirteen Attributes of the Forgiving God," taken from Exodus 34:6–7. The confession begins with the Lord's divine name, acknowledged twice (and counted as two). This name most probably refers to God's self-existence: "He Who Is," "the Existing One," or, in brief, "He Is."[64]

> He Is, He Is, God, Compassionate, and Gracious, Slow to Anger, and Abundant in

The Greater Atonement in the Book of Hebrews

"Now if perfection had been attainable through the Levitical priesthood (for under it the people received the law), what further need would there have been for another priest to arise after the order of Melchizedek, rather than one named after the order of Aaron?" (Heb. 7:11).

"Now even the first covenant had regulations for worship and an earthly place of holiness. For a tent was prepared, the first section, in which were the lampstand and the table and the bread of the Presence. It is called the Holy Place. Behind the second curtain was a second section called the Most Holy Place, having the golden altar of incense and the ark of the covenant.... These preparations having thus been made, the priests go regularly into the first section, performing their ritual duties, but into the second only the high priest goes, and he but once a year, and not without taking blood, which he offers for himself and for the unintentional sins of the people" (Heb. 9:1–7).

"But when Christ appeared as a high priest of the good things that have come, then through the greater and more perfect tent (not made with hands, that is, not of this creation) he entered once for all into the holy places, not by means of the blood of goats and calves but by means of his own blood, thus securing an eternal redemption" (Heb. 9:11–12).

> Devotion, and Truth, Preserving Devotion to Thousands, Bearing Iniquity, and Transgression, and Sin, and Cleansing.

In this confession, we have a delightful picture of the Existing One's gracious desire to be in relationship with his creatures.

 FEAST OF BOOTHS (SUKKOT)

The Feast of Booths, or the Feast of Tabernacles, is the final Torah-mandated feast of the religious year, appearing like a crown at the end of the laity and priestly calendars (Lev. 23:33–43; Num. 29:12–38). The feast lasts seven days, with the first day observed as a festival Sabbath and an eighth day, following the seven, also celebrated as a festival Sabbath. The feast's dominant theme is the command to rejoice. This is clear from the pilgrim calendar, which brackets its instruction with the word *rejoice:*

> Rejoice you shall in your festival, you, your son, your daughter, your servant, your maidservant ... because the Lord your God will bless you in all your produce and in all the work of your hands, and surely you shall be rejoicing. (Deut. 16:14–15)[65]

The laity calendar adds a tangible symbol of life to the command: take "the fruit of splendid trees, branches of palm trees and boughs of leafy trees and willows of the brook and ... rejoice before the Lord your God seven days" (Lev. 23:40). Even the obligation of the second tithe is an occasion to rejoice: "Spend the money [of your tithe] for whatever you desire—oxen or sheep or wine or strong drink, whatever your appetite craves, and you shall eat there before the Lord your God and rejoice" (Deut. 14:26). The sacrifices are no less elaborate. The priestly calendar specifies a total of seventy bulls, fourteen rams, ninety-eight lambs, as well as seven goats as sin offerings, presented over the days of the feast. On the eighth day another bull, a ram, seven lambs, and a goat were offered (Num. 29:12–38).

Two different things are emphasized for the Feast of Booths in the laity calendar:

- The first connects the feast to the completion of the year's harvest: "When you have gathered in the produce of the land, you shall celebrate the feast of the Lord seven days" (Lev. 23:39).
- The second explains the festive instruction to dwell in booths (*sukkot*) for seven days: "All native Israelites shall dwell in booths, that your generations may know that I made the people of Israel dwell in booths when I brought them out of the land of Egypt" (Lev. 23:42–43).

God's provision in the harvest and his protection of Israel through their years in the inhospitable

"You shall take on the first day [of the Feast of Booths] the fruit of splendid trees, branches of palm trees and boughs of leafy trees and willows of the brook, and you shall rejoice before the Lord your God seven days" (Lev. 23:40). An individual overlooks the Temple Mount in Jerusalem holding a lulav used during the festival of Sukkot.

wilderness—"a land of drought and deep darkness, . . . a land that none passes through, where no man dwells" (Jer. 2:6)—are indeed reasons to rejoice.

For the messianic movement, the Feast of Booths is much more than just an agricultural festival or a time to remember Israel's wilderness wanderings. As Israel developed as a nation, the Davidic kingdom and the Jerusalem temple became dominant biblical themes. These were interrupted when the Babylonians destroyed the kingdom of Judah in 586 BC. For this reason, many of the promises of the biblical prophets focus on the restoration of the Davidic kingdom and the temple in the messianic age. Messianic believers understand that the Feast of Booths, the final feast of the calendar year, anticipates this happening.

Many messianic believers build a sukkah in which to celebrate the feast. Others leave their homes and camp outdoors throughout the week. In worship, they also observe the instruction to keep the Feast of Booths with a lulav, made of palm branches and boughs of the myrtle and willow, along with an etrog (Lev. 23:40). The prayers for the feast include the Hallel (Psalms 113–118). Psalm 118 concludes the Hallel and builds messianic expectation of the kingdom. The psalm presents a victorious king who thanks God for the many ways he delivers his people. Toward the end, it points to the Messiah, declaring, "The stone that the builders rejected has become the cornerstone" (Ps. 118:22). This verse is quoted five times in the New Testament to support Yeshua's claim as Messiah.[66] The lulav is waved in

The Western Wall is the most notable retaining wall of the Jerusalem temple complex still standing since the temple's destruction by the Romans in AD 70. Yeshua frequently visited the temple courts, teaching his followers, challenging his critics, and confronting the status quo of the religious leaders of his day. Today, the Temple Mount remains a holy site for Jews, Christians, and Muslims. The Western Wall plaza (shown here) is a place of prayer and Torah reading, and also a public gathering place for celebrating the Jewish holidays. (Photo by Finn stock/Shutterstock)

all directions while the Psalm is read signifying God's omnipresence, but for messianic believers it also evokes God's promises to the patriarchs in the Hebrew Scriptures:

> You shall spread abroad to the west and to the east and to the north and to the south, and in you and your offspring shall all the families of the earth be blessed. (Gen. 28:14)

The fulfillment of God's promises to Abraham, Isaac, and Jacob is significant for messianic believers, who trust that it will be accomplished through our master Yeshua's reign as Messiah over all the earth.

Yeshua and the Feast of Booths

In the New Testament, the apostles applied the themes and events of the Feast of Booths to the life of Yeshua.[67] In the prologue of his gospel, the apostle John states, "The Word became flesh and dwelt among us" (John 1:14). Here, for the word *dwelt,* John uses the Greek word *eskenosen,* which means literally "to pitch a tent" or "live in a tabernacle/tent."[68] In doing so, John implies that "the Word [Yeshua] lived in a tabernacle among us." What does this mean? On the one hand, we can conclude that the Word lived among us in, or as, a sukkah (booth, tent), that is, in a temporary, earthly human body.[69] But there is an additional significance. We recall God's instruction to Israel at Mount Sinai: "Let them make me a sanctuary, that I may dwell in their midst" (Ex. 25:8). Then the Lord showed Moses exactly what the pattern of the tabernacle (*skene*) should be (Ex. 25:9).[70] In the book of Revelation, John offers a future fulfillment of this promise: "The dwelling place [*skene,* tabernacle] of God is with man. He will dwell [*skenosei,* will tabernacle] with them, and they will be his people, and God himself will be with them as their God" (Rev. 21:3). Yeshua dwelt, or tabernacled, in a human body, but he also will dwell *with us.*

The Mishnah records an event that is not mentioned in the New Testament but was held each day of the Feast of Booths. At "cock crow," a trumpet blast signaled the start of a procession from the temple complex down to the lowest part of Jerusalem to draw water from the pool of Siloam. Trumpet blasts marked the movement of the procession through the temple courts and out its gates and then gave the signal to draw water from the pool with a golden flask. After the procession returned to the temple and the participants walked once around the altar, a priest holding the flask ascended the ramp of the altar and poured out the water on the altar. It was a popular event, prompting the Mishnah to state, "He that never has seen the joy of [the water-drawing ceremony] has never in his life seen joy."[71]

On the seventh day of the feast, its "great day" (called Hoshana Rabbah), the people circled the altar not once but seven times before the priest poured out the water.[72] Messianic believers understand this as the setting for Yeshua's dramatic statement about himself that was made "on the last day of the feast, the great day" (John 7:37). We can picture the scene: the people had completed seven processions around the altar. The willow branches with which they were beating the ground during their prayers fell silent. All eyes fixed on the priest's raised hand, holding the golden flask of water. As the flask began to tip, Yeshua stood up and cried out,

> If anyone is thirsty, let him come to me and drink. He who believes in me, as the Scripture said, "From [Messiah's, or the temple's[73]] innermost will flow rivers of living water." (John 7:37–38)[74]

The Mishnah mentions another feature of the festival to which Yeshua alludes. The Court of the Women, located within the temple complex, contained four tall golden candlesticks with a golden bowl atop each. At the end of each day's activities, four young priests climbed to the top of these candlesticks with pitchers of oil to fill the bowls and then lit the wicks to illuminate the courtyard throughout the night. According to the Mishnah, because the candlesticks towered high above the Temple Mount, there was not a courtyard in Jerusalem that was not lit up by the light.[75]

At this same Feast of Booths, Yeshua—we can picture him under the light cast by these candlesticks—proclaimed, "I am the light of the world. Whoever follows me will not walk in darkness, but will have the light of life" (John. 8:12; see also v. 20). Messiah is God's "light for the nations" so that his "salvation may reach to the end of the earth" (Isa. 49:6; see also Isa. 42:6). God promised Israel and those who come to his light, "The sun shall be no more your light by day, nor for brightness shall the moon give you light; but the Lord will be your everlasting light" (Isa. 60:19). The apostle John foresaw this in the New Jerusalem: "The city has no need of sun or moon to shine on it, for the glory of God gives it light, and its lamp is the Lamb" (Rev. 21:23).

The promise of the Feast of Booths for messianic believers is that God will establish his kingdom: the house of the Lord will be built in Zion and nations will flow up to it to be taught God's ways (Isa. 2:2–3; Mic. 4:1–2). Then, all peoples—Jew and gentile—"shall go up year after year to worship the King ... and to keep the Feast of Booths" (Zech. 14:16).

Eighth Day of Assembly

Shemini Atzeret, "the solemn assembly of the eighth [day]," is a term that Jews use to designate the day that follows (or in some cases, concludes) the Feast of Booths. The laity and priestly calendars do not have a special name for this day, calling it only "the eighth day" (Lev. 23:36; Num 29:35). It was to be a "holy convocation" and a "solemn assembly" (*atzeret*) on which food offerings and special sacrifices were made, but no ordinary work was done (Lev. 23:36; Num. 29:35–38).[76] What these calendars don't mention is the reason for the day or how it is connected to the Feast of Booths, a festival that is supposed to last for only seven days (Lev. 23:34–36; Num. 29:12, 35–38). This ambiguity leaves room for speculation.

- The Mishnah refers to the eighth day as the last day of the Feast of Booths, noting that on this day people pray for the seasonal rains to begin, breaking the long drought of summer.[77]

In Luke's account, Yeshua reads from the scroll of Isaiah in the synagogue of Nazareth on the Sabbath, declaring that Isaiah's prophecy about the Messiah is fulfilled in him (Luke 4:16–21). Today, that passage from Isaiah is part of the synagogue readings for the fourth Sabbath in the month of Elul, the last Sabbath of the year. The following month is Tishri when the fall High Holidays occur. If the cycle of synagogue readings was the same in the first century, then Yeshua declared himself to be the fulfillment of Isaiah's prophecy at the cusp of a new year, prompting his disciples to watch for how he would continue to fulfill Scripture in the coming year. (James Tissot, c.1886–1894)

- The Babylonian Talmud also considers the eighth day to be part of the Feast of Booths, joining it to the feast as one of eighteen days in the year when people are obligated to recite the full Hallel.[78]
- The Talmud considers this eighth day to be a festival "unto itself," listing several differences between it and the ways that the Feast of Booths is celebrated.[79]

How this eighth day is celebrated within the messianic movement depends on whether a congregation doubles the festivals or not. The practice of doubling a feast day—celebrating it twice—arose from a curious necessity during the Babylonian exile in the sixth century BC. Because feast dates are tied to specific days of the month, it was important to know when each month began. This was determined by the physical sighting of the new moon in Jerusalem. The problem was how to alert the Jews in Babylon that the new moon had been sighted in Israel, thus signaling the start of the month in which one of the feasts would be held. The news, we are told, spread by signal fires lit in rapid succession. But with the very real possibility of error, tardiness, or malfeasance (the Mishnah mentions malfeasance by the Samaritans in particular) in alerting Jews living far from Israel, the Jewish sages ruled that those communities should double the feast days to ensure it was kept on the correct day: do it twice so that one of the days would bound to be the right one.[80] Today, with the ability to calculate the appearance of the new moon mathematically, this is no longer necessary, but some observant communities outside Israel continue to follow tradition and double the festivals.

Messianic communities who do not double the festivals celebrate the eighth day as it has come to be celebrated in Israel, as Simchat Torah, a day of "Rejoicing in the Torah." On this day, participants read the final portion of Deuteronomy and then roll the Torah scroll all the way back to the beginning to read the first portion of Genesis. In this way, they recognize the ongoing nature of a life devoted to the complete instruction (Torah) of God. For those who double the festivals, Simchat Torah is celebrated the second day.[81]

When we consider the messianic significance of the biblical feasts, this eighth day also holds special promise.

- First with Passover, we remember the Messiah as our Passover Lamb.
- Next, the Day of Firstfruits celebrates his resurrection.
- The Feast of Weeks remembers the giving of Torah and the outpouring of the Holy Spirit.
- The Day of Trumpets is a promise of Yeshua's return and the ingathering of believers.
- The Day of Atonement recognizes the promise of his once-and-for-all atonement in the heavenly temple.

- Then, the Feast of Booths celebrates the promise of the coming kingdom.

Following this sequence, the eighth day of the last feast of the calendar year points messianic believers to consider the end of the kingdom, when Yeshua has asserted his rule and can turn the world that fully recognizes their Creator over to the Father:

> Then comes the end, when he delivers the kingdom to God the Father after destroying every rule and every authority and power. For he must reign until he has put all his enemies under his feet. The last enemy to be destroyed is death. (1 Cor. 15:24–26 citing Ps. 110:1)

This is the fulfillment of the promise of eternal life: believers are presented before the throne of God and of the Lamb, with access to the Tree of Life in a renewed Eden.

"Then the angel showed me [John] the river of the water of life, bright as crystal, flowing from the throne of God and of the Lamb through the middle of the street of the city; also, on either side of the river, the tree of life with its twelve kinds of fruit, yielding its fruit each month. The leaves of the tree were for the healing of the nations. No longer will there be anything accursed, but the throne of God and of the Lamb will be in it, and his servants will worship him. They will see his face, and his name will be on their foreheads. And night will be no more. They will need no light of lamp or sun, for the Lord God will be their light, and they will reign forever and ever." (Rev. 22:1–5)

PURIM (FEAST OF LOTS)

The festivals of Purim and Hanukkah emerge later in biblical history and so do not appear in the festival calendars of the Torah. Both holidays celebrate the Jewish people's deliverance from oppressive kingdoms. Let's begin by looking at Purim.

This holiday is introduced by the book of Esther and its story is set during the reign of the Persian King Ahasuerus, a form of the name for Xerxes, who reigned 486–465 BC. The book narrates the Persian king's choice of Esther, a Jew, as his new queen, but her Jewish lineage was not revealed to either the king or the people. Her cousin Mordecai, on the other hand, was a known Jew at the gate of the palace. Mordecai refused to bow before Haman, a high-ranking official in the king's court. Haman's rage over this affront drove him to plot against the Jews of the Persian Empire, and he cast a lot to determine a day for their destruction. (The name Purim comes from the Hebrew word *pur*, meaning "lot," and so Purim is also called the Feast of Lots.) King Ahasuerus permitted Haman to issue an irrevocable decree for the destruction of the Jews in the empire. Esther then revealed her identity to the king as she informed him of Haman's evil plot. The king promptly issued an edict throughout the empire that permitted the Jewish people to defend themselves. This they did, prompting Mordecai to initiate the festival of Purim.

Messianic believers celebrate Purim in a manner similar to that of Judaism. Many begin with a fast

Hebrew Scroll of Esther with elements from the joyous festival of Purim—a costume mask and noisemaker called a grogger. (Photo by Seth Aronstam/Shutterstock)

on the thirteenth day of the month of Adar, the day before Purim. The day of Purim, however, is a festive time that involves dressing up in costumes, donating charity to the poor, giving gift baskets, having a festive meal, and reading the story of Esther from the scroll which is always accompanied by loud boos and noisemakers to drown out the mention of Haman's name. This boisterous practice leads others to offer cheers for Mordecai and sighs over Esther.

Some messianic believers follow the suggestion that Yeshua's presence in Jerusalem for the unnamed feast of John 5:1 was for the celebration of Purim. John states, "There was a feast of the Jews, and Jesus went up to Jerusalem." John goes on to relate that while there, Jesus healed a paralyzed man at the Pool of Bethesda, then adds, "Now that day was the Sabbath" (v. 9). If this Sabbath healing was on the actual feast day, as the gospel may suggest, then it might be matched with the Purim which fell on the Sabbath in the year AD 28.[82]

HANUKKAH (FEAST OF DEDICATION)

Hanukkah celebrates the cleansing and rededication of the temple in Jerusalem after Jewish freedom fighters had cast off the heavy hand of the Hellenistic (Greek) Seleucid kingdom that had both outlawed Jewish practices and defiled the temple. Hanukkah is set within the days of the Seleucid King Antiochus IV who reigned 175–164 BC. The book of 1 Maccabees records that Antiochus invaded Jerusalem in 169 BC and took the temple's sacred treasures.[83] Josephus records that in 167 BC, Antiochus built a pagan altar over God's altar in the Jerusalem temple, sacrificed swine on it, and forced the Jews to worship pagan gods.[84] Antiochus also attempted to unify his far-flung empire by introducing Hellenistic (Greek) culture throughout his land. When he encountered Jewish resistance to Greek culture, he outlawed Sabbath and circumcision, crucified offenders, and destroyed Torah scrolls.[85]

Mattathias and his five sons, descendants of the priestly Hasmonean family, led a revolt against this oppression. In Mattathias's speech before his death, he passed the military leadership on to his third son, Judas Maccabeus, meaning "Judah the hammer," from which we get the name Maccabees. Roughly three years after the outbreak of the Maccabean Revolt and after intense battles fought on the various ascents to Jerusalem, Judas and his brothers cleansed the temple, built a new altar, set up the menorah and lit the lamps. This happened on the twenty-fifth day of the month of Kislev. The celebration of the dedication lasted for eight days.[86]

Latkes and sufganiyot with dreidels (tops) and other items used in modern Hanukkah celebrations.

Messianic believers celebrate Hanukkah in ways that are similar to the rest of Judaism. For the eight nights of the festival, we bless God as the One who provides miracles of deliverance and we light the Hanukkah menorah. Because oil lamps were used in the temple menorah, oil is a significant part of the celebration, even appearing in some of the festival's foods, such as latkes (potato pancakes) and sufganiyot (jelly donuts), both fried in oil.

Of special significance for messianic believers is the record that Yeshua observed Hanukkah, a festival that celebrates the cleansing and rededication of the Jerusalem temple. The gospel of John records, "At that time the Feast of Dedication took place at Jerusalem. It was winter, and Jesus was walking in the temple, in the colonnade of Solomon" (John 10:22–23). It was during this festival that he was accused of blasphemy, having said, "I and the Father are one" (v. 30). Just over three months later, Yeshua entered the temple precincts again, this time for the festival of Passover. A few days before Passover began, he defended the temple's sanctity by driving out money changers who had made it a den of robbers rather than a house of prayer (Mark 11:15–17). Soon afterward, he was arrested, tried, and crucified. Messianic believers find it significant that Yeshua emphasized the sanctity of the temple in some of his last public acts in Jerusalem, setting an example of dedication to God which we can follow, even after Yeshua showed himself to be the once and for all temple sacrifice.

DEPENDENCE AND TRUST

As messianic believers observe the biblical feasts and do so in holy convocation at God's appointed times, we seek to add a measure of reverence and awe to our walks of faith as disciples of our master Yeshua. In doing so, we learn to look forward, year by year, to gathering with our Father at his appointed times. Together, each spring, we thank

Modern Hanukkah menorah with oil lamps.

God for the work accomplished by Yeshua in his first coming, and every autumn, we embrace anew the promise of his second coming. We search our hearts diligently, knowing that Yeshua will return as judge. Then we celebrate joyfully the prospects of his kingdom and the end of the age. With John at the conclusion of the book of Revelation, we learn to cry out, "Amen. Come, Lord Jesus!" (Rev. 22:20).

People today who are cut off from the harsh geographical realities of the Land of Israel and its constant thirst for rain easily lose sight of the agricultural aspects of the biblical feasts and the lessons they teach us about frailty and our need to depend on God. For the ancient residents of Israel, each year was a renewal of that dependence. God said if his people loved and served him, he would respond by sending rain "in its season"; if not, he would withhold the rain (Deut. 11:13–17). Within this rhythm of seasons—wet then dry, then wet then dry—his people celebrated the feasts, linked not only to Israel's great national story (the exodus, Mount Sinai, wilderness wanderings) but also to the cycle of harvests in their homeland: grain, new wine from the summer vintage, oil from the olive harvest, and grass for their livestock (Deut. 11:14–15). Throughout, we see God's power, mercy, and grace, and our need to depend on and trust in him. To live is to depend on God.

Because many of us do not witness crops growing to harvest or because we take food preservation and storage for granted, we overlook this most essential reminder of who God is.

The opposite of the blessing of rain and harvest is famine and starvation. The prophet Habakkuk closed his short book with a picture of the fragility of life in an arid land, the bald reality of the thin line between plenty and scarcity on which we all tread. What did he conclude? Regardless of which side of that line he stood on, he chose to depend on the Lord and rejoice in him:

> Though the fig tree does not shoot forth its leaves [in the spring],
> nor any fruit be on the vines [in the summer];
> though the [supply of oil from the] olive harvest fail [in the fall]
> and the fields provide no food [for lack of winter rains];
> yea though the pen be empty of sheep and the stalls without cattle,
> yet will I rejoice in the Lord,
> yea, I will rejoice in the God of my salvation.
> (Hab. 3:17–18)[87]

As we celebrate the feasts together, remember our dependence on the God of life. *Ein od!* "There is no other!"

FROM AGRICULTURAL PLENTY TO FAILURE

Yet I will rejoice in the LORD, yea, I will rejoice in the God of my salvation.
—Habakkuk 3:17–18

Courtesy of Biblical Backgrounds

Notes for Chapter 4

1 *Yeshua* is the Hebrew pronunciation of Jesus' name.

2 The declaration in Isaiah 53:12 is the heart of the apostolic message, the culmination of the Song of the Exalted Servant (Isa. 52:13–53:12). Steven P. Lancaster and James M. Monson, "Isaiah's Exalted Servant in the Great Isaiah Scroll," Special Supplement to *Messiah Journal* 107 (2011): 29–33, 48–55.

3 David Rudolph, "Messianic Judaism in Antiquity and in the Modern Era," in *Introduction to Messianic Judaism: Its Ecclesial Context and Biblical Foundations*, David Rudolph and Joel Willitts, eds. (Grand Rapids, Mich.: Zondervan, 2013), 26–33, summarizes the development and growth of modern messianic Judaism.

4 Union of Messianic Jewish Congregations (UMJC), "Defining Messianic Judaism," July 20, 2005. n.p. https://www.umjc.org/defining-messianic-judaism (accessed October 26, 2020).

5 Rudolph, "Messianic Judaism," 34–35. Rudolph's use of the term "Yeshua-believing Gentiles" demonstrates the difficulty of nomenclature for gentiles who embrace the Jewishness of *Yeshua HaMashiach*, Jesus the Christ, and seek to practice the faith of the first-century believers.

6 Boaz Michael, *Tent of David: Healing the Vision of the Messianic Gentile* (Marshfield, Mo: First Fruits of Zion, 2013), 17.

7 Toby Janicki in *God-Fearers: Gentiles & the God of Israel* (Marshfield, Mo.: First Fruits of Zion, 2012), 107, discusses the struggles for gentile identity within the messianic movement and concludes: "Who are the Gentiles practicing Messianic Judaism? We are the God-fearers. We non-Jews in Messiah who are seeking a proper relationship to the Jewish people and the Torah are resurrecting this ancient identity."

8 Messianic Jews by the UMJC's definition (see note above) observe the feasts traditionally while holding loyally to their belief that Yeshua is the Messiah. Carl Kinbar, "Messianic Jews and Jewish Tradition," in *Introduction to Messianic Judaism: Its Ecclesial Context and Biblical Foundations*, 72, however, speaks about a spectrum in messianic Judaism with widely divergent practices. He also summarizes the statements of three Jewish organizations that engage Jewish tradition more seriously (74–80).

9 Marion Bible Fellowship, Marion, Ohio (marionbible.com).

10 Gordon. J. Wenham, *The Book of Leviticus*, New International Commentary on the Old Testament (Grand Rapids, Mich.: Eerdmans, 1979), 300.

11 James M. Monson with Steven P. Lancaster, *Regions on the Run: Introductory Map Studies in the Land of the Bible* (Rockford, Ill.: Biblical Backgrounds, 2019), 6–7.

12 Rabbinic midrash responds variously to this "mixed multitude," but all understand it as gentiles leaving Egypt with Israel. The rabbinic text *Shemot Rabbah* 18:10, an early commentary on the book of Exodus, offers a very positive identification of this mixed multitude: "God made a day of rejoicing for Israel when he redeemed them and He proclaimed, 'All who love my sons may come and rejoice with them.' The virtuous among the Egyptians came, celebrated the Passover with Israel, and went up with them, for it says, 'And a mixed multitude went out also with them;'" from *Exodus,* trans. by S. M. Lehrman, in *Midrash Rabbah*, eds. H. Freedman and Maurice Simon (New York: Soncino, 1983), 226. Dennis Prager provides additional insight: "The Israelites left Egypt with members of several other nations who comprised the lowest classes of Egyptian society;" Dennis Prager, *Exodus: God, Slavery, and Freedom* (Washington, D.C.: Regnery Faith, 2018), 148.

13 Promises made to Abraham: Gen. 12:1–3, 7; 13:14–17; 15:1–21; 17:1–11; 18:18–19; 22:17–18; 24:7; to Isaac: Gen. 26:3–5, 24; and to Jacob: Gen. 28:10–15; 35:11–15; 46:3–4; 48:4.

14 The second redemption is found in many of the letters of the New Testament, including Colossians 1, Ephesians 2, Romans 6 and 11, and 1 Peter 2.

15 Nahum N. Glatzer, ed., *The Passover Haggadah with English Translation and Introduction,* based on commentaries of E. D. Goldschmidt (New York: Schocken, 1969), 9.

16 Glatzer, *Passover Haggadah*, 9. Notice the triple rhymes with *–hatz* endings in the first line and the *–rech* endings in the second line. Both lines conclude with a *–tzah* rhyme.

17 Glatzer, *Passover Haggadah*, 10.

18 *Vine of David Haggadah: Messianic Jewish Passover Seder* (Marshfield, Mo.: Vine of David, 2011), 95, n. 5 explains that although other dippings occur in the Seder, this is the correct place as it must precede the blessing over the bread described in Matthew 26:26 (see also Mark 14:17–22).

19 See also Matt. 26:26; Mark 14:22.

20 "During supper" (v. 2) he "rose from supper" (v. 4) and then "resumed his place" (v. 12; Greek reads "having reclined again," which refers to the leaning on his left side at a low table to begin eating again with his right hand).

21 See also Matt. 26:27–28; Mark 14:23–24.

22 See also Mark 14:26.

23 Peter alludes to a requirement for the Passover Lamb in Exodus 12:5: "Your lamb shall be without blemish." With John's statement "When they came to Jesus and saw that he was already dead, they did not break his legs" (John 19:33), another allusion to the Passover lamb is made: "You shall not break any of its bones" (Ex. 12:46).

24 John, Peter, and Philip use *amnos,* "lamb," which occurs in the Septuagint almost exclusively for the sacrificial language of the Torah. Joseph H. Thayer, *Thayer's Greek-English Lexicon of the New Testament* (Peabody, Mass.: Hendrickson, 2017), 32, observes on the use of amnos in John 1:29, 36; Acts 8:32, and 1 Peter 1:19 that "Messiah is likened to a sacrificial lamb on account of his death, innocently and patiently endured, to expiate sin."

25 Paul uses the word *pasxa* "the Pesach," which means here the animal victim of the Passover: a lamb.

26 The time and order of slaughtering the Passover lamb with respect to the daily offerings, as well as the organization for accomplishing the task quickly, is described in the Mishnah in *m. Pesachim* 5:1, 3, 5–10. During the slaughtering, the Levites sang the Hallel (Psalms 113–118) continuously but never had to repeat it fully the third time before the task was completed.

27 In the Feast of Weeks, however, when Israel brought their firstfruits to the temple, they were instructed to bring two loaves of bread "baked with leaven, as firstfruits to the LORD" (Lev. 23:17).

28 Delwen Samuel, "Bread" in *The Oxford Encyclopedia of Ancient Egypt*, ed. Donald B. Redford (Oxford: Oxford University Press, 2001), 1:197; David Kraemer, "Leavened or Unleavened: A History," n.p. https://forward.com/articles/10411/leavened-or-unleavened-a-history (March 30, 2007).

29 Prager, *Exodus*, 140.

30 The Torah reading in the synagogue on the seventh day of Passover is Exodus 13:17–15:26, which narrates Israel's crossing of the Red Sea and the song of Moses that was sung afterward (cf. *b. Megillah* 31a.) The note accompanying this text in the Soncino Edition of the Talmud says, "Ex. XIII, 17 relating to the passage of the Red Sea which is supposed to have taken place on the seventh day."

31 "Grace After Meals" in *The Complete Art Scroll Siddur*, trans. and ed. by Nossom Scherman with Meir Zlotowitz (Brooklyn, N.Y.: Mesorah, 1997), 197.

32 Aaron Eby, Boaz Michael, Toby Janick, and Daniel Lancaster, *Meal of Messiah: The Wedding Supper of the Lamb* (Marshfield, Mo.: Vine of David, 2010), vi. Vine of David has produced this rich resource for celebrating the Meal of Messiah.

33 Glatzer, ed., *The Passover Haggadah*, 49.

34 Glatzer, ed., *The Passover Haggadah*, 24–28. From four verses in the Torah, the Haggadah introduces four types of children whom the parent answers differently when asked about the reason for celebrating Passover: Deuteronomy 6:20 is the question posed by a wise child; Exodus 12:26 is the question posed by a wicked child; Exodus 13:14 is the question posed by a simple child; and Exodus 13:8 is the answer given a child who does not know how to ask.

35 Paul also uses the metaphor to identify his first convert in Asia (Rom. 16:5) and a household of first converts in Achaia (1 Cor. 16:15), both symbolic of a fuller harvest in these regions to come. Paul also sees believers as the firstfruits of the restoration of the creation (Rom. 8:23). James speaks similarly: "We should be a kind of firstfruits of his creatures" (James 1:18). See also Rom. 11:16; Rev. 14:4.

36 Eckhard J. Schnabel, *Jesus in Jerusalem: The Last Days* (Grand Rapids, Mich.: Eerdmans, 2018), 139–151, 334.

37 Nogah Hareuveni, *Nature in Our Biblical Heritage,* trans. Helen Frenkley (Kiryat Ono, Israel: Neot Kedumim, 1980), 59–60.

38 *m. Bikkurim* 3:1–12.

39 The firstfruits could be brought any time from the Festival of Weeks until the end of the Festival of Tabernacles; *m. Bikkurim* 1:10.

40 Many messianic believers understand the "house" mentioned in Acts 2:2 to be "the house of God/the LORD," i.e., the temple. Of the 365 times that the Hebrew Scriptures use the expression *ha-bayit,* "the house," many apply to the temple (42 in Ezekiel 40–48 alone). More specifically, the phrase *bēt elohim/Ha-Shem*, "house of God/the LORD," which appears 408 times, always refers to the temple. Rabbinic literature typically refers to the temple as *ha-bayit,* "the house," and throughout Jewish history scholars have used the terms *bēt rishon* and *bēt shenī* to express "First Temple" and "Second Temple."

41 Luke, the presumed author of the book of Acts, presents the apostolic community as a temple community. After the ascension, they "were continually in the temple blessing God" (Luke 24:53). They attended temple together (Acts 2:46), devoting themselves to "the prayers" there (Acts 2:42). Peter and John went up to the temple at the time of prayer to join in the afternoon prayer (Acts 3:1). Peter preached in Solomon's Portico, the eastern colonnaded porch of the temple (Acts 3:11), which was a common gathering place for the disciples (Acts 5:12) and where he and John were arrested (Acts 4:1).

42 Paul H. Wright, "Geography of the Nations in Jerusalem for Pentecost," in *Lexham Geographic Commentary on Acts through Revelation,* ed. Barry J. Beitzel (Bellingham, Wash.: Lexham, 2019), 105–114.

43 *b. Shabbat* 86b–87a.

44 Author's translation.

45 *Shemot Rabbah* 5:9 in *Exodus*, trans. by S. M. Lehrman, in *Midrash Rabbah*, 86. Lehrman translated *ha-qol* and *ha-qolot* as "the thundering" and "the thunderings;" the author used the more literal translation, "the voice" and "the voices" as in Psalm 29:3.

46 *b. Shabbat* 88b.

47 *b. Shabbat* 88b, n. 2.

48 *Shir HaShirim Rabbah* 1:2 in Song of Songs, trans. by Maurice Simon, in *Midrash Rabbah* (New York: Soncino, 1983), 23.

49 Author's translation.

50 *b. Shabbat* 88b.

51 H. B. Hackett as quoted by A. T. Robertson in *Word Pictures in the New Testament*, vol. 3 (Nashville, Tenn.: Broadman, 1930), 21.

52 Amos 9:11, as applied by James the Just in Acts 15:13–18; author's translation of Amos 9:11.

53 *Teru'ah* is grammatically singular but in practice is more than one blast of the shofar.

54 *b. Rosh HaShanah* 27a. *m. Rosh HaShanah* 1:1 identifies four New Years in Judaism. The civil new year begins on 1 Tishri, which the biblical calendar calls the seventh month.

55 John Fischer, *Messianic Services for the Festivals and Holy Days* (Palm Harbor, Fla.: Menorah Ministries, 2006), 10.

56 *m. Rosh HaShanah* 1:2.

57 The first verse of the hymn *Adon Olam*, "Lord of the World," which is part of the Sabbath liturgy, expresses delightfully that after creation, God received the title King: "Lord of the world, who reigned supreme, before creation's form was framed. When all was finished by his will, his name as King was proclaimed."

58 *m. Yoma* 1:1–8; 3:3–7:1.

59 D. Thomas Lancaster, *What About the Sacrifices?* (Marshfield, MO: First Fruits of Zion, 2011), 45–75 presents the *protos* (first) and *deuteros* (second) covenant, two priesthoods, two temples, and two eras.

60 D. Thomas Lancaster, *Restoration: Returning the Torah of God to the Disciples of Jesus* (Marshfield, Mo.: First Fruits of Zion, 2009), 95.

61 *b. Rosh HaShanah* 16b; cf. 32b.

62 Isa. 13:9–10; 24:21–23; Joel 2:30–31; 3:14–15; Amos 5:20; 8:9; Zeph. 1:14–16; Matt. 24:29.

63 J. K. McKee, *Moedim: The Appointed Times for Messianic Believers* (McKinney, Tex.: Messianic Apologetics, 2013), 23.

64 E. Schild, "On Exodus iii.14—'I Am That I Am,'" *Vetus Testamentum* 4 (1954): 296–302.

65 Author's translation.

66 Yeshua used Psalm 118:22 as a conclusion to his parable of the vineyard (Matt. 21:42; Mark 12:10; Luke 20:17). Peter applied it in the same way in Acts 4:11. In his first epistle, Peter uses the verse as a metaphor of Messiah Yeshua the chief cornerstone of a living temple (1 Peter 2:7).

67 The New Testament follows the Septuagint's choice to translate the Hebrew word *sukkot* ("booths") in Leviticus 23 by the Greek word *skenon* ("tabernacle").

68 Thayer, *Thayer's Greek-English Lexicon of the New Testament*, 578.

69 Paul also uses the word *skene*, "tabernacle" for our earthly bodies (2 Cor. 5:1, 4).

70 Septuagint translation.

71 *m. Sukkah* 5:1, 4–5.

72 For a presentation of the ceremony in narrative form, see D. Thomas Lancaster, *King of the Jews: Resurrecting the Jewish Jesus* (Littleton, Colo.: First Fruits of Zion, 2006), 131–138.

73 The citation is puzzling, with interpreters identifying the pronoun *auton*, "his," in v. 38 as the believer, the Messiah as in Isaiah 12:3, or the temple as in Ezekiel 47:1–12 and Zechariah 14:8.

74 Author's translation.

75 Blackman (*Sukkot* 5:2, n. 5 in *Order Moed*, vol. 2 of *Mishnayoth*) states the candlesticks were "each fifty cubits [75 feet] high and from the Temple Mount overlooked the whole of Jerusalem." *m. Sukkot* 5:2–3.

76 *Atzeret*, often translated "assembly," derives from the Hebrew verb *atzar*, "to restrain, retain, stop," likely referring to the cessation of ordinary work on days dedicated to the Lord (Lev. 23:36; Deut. 16:8).

77 *m. Ta'anit* 1:1–2.

78 *b. Ta'anit* 28b.

79 *b. Sukkot* 47b–48a.

80 *m. Rosh HaShanah* 1:3–2:9.

81 The postponement of reading the last portion of the Torah until the second day by communities in the Diaspora is stated in *b. Megillah* 31a.

82 John J. Parsons, "Purim—Feast of Lots," https://www.hebrew4christians.com/Holidays/Winter_Holidays/Purim/purim.html and Gordon Franz, "Jesus Celebrated Purim," https://www.lifeandland.org/2008/12/jesus-celebrated-purim.

83 1 Maccabees 1:21–23; cf. Josephus, *Antiquities* 12.249-250/v.4. While the books of Maccabees are part of the Apocrypha rather than Scripture, they preserve a history of the Jewish struggle against the Seleucids in the second century BC.

84 *Antiquities* 12.253–254/v.5.

85 *Antiquities* 12.254-256/v.5; 1 Maccabees 1:41–61.

86 1 Maccabees 2–4.

87 Translation by James M. Monson, *The Land Between: A Regional Study Guide to the Land of the Bible* (Jerusalem, Israel: James M. Monson, 1983), 15; and *Regions on the Run: Introductory Map Studies in the Land of the Bible* (Rockford, Ill.: Biblical Backgrounds, Inc., 1998–2019), 5.

CHAPTER 5

Feasts of the Bible and the Church

Heidi Kinner

Since the earliest days of the church, followers of Jesus have struggled to understand which Jewish observances of Old Testament practices gentile Christians should keep. The record of the Jerusalem Council in Acts 15, as well as the letters of Paul, describe many of these decision points, but no mention is made of the feasts of the Bible, even though by the time of the New Testament these were becoming important markers of what it meant to be Jewish. While Jewish followers of Jesus continued to observe the feasts,[1] it does not seem that the apostles required gentiles to do the same. As they oversaw an increasingly gentile church, gentile leaders in the generations that followed observed only the feasts that had clear connections to Jesus. In the process, they reframed the Jewish feasts to focus on Jesus' saving work.

The biblical feasts were—and remain—an important gateway into understanding the Jewish roots of our Christian faith. And learning about them certainly helps us gain a deeper appreciation of our Jewish neighbors and the shared culture in which we live. But how should Christians today approach the feasts of the Bible? Should believers in Jesus celebrate Jewish festivals? Should the feasts be embraced? Reimagined? Abandoned? Some Christians say that believers in Jesus are free to celebrate the biblical feasts if they wish but doing so is not necessary. Others believe that participating in the feasts is a matter of discipleship, an important way to pattern their lives after Jesus' life. Still others argue that Christians should not celebrate them at all. A look into how the early Christians approached the Jewish feasts can help us make informed decisions and become more aware of why we choose to celebrate the feasts or why we choose not to.

It did not take long for Christianity to become a very diverse movement, even in its early centuries. In order to avoid getting too complex too quickly,

This depiction of Jesus' seaside breakfast with his disciples, recorded in John 21, adorns an interior wall of the Greek Orthodox Church of the Holy Apostles at Capernaum. Both the event—it happened after Jesus' resurrection—and its position as the last story in the Gospels make this meal a bridge to the communal meals of the early church (Acts 2:46). (Photo by Paul H. Wright)

we will focus our discussion in this chapter on the Western church, rather than the interesting diversity of the Eastern churches. And we'll start with the most frequent, and primary, Jewish celebration—the weekly Sabbath.

 THE SABBATH AND SUNDAY

The Sabbath (Saturday) is a day of rest, the first celebration given by God, and it serves as a reminder of his sovereignty and care. Today, many Christians wonder whether they should observe the Sabbath or keep Sunday as the main holy day of the week instead. (Indeed, some call Sunday "the Sabbath.") This is a good question and an ancient one that early Christians, both Jewish and gentile, debated.

The story of Paul preaching until midnight, with the result that Eutychus, who had fallen asleep, fell from his window perch, took place "on the first day of the week," literally "on the first [day] of the Sabbaths" (Acts 20:7). This phrase suggests a compromise position among the first Christians. Jewish followers of Jesus could keep their weekly Sabbath observance and then immediately gather for a Christian worship service on Saturday evening, after sundown, which was the start of Sunday according to the Jewish pattern of counting days.[2]

As more gentiles joined the church and the divisions between Jews and gentiles increased, the observance of the Sabbath was often discouraged and the main weekly Christian worship gathering began to shift to Sunday morning. This followed the pattern of considering the start of a day at midnight, as was common in the Roman world. For example, around the year 100, the early Christian leader Ignatius of Antioch wrote, "Those, then, who lived by ancient practices arrived at a new hope. They ceased to keep the Sabbath and lived by the Lord's Day [Sunday], on which our life as well as theirs shone forth."[3] By the middle of the third century, Sunday morning had become the standard time for worship in most churches.[4]

The early Christians used three main names for Sunday:

- The most common name was **"the first day of the week"** (Acts 20:7).[5] By continuing to use this Hebrew phrase for Sunday, they emphasized not only creation, but also the first day of the new creation that begun at Jesus' resurrection: "Therefore, if anyone is in Christ, he is a new creation. The old has passed away; behold, the new has come" (2 Cor. 5:17; see also Rev. 21:5).
- Early Christians also called Sunday the **"eighth day,"** linking Jesus' resurrection to his return in glory as the full realization of the new creation, something that will surpass our present seven-day creation. So we read in one early second-century Christian writing: "Moreover [God] says to them, 'I cannot stand your new moons and Sabbaths' [Isa. 1:13]. You see what he means: It is not the Sabbaths of the present time that are acceptable to me, but the one I have made, in which I will give rest to all things and make a beginning of an eighth day, which is the beginning of another world."[6]
- The end-times focus of Sunday as the eighth day is also reflected in the term **"the Lord's day,"** first used in Revelation 1:10: "I was in the Spirit on the Lord's day, and I heard behind me a loud voice like a trumpet." "The Lord's day" evokes the phrase "the Day of the LORD" that is used throughout the Old Testament to refer to the dramatic, decisive, future moment when God will restore Israel, judge the nations, and set all things right (Isa. 13:6, 9; Ezek. 30:3; Joel 2:1, 11, 31; Amos 5:18; Zeph. 1:7, 14). Drawing on these ideas, the author of Revelation gives the term a distinctly Christ-centered orientation that connects Jesus' resurrection to his return in glory.

Christian Views of the Sabbath

Some Christians believe that since the Sabbath is grounded in the seventh day of creation and is one of the Ten Commandments, it applies to all people for all time (Gen. 2:1–3; Ex. 20:8–11). "For in six days the LORD made the heaven and earth, the sea, and all that is in them, and rested on the seventh day. Therefore the LORD blessed the Sabbath day and made it holy" (Ex. 20:11).

Others take their cue from early Christians who believed that the first Easter Sunday was the first day of a new creation. This makes every day a type of Sabbath. This implies that we do not need to observe the seventh day as holier or different from other days of the week, since all days, like all people and activities that are in Christ, are part of the new creation.

Sunday, however, can also be seen as a type of weekly Easter celebration that reminds us of Christ's resurrection and our salvation, a day that celebrates our new life in him. Gathering and worshiping on Sunday need not rule out some sort of Sabbath observance as well, although for those in Christ, this is not necessary. Some Christians choose to worship on Sunday and spend the remainder of the day as a time of rest and prayer. Others choose to follow the pattern of the early church and observe the Sabbath on Saturday while worshiping on Sunday. This position, which holds appeal in our often too-busy world, is reflected in a prayer for Saturday from the Anglican tradition:

> Almighty God, who after the creation of the world rested from all your works and sanctified a day of rest for all your creatures: Grant that we, putting away all earthly anxieties, may be duly prepared for the service of your sanctuary, and that our rest here upon earth may be a preparation for the eternal rest promised to your people in heaven; through Jesus Christ our Lord. Amen.[7]

PASSOVER AND THE CHRISTIAN PASCHA

God's intervention in human history at Passover is a defining event for the people of Israel. Jesus' death and resurrection are the defining events for Christians. That Jesus' death occurred at the time of the Passover celebration was of great significance for his followers, who understood the events of Passover as foreshadowing his saving work. Jesus was the unblemished lamb who gave his life to save his people and whose resurrection opened the way through the waters of death into the kingdom of God, the ultimate promised land. The apostle Paul clearly expressed this when he wrote, "Christ, our Passover lamb, has been sacrificed" (1 Cor. 5:7). Passover, as fulfilled by Jesus, so completely defined the faith of the church that for almost one hundred and fifty years it was the only annual Christian celebration.[8]

Until the early second century, Christians celebrated their version of Passover at the same time as the Jews, on the fourteenth and fifteenth days of the Hebrew month of Nisan. The followers of Jesus fasted during the day of the fourteenth and then at sunset (the beginning of the fifteenth of Nisan) gathered for a worship service that included the Lord's Supper. Their worship ended late at night with a celebratory meal.[9]

Not surprisingly, the main focus of the Christianized Passover was Jesus' passion and death on the cross as the ultimate Passover lamb of Exodus 12. This can be seen in the Greek word *pathein*, "to suffer," which was chosen by early church writers to translate the Hebrew word *pesach* (Passover).[10] This was not a literal translation (*pesach* means "to pass" or "spring over"), but it conveyed a key idea by association: Jesus *suffered* as the Passover (Paschal) Lamb in order to free humanity who were *suffering* under the rule of sin and death.[11]

So Bishop Melito of Sardis (c. 160) wrote in his sermon, *On the Pascha*:

> What is the Pascha? Its name is taken from an accompanying circumstance: *paschein* (to keep Pascha) comes from *pathein* (to suffer).... For having been himself led as a lamb and slain as a sheep, he ransomed us from the devil's slavery as from the hand of Pharaoh; and he marked our souls with his own Spirit, and the members of our body with his own blood.[12]

Although the suffering and passion of Christ was the central emphasis of this Christianized Passover, it was not the only focus. All the key redemptive acts of Jesus' life were remembered and given meaning through the lens of the cross. Melito of Sardis also wrote:

> [Jesus] is the lamb being slain; he is the lamb that is speechless; he is the one born from Mary the lovely ewe-lamb; he is the one taken from the flock and dragged to the slaughter and sacrificed at evening and buried at night; who on the tree was not broken, in the earth was not dissolved, arose from the dead, and raised mortals from the grave below.[13]

By the mid-second century, some Christians had moved their Passover celebration from the fourteenth and fifteenth of Nisan to the first Sunday after that date.[14] This change seems to have begun in Jerusalem following the Bar Kokhba revolt in the early second century when the Roman emperor Hadrian expelled the Jews (including the Jewish Christians) from the city. The result was described by the great early church historian Eusebius of Caesarea:

> Thus when the city [of Jerusalem] came to be bereft of the nation of the Jews, and its ancient inhabitants had completely perished, it was colonized by foreigners.... The church, too, in it was composed of Gentiles.[15]

Given the Roman hostility to the Jews following the rebellion, the new gentile church leaders felt that they had to distance themselves from the Jews and their Jewish-Christian brethren in order to protect the churches in Jerusalem. One way that they did this was by only celebrating the Passover on Sunday to make a distinction between the Jewish celebration and that of the Christians. This change spread quickly since congregations were already accustomed to worshiping on Sunday. In the year 325, the Council of Nicea made official the switch to a Sunday Passover observance for all Western churches.[16]

Christians in Jerusalem today celebrate the start of Holy Week with a joyous Palm Sunday walk from Bethany, down the Mount of Olives, and into Jerusalem. The route remembers Jesus' entrance into the city on the Sunday prior to Passover: "So they took branches of palm trees and went out to meet him, crying out, 'Hosanna!'" (John 12:13). (Photo by Paul H. Wright)

This change in date shifted the emphasis of the early church's Passover from the crucified sacrificial Lamb to the resurrected Christ, and by extension the resurrection of the faithful through him. This shift was reflected in yet another translation for the Hebrew word *pesach*, the Latin word *transitus*, "passage,"[17] as illustrated by Augustine (c. 400):

> Careful scholars have discovered that *Pascha* is a Hebrew word, and they do not translate it with "suffering" but with "passage." For by suffering the Lord made the passage from death to life and opened a way for us who believe in his resurrection by which we too might pass from death to life.[18]

Around the same time, Jerome—who learned Hebrew and translated the Hebrew Scriptures into Latin—agreed with Augustine. Using the word *pascha*, an Aramaic form of *pesach*, Jerome wrote:

> The Pascha … does not get its name from *passio* [Latin for "suffering"], as many people think, but from "passage."[19]

In learning Hebrew, Jerome immersed himself in the thought patterns of ancient Israel. As a result, he saw his translation as more closely reflecting the theme of God's passing over the Israelites in Exodus 12 and so sparing their firstborn sons from death.

This new focus on the resurrection was meant to express more fully the events of Good Friday *and* Easter Sunday, but instead it ended up lessening the focus on Jesus' passion and death.

Sometime between the second and fourth centuries, a pilgrim drew this Roman ship on a wall that is now part of the Chapel of Saint Vartan in the lower level of the Church of the Holy Sepulchre. The inscription reads *Domine Ivimus,* "Lord, we have come." It is one of the earliest pieces of evidence of Christian pilgrimage to Jerusalem. (Photo by Becca McDonald)

To bring these different emphases back into balance, Christians developed what is called the *Triduum Sacrum*, the Sacred Three Days. This is a three-day worship cycle from Thursday night to early Sunday morning that follows the arrest, crucifixion, burial, and resurrection of Jesus. It is important to note that these three days functioned as a single worship event in the early church. Christians were (and still are) encouraged to participate in all the services during these three days to embrace, rather than skew, the fullness of Christ's redemptive work.

Some of the earliest information that we have about these worship services comes from the diary of Egeria, a nun who traveled to the Holy Land as a pilgrim and representative of her convent in Spain (c. 381–384). Though Egeria's diary only survives as fragments today, her descriptions of these services in Jerusalem can help us understand the growth of distinctly Christian forms of worship in the early church.

S. HIERONYMUS

This statue of Jerome is in the courtyard of the Church of Saint Catherine, next to the Church of the Nativity, in Bethlehem. For the last thirty years of his life, Jerome lived in Bethlehem where he translated the Old Testament from Hebrew into Latin (the Vulgate). (Photo by Paul H. Wright)

Old City Jerusalem

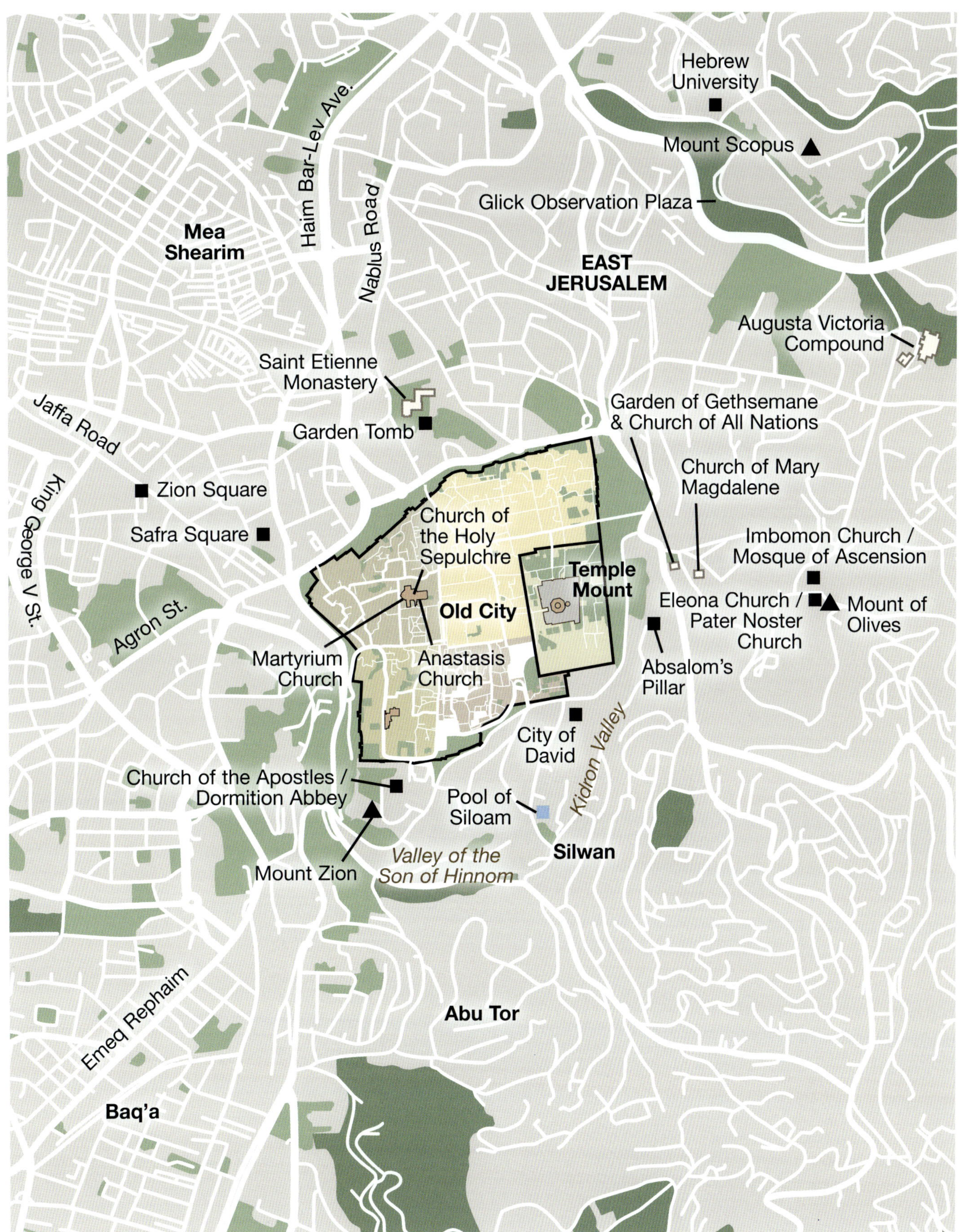

 YOM KIPPUR AND GOOD FRIDAY

According to the pilgrim Egeria, the Good Friday worship service began on Thursday evening after sunset.[20] This was in keeping with the Jewish custom of counting days from sunset to sunset.

The faithful gathered at 7:00 p.m. at the Eleona ("olive grove") Church on the crest of the Mount of Olives, the site of today's Pater Noster Church. The service there included many Scripture readings interspersed with hymns and psalms, ending with John's account of the Last Supper (John 13:1–18).

About midnight, everyone walked to the nearby Imbomon ("on the hill") Church, remembering the place where Jesus ascended into heaven. (Today the site is marked by the Mosque of Ascension.) Here the service focused on reading John 13:16–18:1, Jesus' farewell discourse and prayer for his disciples.

Although it is not possible to pinpoint the location of the garden of Gethsemane, this compound belonging to the Church of All Nations preserves a memory of the event that traces from the time of Egeria. Gethsemane means "olive press." The oldest of the olive trees still standing here dates to the time of the Crusades, around the twelfth century. (Photo by Paul H. Wright)

In the darkness just before dawn, the worshipers walked to "the place where the Lord prayed," where Egeria mentions "a graceful church" (its location is unknown today). There, they read about Jesus' prayers in Gethsemane. Then they followed a candle-lit procession down the steep slope—Egeria quite correctly says "a very big hill to come down"—to the garden of Gethsemane, where after a prayer and a hymn the Scripture reading concluded with the account of Jesus' arrest (John 18). She reports that the pilgrims were moved to tears hearing the passage read in that place: "By the time it has been read everyone is groaning and lamenting and weeping so loud that people even across in the city can probably hear it all."[21]

Just before dawn, the pilgrims walked back into Jerusalem to the courtyard of the Martyrium ("martyr" or "witness") Church, marking the site of Jesus' crucifixion. Here the bishop of Jerusalem blessed them before sending them home for a brief rest.

When the pilgrims returned at 8:00 a.m. on Friday, the bishop showed them "the holy Wood of the Cross that, as every one of us believers, helps us attain salvation."[22] According to one contemporary tradition, Helena, the mother of Emperor Constantine, had been led by the Holy Spirit to find the True Cross near the rock of Golgotha during her visit to Jerusalem (c. 325).[23] Although we may doubt the story behind the True Cross, it was nonetheless a powerful symbol of Christ's sacrifice in Egeria's time, and many of the faithful were deeply moved as they thought of Jesus' great love when they saw it.

At noon on Friday, everyone gathered in the courtyard between the Martyrium and Anastasis ("resurrection," marking the site of the tomb of

Jesus) churches. Today, both are part of Jerusalem's Church of the Holy Sepulchre, a structure that Eastern Orthodox congregations still call the Church of the Resurrection, preserving its ancient Anastasis name.[24] Here the early pilgrims participated in a three-hour service, as described by Egeria:

> And in this way they continue the readings and hymns from midday till three o'clock, demonstrating to all the people by the testimony of the Gospels and the writings of the Apostles that the Lord actually suffered everything the prophets had foretold. For those three hours, then, they are teaching the people that nothing which took place had not been foretold, and all that was foretold was completely fulfilled; and between all the readings are prayers, all of them appropriate to the day.[25]

The service concluded with John 19:30: "[Christ] gave up his spirit." Egeria freely tells us that the gathered pilgrims found this service profoundly moving:

> It is impressive to see the way all the people are moved by these readings, and how they mourn. You could hardly believe how every single one of them weeps during the three hours, old and young alike, because of the manner in which the Lord suffered for us.[26]

The services for the day ended before sunset with the pilgrims gathered back in the Anastasis to hear and ponder the account of Joseph of Arimathea burying Jesus "in his own new tomb" (Matt. 27:60). Egeria noted that those who "have the energy" spent all night in prayer before the tomb of Jesus.[27]

The *Old Armenian Lectionary,* a text dating to the early fifth century that preserves the ancient liturgical practices of the Jerusalem church, adds to Egeria's account by telling us that all four gospel accounts of Jesus' arrest and crucifixion were read during these services. Curiously, the story of Passover (Ex. 12) was not read on Good Friday in Jerusalem in Egeria's day but transferred instead to the Easter Vigil service on Saturday night through

The interior of the great dome over the Anastasis, the portion of the Church of the Holy Sepulchre that encloses the traditional site of Jesus' tomb. The round window at its top signifies the light of Christ, the twelve rays depict the twelve apostles, and the stars to which they point represent the church worldwide. (Photo by Belikova Oksana/Shutterstock)

Pictured here is the Aedicule, a stone structure enclosing the traditional location of the tomb of Jesus. The walls behind are those of the great rotunda of the Anastasis, part of the Church of the Holy Sepulchre. The Aedicule was built over the remains of a cave tomb that was originally hewn from bedrock and dates to the first century. In Egeria's time, as today, a lamp is kept burning as a sign of the light of Christ. The lamp is extinguished on Good Friday, a sign of Jesus' death, and according to tradition it is lit again miraculously on Easter, a sign of Jesus' resurrection. (Photo by Belikova Oksana/Shutterstock)

early Sunday morning. This reflects the idea (as mentioned earlier) that Passover is a *transitus,* "passage," from death to life.

Additional Scripture passages that were read on Good Friday included Isaiah 52:13–53:12 (the Suffering Servant) and large portions of Hebrews 9 and 10. These emphasize the sacrifice of Christ. They are interesting choices, since they are more closely related to the themes of Yom Kippur (the Day of Atonement) than Passover.

For the early Christians, Jesus' death at Passover showed that he was the Passover Lamb. They also believed that, with his self-giving death, Jesus atoned for the sins of the people, thus fulfilling the events of Yom Kippur. Jesus is both the perfect high priest who is worthy to intercede for people and the unblemished sacrifice who willingly gave his life to atone for their sins:

> For Christ has entered, not into holy places made with hands, which are copies of the true things, but into heaven itself, now to appear in the presence of God on our behalf. Nor was it to offer himself repeatedly, as the high priest enters the holy places every year with blood not his own, for then he would have had to suffer repeatedly since the foundation of the world. But as it is, he has appeared once for all at the end of the ages to put away sin by the sacrifice of himself. (Heb. 9:24–26)

One early second-century Christian writing described Jesus as the scapegoat of Leviticus 16:20–22, who carried away the sins of the people on Yom Kippur:

> Pay attention to what [the Lord] commands: "Take two fine goats who are alike and offer them as a sacrifice; and let the priest take one of them as a whole burnt offering for sins." But what will they do with the other? "The other," he says, "is cursed." Pay attention to how the type of Jesus is revealed. "And all of you shall spit on [the scapegoat] and pierce it and wrap a piece of scarlet wool around its head, and so let it be cast into the wilderness." And so, what does this mean? Pay attention: "The one they take to the altar, but the other is cursed," and the one that is cursed is crowned. For then they will see him in that day wearing a long scarlet robe around his flesh, and they will say, "Is this not the one we once crucified, despising, piercing, and spitting upon him? Truly this is the one who was saying at that time that he was himself the son of God."[28]

While the early Jewish followers of Jesus may have continued to observe both Passover and Yom Kippur, gentile Christians observed only Good Friday and Easter since that weekend became, for believers in Jesus, the new Passover and Yom Kippur.

The Greek Orthodox altar of Calvary in the Church of the Holy Sepulchre. The altar stands above a portion of bedrock that marks the traditional spot of Jesus' cross. In Egeria's day, this location was enclosed in the Martyrium Basilica. (Photo by Paul H. Wright)

THE SABBATH AND HOLY SATURDAY

Egeria reports that only two brief prayer services happened on Holy Saturday after the long day of worship on Good Friday.[29] This was primarily a day of rest and private prayer for the weary pilgrims, mirroring Jesus' time in the tomb, which in turn was his fulfillment of the Sabbath rest of Exodus 20:8–11 (see also Gen. 2:1–3). Gregory of Nyssa (c. 335–395), bishop in Cappadocia, articulated this understanding of Holy Saturday beautifully:

> Behold the blessed Sabbath of the first creation of the world, and in that Sabbath recognize this Sabbath, the day of the Repose, which God has blessed above the other days. For on this day the only-begotten God truly rested from all his works, keeping Sabbath in the flesh by means of his death; and, returning to what he was before through his resurrection, he raised up with himself all that lay prostrate, having become Life and Resurrection (John 11:25) and East and Dawn and Day "for those in darkness and the shadow of death" (Luke 1:79).[30]

PASSOVER AND EASTER VIGIL

One of the strange things about Egeria's diary is that she gives very little information about the most important worship service of the Christian church year: the Easter Vigil. Beginning Saturday after sunset and lasting into the early hours of Sunday morning, this was the main celebration of Christ's resurrection in the early church. Egeria wrote only two short paragraphs about this lengthy service, summarizing it simply as "like us … they follow the same order as people do everywhere else."[31] Her comment indicates how widespread the Easter Vigil already was by her day and how uniformly it was celebrated around the Christian world.

Although Egeria did not provide very much detail, scholars have been able to reconstruct the order of the service from information found in the *Old Armenian Lectionary*.[32] The Easter Vigil service began after sunset on Saturday evening, a time that coincided with the start of Sunday, the first day of the week in the Jewish calendar (see John 20:1). The service began with a ceremonial lighting of the church lamps from a flame that burned continually in Jesus' burial cave, located in the Anastasis.[33] While this service of lighting the lamps was held each evening, it carried heightened significance on Easter, representing Jesus' resurrection: light out of darkness; life out of death. After the lamps were lit, the congregation gathered in the Martyrium to listen to the reading of twelve passages from the Hebrew Scriptures that traced the unfolding of salvation from creation to the exodus to prophecies about Jesus. This echoed the Jewish tradition of reciting the exodus event at the Passover Seder.

Around midnight, the congregation returned to the Anastasis, giving the pilgrims a sense of connection to Jesus' disciples who went to the tomb early on Easter morning. This movement between the Martyrium (the remembered spot of the crucifixion) and to the tomb in the Anastasis reminded the pilgrims of their salvation through Jesus' death on the cross and underscored the promise that in him, they too would "pass over" from the old life of sin and death to rise to a new and eternal life. They listened to readings of the resurrection (Matt. 28:1–10; 1 Cor. 15:1–11) and then participated in the celebration of Holy Communion.

The conclusion of the Easter Vigil after midnight held great significance for the early Christians. It was seen, first, as a fulfillment of the exodus Passover, since an angel of death had struck down the Egyptians but passed over the homes of the Israelites at midnight (Ex. 12:29–30).[34] Second, it anticipated Jesus' return in glory, a future midnight event illustrated in his parable about the wise and foolish bridesmaids (Matt. 25:1–13). The close of the Easter Vigil service, at midnight, was an especially expectant moment for the gathered community to watch for his imminent return. Toward the close of the fourth century, the church father Jerome expressed this expectation and hope in his commentary on the parable:

> At midnight came the cry: Here comes the Bridegroom, go out to meet him! Yes, it will be very late at night, when everyone is fast asleep, without a care in the world, that Christ will make his coming heard through the shouts of angels and the trumpets of powers which go before him. Perhaps it will help the reader to know that Jewish tradition tells us that the messiah will come at midnight, as happened in Egypt, when they celebrated the Pascha, and the Exterminator came, and the Lord passed over the dwellings, and the doorposts of our foreheads were consecrated with the lamb's blood. This is why I think we also have an apostolic tradition that on the day of the paschal vigil the people should not be dismissed before midnight while they await the coming of Christ.[35]

The Easter celebrations continued the next day with a morning service, followed by a series of services beginning at 3:00 p.m.[36] The first of these afternoon worship services in Jerusalem, according to the account of Egeria, was held in the Eleona Church on the Mount of Olives, the place where Jesus was remembered to have taught the disciples the Lord's Prayer. This service was aimed especially at those who had been baptized the day before and included additional instructions in the faith. Services of hymns, prayers, and readings in the Martyrium and Anastasis followed. Then as evening approached, there was a joyful procession to the Church of the Apostles, where:

> They have hymns suitable to the day and the place, a prayer, and the Gospel reading which describes the Lord coming to this place on this day, "when the doors were shut," for this

Easter sunrise on the Mount of Olives, overlooking the Judean wilderness. This is the direction from which Jesus came to Jerusalem to celebrate Passover. "Arise, shine, for your light has come, and the glory of the LORD has risen upon you" (Isa. 60:1). (Photo by Paul H. Wright)

> happened in the very place where the church of Sion [Zion] now stands. This is when one disciple, Thomas, was not present.[37]

Egeria's account of the Sacred Three Days gives us a sense of the joy and richness of early church worship. Moving among the various church buildings in and around Jerusalem while listening to the corresponding Scripture passages being read helped the faithful walk with Jesus spiritually through the events of Holy Week and Easter. This pattern of worship spread throughout the Christian world. Churches set up small chapels within a church building or designated places on church grounds to represent the different locations in Jerusalem where pilgrims would have visited. In this way, even those who would never set foot in the Holy Land could make the pilgrimage spiritually. These "rememorative" observances were very like the experience of the Passover Seder, in which storytelling is enhanced by physical actions that enliven the connection between participants and the historic event they are remembering.[38]

Easter decorations at the corner of Christian Quarter and Greek Orthodox Patriarch roads in the Old City of Jerusalem. (Photo by Paul H. Wright)

HOLY WEEK TODAY

Through the centuries, the celebration of the Sacred Three Days continued to grow. In some cases, lengthy services and excessive pageantry obscured the biblical events being celebrated. This greatly disturbed the Protestant reformers of the sixteenth and seventeenth centuries, including Martin Luther. He objected to practices such as "chanting the four passions, [and] preaching on the passion for eight hours on Good Friday."[39] As a result of the Reformation, liturgical celebrations of prayer and Bible readings about the passion and resurrection became simpler and more somber. This back-to-basics approach was helpful in reclaiming the heart of the events, but in extreme cases it led to Good Friday and Easter services that were no different from those of ordinary Sundays.

As a corrective, many Protestant churches in recent decades have reexamined the worship patterns of the early church to reclaim something of their memory of the events of salvation brought by Christ and to use that memory to learn to walk more closely with him. For example, Maundy Thursday services remember the Last Supper—probably a Passover meal—and Jesus' words to his disciples huddled around the table: "A new commandment I give to you, that you love one another: just as I have loved you, you also are to love one another" (John 13:34).[40]

These services, held on the Thursday evening of Holy Week, usually include readings from Exodus 12 and John 13, a symbolic foot washing, Holy Communion, and a community meal. At the end of the service, the lights are dimmed and people exit in the dark, a reminder of Jesus and his disciples walking to Gethsemane through the darkened streets and quiet plots of Jerusalem. Some

Chrism Mass, a Maundy Thursday morning service, being held in the rotunda of the Anastasis in the Church of the Holy Sepulchre, Jerusalem. (Photo by Paul H. Wright)

churches re-create the garden of Gethsemane on their grounds with flowers, palm fronds, and olive branches; here, worshipers can pray through the night and ponder the events of the Passion.

On Good Friday, many Christians fast as a way of remembering Christ's suffering, an act reminiscent of the high fast on Yom Kippur, the Day of Atonement. Churches hold services from noon to 3:00 p.m. that recall Jesus' last words from the cross. Some install a large wooden cross as a visual reminder of the crucifixion, echoing the display of the True Cross to early Christians in Jerusalem.

The Easter Vigil is a nighttime service beginning on Holy Saturday and commences with lighting a small bonfire that, like the lamp lighting ceremony in the days of Egeria, represents the resurrection. From that fire, a Paschal Candle representing the risen Lord is lit and the congregation sings "Exsultet," an ancient hymn about the resurrection. The flame from the Paschal Candle is used to light many smaller candles held by the congregation as a reminder of their commission to take the light of Christ into the world. The congregation then moves into the church, lit only with candles, for a service from the Old Testament that traces salvation history and prophecies about Jesus.[41] After the last reading, all the lights are turned on and a church leader declares the ancient Easter greeting, "Alleluia, Christ is risen!" The congregation replies, "The Lord is risen indeed. Alleluia!" The service continues with a hymn, Scripture readings about the resurrection, and then Holy Communion as a foretaste of the heavenly banquet. Many churches celebrate with an Easter feast following the service.

This depiction of Jesus' Last Supper is at the Coptic Monastery of Saint Zacchaeus (Mar Zakka) in Jericho. Judas appears on the far left, his back turned toward the others. (Photo by Heidi Kinner)

A Christian Seder: Some Things to Consider

Since the 1970s some churches have hosted Seder meals, often on Maundy Thursday evening, as reenactments of the Last Supper. These Seders combine elements of the modern Jewish Passover Seder with elements of the Last Supper and other Christian teachings. (There are numerous available resources that serve as guides.)[42] Although these Christianized Seders can provide a glimpse into the importance of Passover for Judaism and help us make some connections between Jesus and Passover, there are several reasons why Christians should think carefully before holding one—and especially *instead* of celebrating the feasts and holidays of Holy Week.

First, Christianized Seders can diminish the fullness of the Christian understanding of salvation in Jesus. The celebrations of the Sacred Three Days developed in large part because one festival or worship event was insufficient to contain the wonder and complexity of salvation and redemption in, and through, Jesus' death and resurrection. Frank Senn puts this way: "The point is that the true Christian Passover is the Easter Vigil, and it expresses both Christian continuity and discontinuity with the Jewish Passover."[43]

Second, the modern Jewish Passover Seder, upon which many reenactments of the Last Supper are based, developed over the centuries and looks quite different from the Passover observances that Jesus would have known, if for no other reason than that the temple, which was the focus of the feast in Jesus' day, was destroyed in AD 70.[44] Indeed, it is not clear, at least from the gospel of John, if Jesus' Last Supper meal even was a Passover Seder.[45] If our hope is to connect with the historical Jesus and the events of his passion, these meals may not be the best means to do that. We might be better served by celebrating the Lord's Supper as Paul described it in 1 Corinthians 11:23–26, accompanied by readings from John 13–18, as the early church did in Jerusalem.

Third, no matter how sincere Christians might be in celebrating Passover Seders, many Jews feel that doing so is insensitive to their faith. Given the long and terrible history of the Christian persecution of Jews, Christianized Seders can imply that the Jewish Seder is somehow inadequate and that Christians have "fixed" it. The irony is that although Christians often hold Seders with every intention of learning more about the Jewishness of Jesus and Jewish cultural practices within the Christian faith, by doing so we may be lessening both faiths and increasing divisions between Christians and Jews.

Instead of holding Passover Seders, Christians might consider inviting a Jewish friend or local rabbi to give a teaching about Passover's history and meaning within Judaism. This would help us better understand and appreciate the themes of Passover in the Jewish tradition. It also would help us become more aware of the ways that the Passover celebration already has shaped and informed the celebrations of the Sacred Three Days in the early church.

The types of worship adopted by the early church reinterpreted elements of the Jewish Passover in ways that centered on the redemptive work of Jesus and its meaning for all followers of Christ. Certainly, the church was in awe of the work of God's mighty hand during the first Passover in Egypt, but it reinterpreted that event as pointing to and being fulfilled by the death and resurrection of Jesus. For this reason, it was unthinkable that the early Christians would simply continue to observe a purely Jewish celebration. Their celebrations had to point to the saving work of Jesus.

SHAVUOT AND PENTECOST

The Benedictine Dormition Abbey, built by Kaiser Wilhelm II just before the First World War, stands on the site of the Church of the Apostles, the highest part of Mount Zion. This view is from its bell tower looking east toward the Mount of Olives. The golden Dome of the Rock, built over the site of the temple visited by Jesus and his disciples, is visible just to the left of the conical roof of the abbey's rotunda. (Photo by Paul H. Wright)

Shavuot, the Jewish Feast of Weeks, occurs seven weeks after the day following Passover (Lev. 23:15–16). In the Old Testament, this feast was simply a harvest festival, but by the time of the New Testament, it had become a celebration of God's covenant with Israel at Mount Sinai. The period between the feasts of Passover and Shavuot, known as Counting the Omer (*omer* means a sheaf of grain), spans the time from the barley harvest to the wheat harvest. According to Jewish tradition, these seven weeks also cover the period from Israel's escape from Egypt to the sealing of God's covenant at Sinai. The entire season, bookended by feasts, was one long celebration of freedom, ingathering, and covenant.

For Christians, Shavuot is better known as Pentecost, from the Greek *pentekoste*, meaning "fiftieth." Pentecost falls on the fiftieth day after Passover. It is the day when Christians celebrate the gift of the Holy Spirit, who "will teach you all things and bring to your remembrance all that [Jesus had] said" (John 14:26), just as Shavuot celebrates God giving Torah (literally "instruction") to his people. Augustine wrote:

> Why do the Jews celebrate Pentecost? This is a great mystery, brethren, and quite wondrous. Consider this: on the day of Pentecost they received the Law written by the finger of God, and on the day of Pentecost the Holy Spirit came.[46]

Some Christians regard Pentecost as the birthday of the church, just as the covenant at Sinai can be considered the birthday of the nation of Israel. And just as the period from Passover to Shavuot was a single festival season, Easter to Pentecost was one long celebration in the early church, bookended by the resurrection and the gift of the Holy Spirit, and filled with remembrances of the appearances of the risen Lord.[47] The early Christians drew many spiritual connections between this Jewish season and the work of Jesus and the Holy Spirit. For example, Eusebius, bishop of Caesarea, compared the ingathering of the barley and wheat harvests in Israel during that season with Jesus gathering in the faithful and presenting them to God as "new loaves."[48]

Since the early Christians understood Shavuot to have been given such important, and new, significance by the work of Christ and the gift of the Holy Spirit, they felt that it could no longer be celebrated by following Jewish tradition alone. Eusebius explained: "We have learned to celebrate a festival still more splendid, as though we were already gathered to the Savior and shared his kingdom."[49]

So how did the early church celebrate Pentecost? Again, the writings of the pilgrim Egeria provide some insight.[50] The worship services began the night before with a vigil similar to the Easter Vigil. At dawn the next morning, there was a service in the Martyrium, followed by a procession to the Church of the Apostles. The service there included Holy Communion and the Pentecost reading from Acts 2. That afternoon, everyone met at the Imbomon Church on the Mount of Olives, until, as Egeria reported, "There is not a Christian left in the city."[51] The service there focused on Jesus' ascension. This was followed immediately by an evening prayer service in the Eleona Church. After dark, the congregation walked in procession with lamps and song into Jerusalem for two more worship services, one in the Martyrium and the other in the Anastasis, before walking back to the Church of the Apostles for a final service that ended after midnight.

The churches visited on this long day of celebratory worship tell us something about how the early Christians understood Pentecost.

- The day began at the two churches associated with Christ's death and resurrection, the lynchpin of the faith and main content of the church's witness to the world.
- Twice the worshipers visited the Church of the Apostles, the spot that remembered the upper room, the Last Supper, the place where the risen Lord breathed his spirit onto his disciples on Easter evening, and where the disciples gathered on a regular basis, including at Pentecost. (Indeed, this Church of the Apostles laid claim to being the first church in the world.)
- The Imbomon Church remembered Jesus' ascension to heaven and anticipated his return in glory.
- The Eleona Church marked the place where Jesus regularly taught his disciples (John 18:1–2).

So the theme of the day, driven home by the Scripture readings and the churches visited, was how to be the church, the body of Christ, in the world until Christ comes again in glory.

These ideas, as Eusebius explained, went beyond the covenant at Sinai; the early church would not, or could not, celebrate Pentecost according to the Jewish tradition of Shavuot. Instead, they

This is the southern, outside wall of the upper room. The arched windows are those of the upper room. The large, square stones forming the lower section of the wall date to as early as the second century. Their size suggests that they were part of a building suitably large enough to be a gathering place for the early church. They may have been incorporated into the Church of the Apostles mentioned by Egeria, which was built on or adjacent to the site. (Photo by Diane Wright)

worshiped on Pentecost with uniquely Christian celebrations.

The feast of Pentecost ended the only annual festival season observed in the first two hundred years of Christianity. From the perspective of the early Christians, this season from Good Friday to Pentecost was the only festival season that was needed, since it encompassed the main events of salvation and the formation and commission of the church. However, it wasn't long before new feasts appeared in the calendar, perhaps out of a desire to compete with Jewish or pagan feasts celebrated in Jerusalem and across the Roman world, or perhaps simply to allow Christians to celebrate their faith throughout the entire year. We'll next look at several of these other Christian holy days and how they related to the Jewish feasts.

The interior of the traditional site of the upper room, today preserved as a structure from the Crusader era. A mihrab (center) shows that the room was used as a mosque during the Ottoman Turkish and British Mandate periods (1524–1948). (Photo by Richard Sevcik/Shutterstock)

ROSH HASHANAH AND ADVENT

Rosh HaShanah, the autumn New Year's Day in the Jewish calendar, recalls how God created and rules over the world. It also marks the beginning of the Days of Awe, a ten-day period during which, in response to God's rule, people are called to repent, make amends for wrongs committed in the previous year, and perform acts of charity. The ten days conclude with Yom Kippur, the solemn day when God judges each person for the past year and seals their fate for the coming year. Perhaps because Rosh HaShanah was also linked to the agricultural cycle of the land of Israel, it was not celebrated by gentile Christians living across the Roman world. Nor did early Christians interpret Rosh HaShanah as having any connection to Jesus' saving work on the cross.

While Rosh HaShanah did not become part of the Christian calendar, the season of Advent echoes some of its themes. From the Latin *adventus* ("coming"), Advent is a relatively late addition to the Christian calendar, with references to Advent appearing in writings only as early as about the year 380. Its origins are found in the period of preparation for those who would be baptized on the Feast of Epiphany, January 6.[52] Advent didn't gain its current form as a four-week time of preparation for Christmas until around the year 600.[53] Despite this late date, Advent clearly has become an important season in the Christian calendar.

In many Christian traditions, Advent is the beginning of the Christian New Year, a time when we as believers in Jesus are called to repent and renew our commitment as disciples, and to think about and prepare for Jesus' second Advent "to

Jesus' Advent visit by the magi (the wise men) on Epiphany, depicted in stained glass in the sanctuary of the Church of Saint Catherine, Bethlehem. (Photo by Paul H. Wright)

judge the living and the dead" (1 Peter 4:5).[54] This theme is seen in many of the Scripture passages appointed for the season (for example, Zech. 14; Matt. 24; Mark 13; Luke 21).[55] But Advent is also the season to prepare for the celebration of Jesus' first Advent, his birth in Bethlehem. Christmas preparations remind us of God's great love, even as we look for Christ's return in glory to judge the world. This twofold nature of Advent helps Christians begin their new year with a clear understanding of the sovereignty and loving kindness of the Lord. In light of this, Advent has both aspects of penitence and hopefulness, as Christians are encouraged to take time to evaluate their lives, repent of sin, make amends, perform charitable acts, and generally think about ways that they can better serve as "ambassadors for Christ" (2 Cor. 5:20). In this sense, Advent reflects the Jewish Days of Awe but with a uniquely Christian outlook rooted in the person and work of Jesus.

As all of the candles on the Advent wreath are lit on the fourth Sunday of Advent, we remember that Jesus is the light of the world. The season of Advent is also a good time to consider that our present life with Christ is, in the words of Bernard of Clairvaux—*the* Saint Bernard (1090–1153)—actually a third coming of Christ:

> We have come to understand a threefold coming of the Lord.... In the first coming the Lord was seen on earth, dwelling among us.... In his final coming "all flesh shall see the salvation of our God."... The intermediate coming is hidden, in which only his chosen recognize his presence within themselves and their souls are saved.... This intermediate coming is like a road on which we travel from his first coming to his last. In the first, Christ was our redemption; in the last, he will appear as our life; in his intermediate coming, he is our comfort and our rest.[56]

A three-camel caravan approaches Bethlehem in the early part of the twentieth century. Such images remind us of the Christmas story two thousand years earlier. (Library of Congress/ Matson Photograph Collection)

YOM KIPPUR AND HOLY CROSS DAY

Yom Kippur (the Day of Atonement) begins as the most solemn day in the Jewish calendar as Jews pray to God for forgiveness. It ends joyfully, confident in God's forgiveness and mercy. Before the Jerusalem temple was destroyed in AD 70, the high priest offered animal sacrifices on behalf of the people and then laid their sins on a scapegoat, so they could once again be restored to a right relationship with God (Lev. 16:20–22).

While Yom Kippur, a somber day of fasting, did not enter the church calendar, its theology most definitely did as part of the liturgy of Good Friday. As we have seen, the early Christians understood Jesus as both the Passover Lamb and the scapegoat of Yom Kippur, and because they observed Jesus' death on Good Friday, they did not need to keep Yom Kippur. But in a way, another Christian feast took Yom Kippur's place in the autumn calendar.

Rosh HaShanah and Yom Kippur typically fall in mid to late September. By the mid-300s, the church in Jerusalem had added a feast to their calendar on September 14, roughly corresponding to the time of these Jewish holy days. Its purpose was to celebrate the finding of the True Cross beside the rock of Golgotha. The earliest known mention of the finding of the cross is in a letter written by Cyril of Jerusalem to Constantius in 351; Cyril reported that a portion of cross was found during the reign of the Emperor Constantine.[57] Regardless whether the wood that was found was actually part of Jesus' cross, it nonetheless quickly became a symbol that held great spiritual value for Christians. Its discovery, said to have been made on September 14, was celebrated as a type of mini-Good Friday.[58] The discovery was also interpreted as a sign from God confirming the Christian presence in Jerusalem and as a warrant to build the Martyrium Church on the site where it was found.[59] This is reflected in the epistle reading for the day, 1 Corinthians 1:18–25, especially verse 18: "For the word of the cross is folly to those who are perishing, but to us who are being saved it is the power of God." In this way, the Feast of the Holy Cross became a Christ-focused and distinctly Christian counterpoint to Yom Kippur in both theme and in date.

The celebration eventually spread throughout the church and continues to be observed by many Christian denominations today. Renamed Holy Cross Day and still observed on September 14, it marks a time for Christians to rejoice in our redemption through Jesus. For Christians, remembering the traditions of Holy Cross Day can serve as a midyear pause to ponder and give thanks for Jesus' atoning self-sacrifice.

Where Is the True Cross Today?

Pieces of the True Cross made their way to churches all around the Byzantine and Roman Empires, with the largest pieces held in Jerusalem and Constantinople. After the fall of Jerusalem to the Muslim invasion, reclaiming the pieces of the True Cross became one of the goals of the early Crusades.

Today, small fragments can still be found around the world, primarily in Orthodox and Roman Catholic churches and monasteries. Whether they are part of the wood found in Jerusalem in the 300s is debatable. Protestant Reformer John Calvin noted in *A Treatise on Relics*, "If we were to collect all these pieces of the true cross exhibited in various parts, they would form a whole ship's cargo." On the other hand, in 1870 the French architect Charles Rohault de Fleury catalogued all of the known pieces of the true cross available to him and calculated that together they would form only one-third of the actual cross on which Jesus died.

SUKKOT, HANUKKAH, AND ENCAENIA

This model of the Church of the Holy Sepulchre as it looked in Byzantine Jerusalem stands on the grounds of the Saint Peter in Gallicantu ("cock's crow") Church on the southeastern slope of Mount Zion. The Holy Sepulchre was really two churches: the Martyrium Basilica (right) which enclosed the traditional site of Jesus' crucifixion and the domed Anastasis (left) which preserved the spot of his tomb. They were joined by an open courtyard between them. This view looks toward the northwest. (Photo by Paul H. Wright)

The autumn feast of Sukkot (Booths or Tabernacles) incorporates several biblical themes:

- It celebrates the ingathering of the last harvest of the year (Deut. 16:13–15).
- It remembers God's presence and provision for Israel during their years of wilderness wandering after the exodus (Lev. 23:43).
- And it was the time when Solomon dedicated the first temple in Jerusalem (1 Kings 8:1–2).

Sukkot did not enter the early Christian calendar because it was not tied directly to Jesus' crucifixion and resurrection. However, later Christian celebrations echo some elements of Sukkot. For example, the agricultural aspects of Sukkot are similar to those found in the Thanksgiving or harvest festival services of many churches today. These services give thanks to God for the produce of the earth; and prayers are said for rain, the crops of the next year, and everyone involved in food production and distribution. As a tangible sign of God's love and provision, many of these church festivals include collections of food to be distributed to people in need.

Perhaps one of the most interesting early Christian feasts with a connection to Sukkot was an eight-day pilgrim celebration in Jerusalem called *Encaenia,* which means "dedication." Encaenia celebrated the inauguration of the Martyrium and the Anastasis, the two churches that together comprise the Church of the Holy Sepulchre.

Celebrated for the same number of days and at roughly the same time of year as Sukkot, Encaenia connected the dedication of Solomon's temple with the dedication of the two churches that lay at the heart of early Christian worship. As the pilgrim Egeria noted:

> You will find in the Bible that the day of Encaenia was when the House of God [the temple] was consecrated, and Solomon stood in prayer before God's altar, as we read in the Books of Chronicles [2 Chron. 6:12].[60]

With this feast, Christians in Jerusalem connected their faith with the Jewish temple. They also signaled that the churches built on top of the site of Jesus' death and resurrection were now the focal point of God's greatest self-revelation and provision

Gilded light illuminates the interior of the Church of the Nativity, Bethlehem. (Photo by Atosan/Shutterstock)

of salvation and life.[61] Christians today who choose to celebrate Sukkot should take care that it not eclipse the celebrations of Holy Week, the core expressions of the Christian faith.

In Encaenia, we also see reflections of the Jewish festival of Hanukkah, which also means "dedication." The gospel reading on the first day of Encaenia was John 10:22–42, the account of Jesus teaching in the temple during Hanukkah, "the Feast of Dedication" (John 10:22). This Jewish festival celebrated the rededication of the Jerusalem temple by the Maccabees in 164 BC, following its desecration by the Seleucid king Antiochus IV Epiphanes three years earlier.[62] The Martyrium and Anastasis churches were built over the sites believed to be Golgotha and Jesus' tomb, respectively, replacing Roman pagan temples that had been built there in the second century.[63] In this way, the Christian Jerusalem community claimed that just as God had won the victory over pagans in the days of the Maccabees, so he had now won victory over pagans for the church.

The feast of Encaenia did not spread very far beyond Jerusalem and is no longer observed. It remains important, however, as a testimony that Christians in Jerusalem saw the two churches of the Holy Sepulchre as a new temple, built upon the foundation of Jesus Christ. And if we take seriously Paul's statement in Ephesians 2:19–22 that Christians are the new "holy temple in the Lord" with "Christ Jesus himself being the cornerstone," then every day of our lives is a kind of Hanukkah, a dedication to him and lived in his presence.

HANUKKAH, CHRISTMAS, AND EPIPHANY

Although Jesus came to Jerusalem for Hanukkah, the festival was not observed by the early gentile Christians, who apparently viewed it as a national Jewish holiday. Later Jewish tradition linked Hanukkah with God's miraculous provision of holy oil to keep the lamps of the newly restored temple lit until a new supply of oil could be pressed.

As we've just seen, some of Hanukkah's themes were reflected in the Christian feast of Encaenia, but there are also faint echoes of it in the celebrations of Christmas and Epiphany. Hanukkah's theme of God's provision of light is a key element in Christmas and Epiphany, which celebrate Jesus as the light of God in the world. These two holy days are also something of a counterpoint to the nationalism of Hanukkah, announcing that Jesus saved from sin, not one nation from a single earthly empire, but the world.

Here it is important to note the connection made by the early church between Christmas and the crucifixion. The Gospels do not provide an exact birth date for Jesus, so the church had some freedom in choosing when to celebrate the nativity. The date chosen by the western, Roman church was December 25. This may have been to compete with the Roman festival of the Invincible Sun, *Sol Invictus*, which coincided with the winter solstice.[64] However, it has also been suggested that this date was chosen because it was nine months after the date of the crucifixion, thereby linking Jesus' conception and birth to his atoning death on the cross and victory over sin.[65]

Egeria wrote about the Epiphany celebrations in Jerusalem and Bethlehem in the late fourth century.[66] The feast began on January 6 and combined the events of the nativity with the visit of the magi. (In Egeria's day, the birth of Jesus was also celebrated on Epiphany.) The celebrations began at about 4:00 p.m. on January 5, the eve of Epiphany, with a service in the traditional location of Shepherds' Fields, most likely the Greek Orthodox site in Beit Sahour, east of Bethlehem. This was followed by a procession to the Church of the Nativity in Bethlehem. There, Matthew's account of the visit of the magi (Matt. 2:1–12) was read in the cave beneath the church that was believed to be the place where Jesus was born.[67] Then followed a vigil service similar to the Easter Vigil, though with readings focused on prophecies about the birth of the Messiah (for example, Mic. 5:2–7; Isa. 9:6–7). The celebrations continued for eight joyous days, prompting Egeria to write:

> The decorations are really too marvelous for words. All you can see is gold and jewels and

Like Hanukkah, Christmas is a festival of lights. This display celebrates the birth of Jesus at Manger Square, Bethlehem, leading pilgrims toward the Church of the Nativity. (Photo by Paul H. Wright)

> silk; the hangings are entirely silk with gold stripes, the curtains the same, and everything they use for services at the festival is made of gold and jewels. You simply cannot imagine the number, and the sheer weight of the candles and the tapers and lamps, and everything else they use for the services.[68]

In this way, the churches in the Holy Land welcomed the King of Kings by offering their gifts of gold and silk to make the worship beautiful, and they celebrated with candles and lamps to demonstrate the coming of the true Light of the World who cannot be overcome by darkness.

Over the centuries, the celebration of Christmas on December 25 has come to eclipse Epiphany in Western Christianity. In the Eastern Orthodox family of churches, Epiphany remains an important holy day. In recent decades, Hanukkah, which is also a December event, has taken on some of the forms of Christmas decorations in many Western Jewish homes.

Hanukkah and Christmas are joyous celebrations that often coincide in the calendar and, for many people, have come to set the tone of a commercialized, holiday season. Of all the major Jewish feasts, Hanukkah is the one with the loosest connections to the salvation events of the life of Jesus. Christians today can be enriched by keeping their focus during this season on Christmas and Epiphany with the full, Jesus-centered joy that the early church did. During the Advent season, we can prepare our hearts with introspection and then celebrate the twelve days from Christmas to Epiphany with daily meals, candle lighting, Scripture reading, and perhaps even gift giving. In doing so, many Christians have found that this helps them move away from the commercialized version of the season and to refocus on Jesus and his choice to dwell with and in us.

SOME FINAL THOUGHTS

Christian worship is rooted in the Bible, so it shares a heritage out of which Jewish worship and the feasts developed. But as the church became largely gentile, Christians developed their own ways to worship and celebrate the magnitude of Jesus' incarnation, crucifixion, and resurrection. Over the centuries, both Christian and Jewish worship have cultivated ways that best define, reflect, and express their own identities and core beliefs. Ours are related faiths, so we must seek to learn from each other, yet take care to hold fast to what is most important in each of our understandings of God's revelation to humankind. Just as the Jewish feasts are an annual journey through key events in the history of Israel that help Jewish people remember and live out who they are as God's chosen people, so the Christian feasts are an annual journey with Jesus through the key events of his life that helps us remember who we are as God's adopted children.

Christians may celebrate the Jewish feasts but should carefully consider the reasons for doing so, especially as a regular part of worship. The early Christians wrestled with this issue and concluded that to continue celebrating the Jewish feasts was to deny the sufficiency of Jesus' saving work, thus denying him as Savior and Lord. As a result, they developed celebrations that were entirely Christ-centered.

Instead of trying to celebrate the Jewish feasts or to re-create them in a Christian context, we might prefer to learn more about our Christian heritage and reclaim the joy and richness of the ways that the early Christians found to celebrate their salvation and new life in Jesus. We can grow stronger in our Christian faith—and more thankful for our roots in Judaism—by considering how Christianity has developed its own Christ-centered expressions and celebrations and by identifying ways that the life, death, and resurrection of Jesus fulfilled the biblical feasts. In this way, we can appreciate our shared heritage and the unique aspects of both of our faiths, respecting what is different, embracing what is unique, and learning from each other.

Notes for Chapter 5

1 For example, Acts 20:16 reports that Paul traveled to Jerusalem to celebrate Pentecost. "The Fast" (the Day of Atonement, Yom Kippur) is a significant calendar marker in Acts 27:9, with the implication that even late in Paul's Christian ministry, he (and possibly also Luke) observed it according to Jewish tradition.

2 Paul F. Bradshaw and Maxwell E. Johnson, *The Origins of Feasts, Fasts and Seasons in Early Christianity* (Collegeville, Minn.: Liturgical Press, 2011), 10.

3 Ignatius of Antioch, "Letter to the Magnesians," 9:1, in *Early Church Fathers,* ed. Cyril C. Richardson, vol. 1, *The Library of Christian Classics* (New York: Touchstone, 1996), 96.

4 Bradshaw and Johnson, *The Origins of Feasts*, 11–24.

5 Justin Martyr, an early Church father from the second century, used the phrase "the first day after the Sabbath ... the first of all the days" in *Dialogue with Trypho* 41:4.

6 *Epistle of Barnabas* 15:8. This early Christian text (c. AD 100–135) was written as a polemic using allegory and secret knowledge (*gnosis*) to try to convince readers that Christians were the true heirs of God's covenant. It was likely written not long after the destruction of the temple by Rome, when defining the differences between Christians and Jews was a live issue.

7 *The Book of Common Prayer and Administration of the Sacraments and Other Rites and Ceremonies of the Church: Together with the Psalter or Psalms of David according to the Use of the Episcopal Church* (New York: Church Hymnal Corp., 1979), 99.

8 By the end of the second century, a specifically Christian version of Pentecost was being celebrated, the second Christian feast to develop. This was followed by Epiphany in the early third century and Christmas by the mid-fourth century. See Bradshaw and Johnson, *The Origins of Feasts,* 70, 123, 137.

9 Bradshaw and Johnson, *The Origins of Feasts*, 41–43.

10 Raniero Cantalamessa, *Easter in the Early Church: An Anthology of Jewish and Early Christian Texts,* trans. and ed. James M. Quigley and Joseph T. Lienhard (Collegeville, Minn.: Liturgical Press, 1993), 16–17.

11 Bradshaw and Johnson, *The Origins of Feasts*, 45.

12 Melito of Sardis, "On the Pascha," in Cantalamessa, *Easter in the Early Church*, 43–44, 46, 67. Melito also connects Jesus as the Passover Lamb with the lamb of the Suffering Servant song in Isaiah 53.

13 Melito of Sardis, "On the Pascha," 16–17.

14 Oskar Skarsaune, *In the Shadow of the Temple: Jewish Influences on Early Christianity* (Downer's Grove, Ill.: InterVarsity, 2002), 389–391.

15 Eusebius, *Ecclesiastical History* IV.vi.4.

16 Bradshaw and Johnson, *The Origins of Feasts*, 48–59.

17 Cantalamessa, *Easter in the Early Church*, 16–21.

18 Augustine of Hippo, "Exposition of Psalm 120 (Sermon Preached on the Feast of St. Crispina, Martyr), 6," in Cantalamessa, *Easter in the Early Church*, 109.

19 Jerome, "Commentary on the Gospel of Matthew 4, on Matthew 26:2," in Cantalamessa, *Easter in the Early Church*, 99.

20 For Egeria's descriptions of the Good Friday services, see John Wilkinson, *Egeria's Travels to the Holy Land,* rev. ed. (Jerusalem: Ariel, 1981), 74–75, 134–138.

21 Wilkinson, *Egeria's Travels*, 136.

22 Wilkinson, *Egeria's Travels*, 136.

23 The first to mention the discovery of the True Cross was Cyril of Jerusalem in his *Letter to Constantius* (351), but he made no mention of Helena. The first to attribute its discovery to Helena was Ambrose of Milan in his funeral sermon for Emperor Theodosius in 395. See Wilkinson, *Egeria's Travels*, 240–241.

24 For the history of the Holy Sepulchre, see Justin L. Kelley, *The Church of the Holy Sepulchre in Text and Archaeology* (Oxford: Archaeopress, 2019); and "The Holy Sepulchre in History, Archaeology and Tradition," *Biblical Archaeology Review* 47/1 (2021): 34–43.

25 Wilkinson, *Egeria's Travels*, 137–138.

26 Wilkinson, *Egeria's Travels*, 138.

27 Wilkinson, *Egeria's Travels*, 138.

28 *Epistle of Barnabas* 7:6–9.

29 Wilkinson, *Egeria's Travels*, 76, 138.

30 Gregory of Nyssa, "On the Three-Day Interval between Our Lord's Death and Resurrection," in Cantalamessa, *Easter in the Early Church*, 77.

31 Wilkinson, *Egeria's Travels*, 139.

32 Bradshaw and Johnson, *The Origins of Feasts*, 65–68.

33 This ceremony is called a Lucernarium.

34 Thomas Talley, *The Origins of the Liturgical Year* (Collegeville, Minn.: Liturgical Press, 1991), 48–49.

35 Jerome, "Commentary on the Gospel of Matthew 4, on Matthew 25:6," in Cantalamessa, *Easter in the Early Church,* 99.

36 Wilkinson, *Egeria's Travels,* 76, 139–140.

37 Wilkinson, *Egeria's Travels*, 140.

38 Rememorative celebrations are less than reenactments but more than simple retelling of events. They engage the participant physically, mentally, and spiritually, even though the events being remembered are not actually acted out as they are in, for instance, Passion plays or living nativities. The term *rememorative* was popularized by Kenneth Stevens, *Jerusalem Revisited: The Liturgical Meaning of Holy Week* (Washington, D.C.: Pastoral Press, 1988), 9.

39 Robin A. Leaver, "Passiontide Music," in *Passover and Easter: The Symbolic Structuring of Sacred Seasons*, eds. Paul F. Bradshaw and Lawrence A. Hoffman, vol. 6, *Two Liturgical Traditions* (Notre Dame: University of Notre Dame Press, 1999), 152.

40 *Maundy* comes from Latin *mandatum*, "command."

41 For instance, in the Anglican tradition, the Scripture readings for the Easter Vigil are usually Gen. 1:1–2:2 (creation); Gen. 7:1–18; 8:6–18; 9:8–13 (flood and covenant); Gen. 22:1–18 (the binding of Isaac); Ex. 14:10–15:1 (Israel's deliverance at the Red Sea); Isa. 4:2–6 (God's presence renewed in Israel); Isa. 55:1–11 (salvation freely offered to all); Ezek. 36:24–28 (the new heart and new spirit); Ezek. 37:1–14 (the valley of dry bones); and Zeph. 3:12–20 (the gathering of God's people).

42 Examples are plentiful and include *Christ in the Passover* (Rose Publishing, 2008); Ceil and Moishe Rosen, *Christ in the Passover*, new ed. (Chicago: Moody Press, 2006); and Martha Zimmerman, *Celebrating Biblical Feasts: In Your Home or Church* (Bloomington, Minn.: Bethany House, 2004).

43 Frank C. Senn, "Should Christians Celebrate the Passover?" in Bradshaw and Hoffman, eds., *Passover and Easter,* vol. 6 (University of Notre Dame Press, 1999), 201–202.

44 Senn, "Should Christians Celebrate the Passover?" 186–189.

45 Senn, "Should Christians Celebrate the Passover?" 190–193.

46 Augustine of Hippo, "Sermon Mai 158m 4," in Cantalamessa, *Easter in the Early Church*, 113.

47 Bradshaw and Johnson, *The Origins of Feasts*, 71.

48 Eusebius of Caesarea, "On the Paschal Solemnity 5," in Cantalamessa, *Easter in the Early Church,* 67–68.

49 Eusebius of Caesarea, "On the Paschal Solemnity 5," 67–68.

50 Wilkinson, *Egeria's Travels*, 78–79, 141–143.

51 Wilkinson, *Egeria's Travels*, 142.

52 Epiphany remembers the arrival of the magi (wisemen) to Bethlehem. In many Christian denominations, it also celebrates Jesus' baptism, and as such it is one of the principal occasions for baptism in the calendar year.

53 Bradshaw and Johnson, *The Origins of Feasts*, 158–168.

54 Episcopal Church, *The Book of Common Prayer*, 96.

55 See for example, Episcopal Church, *The Book of Common Prayer*, 888–921.

56 Bernard of Clairvaux, "Sermon 5 'On Advent,'" in *Celebrating the Seasons: Daily Scriptural Readings for the Christian Year,* ed. Robert Atwell (Harrisburg, Penn.: Morehouse, 2001), 4.

57 Wilkinson, *Egeria's Travels*, 240–241.

58 Michael A. Fraser, "The Feast of Encaenia in the Fourth Century and in the Ancient Liturgical Sources of Jerusalem" (PhD diss.: University of Durham, 1995), 243.

59 Fraser, "The Feast of Encaenia," 219–221.

60 Wilkinson, *Egeria's Travels*, 146 (see also 79).

61 Fraser, "The Feast of Encaenia," 219–223; Timothy Wardle, *The Jerusalem Temple and Early Christian Identity* (Tübingen: Mohr Siebeck, 2010), 206–226, 231–233.

62 Fraser, "The Feast of Encaenia," 243.

63 Kelley, "The Holy Sepulchre in History, Archaeology and Tradition," 37.

64 Bradshaw and Johnson, *The Origins of Feasts*, 124.

65 For a discussion of the date of Christmas, see Talley, *The Origins of the Liturgical Year,* 91–99.

66 Wilkinson, *Egeria's Travels*, 126–128; see also 81–82.

67 A portion of Egeria's diary describing the events of Epiphany is missing, but the *Old Armenian Lectionary* provides information that has helped scholars reconstruct the worship services. See Wilkinson, *Egeria's Travels*, 81; and Bradshaw and Johnson, *The Origins of Feasts*, 147.

68 Wilkinson, *Egeria's Travels*, 127.

Bibliography

Abudarham, David Ben Joseph. *The Complete Book of Abudarham: Commentary on the Blessings and Prayers.* (Warsaw: Shriftgissen, 1877), 73r, column 145. This is an edition of a book that was first written in the fourteenth century and its author, Abudarham, seems to be the last person to have read Saadia Gaon's original text. It has since been lost

Agnon, Shmuel Yosef. *Days of Awe.* New York: Schocken, 1965.

Agnon, Shmuel Yosef. *Present at Sinai: The Giving of the Law.* Trans. and ed. by Michael Swirsky. Philadelphia: Jewish Publication Society, 1993.

Ahituv, Shmuel. *Echoes from the Past: Hebrew and Cognate Inscriptions from the Biblical Period.* A Carta Handbook. Jerusalem: Carta, 2008.

Atwell, Robert, ed. *Celebrating the Seasons: Daily Spiritual Readings for the Christian.* Harrisburg, Penn.: Morehouse, 2001.

Augustine of Hippo. "Exposition of Psalm 120 (Sermon Preached on the Feast of St. Crispina, Martyr), 6." In Cantalamessa, Raniero. *Easter in the Early Church: An Anthology of Jewish and Early Christian Texts.* Trans. and ed. by James M. Quigley and Joseph T. Lienhard, 109. Collegeville, Minn.: Liturgical Press, 1993.

Augustine of Hippo. "Sermon Mai 158m 4." In Cantalamessa, Raniero. *Easter in the Early Church: An Anthology of Jewish and Early Christian Texts.* Trans. and ed. by James M. Quigley and Joseph T. Lienhard, 113. Collegeville, Minn.: Liturgical Press, 1993.

Averbeck, Richard E. "Sacrifices and Offerings." In *Dictionary of the Old Testament: Pentateuch.* Ed. by T. Desmond Alexander and David W. Baker, 706–733. Downer's Grove, Ill.: InterVarsity, 2003.

Barnabus. Epistle of Barnabas. Trans. and ed. by Bart D. Ehrman. In *The Apostolic Fathers.* Vol. 2. Loeb Classical Library 25N, 1–84. Cambridge, Mass.: Harvard University Press, 2003.

Beck, John A. *The Baker Illustrated Guide to Everyday Life in Bible Times.* Grand Rapids, Mich.: Baker, 2013.

Benovitz, M. "Herod and Hanukkah." *Zion* 68 (2003): 5–40 (Hebrew).

Berkowitz, Matthew L. *The Lovell Haggadah.* Jerusalem: The Schechter Institute of Jewish Studies, 2008.

Bernard of Clairvaux. "Sermon 5 'On Advent.'" In *Celebrating the Seasons: Daily Scriptural Readings for the Christian Year.* Ed. by Robert Atwell, 4–5. Harrisburg, Penn.: Morehouse, 2001.

Blackman, Philip, ed. *Mishnayot.* 6 vols. New York: Judaica Press, 1963–1964, 1983.

Bloch-Smith, Elizabeth. "The Cult of the Dead in Judah: Interpreting the Material Remains." *Journal of Biblical Literature* 3/2 (1992): 213–244.

Block, Abraham P. *The Biblical and Historical Background of Jewish Customs and Ceremonies.* New York: KTAV, 1980.

Borowski, Oded. *Agriculture in Iron Age Israel.* Boston: American School of Oriental Research, 2002.

Borowski, Oded. *Daily Life in Biblical Times.* Leiden: Brill 2003.

Bottéro, Jean. *Religion in Ancient Mesopotamia.* Trans. by Teresa Lavender Fagan. Chicago: University of Chicago Press, 2001.

Bradshaw, Paul F., and Lawrence A. Hoffman, eds. *Passover and Easter: The Symbolic Structuring of Sacred Seasons.* Vol. 6, *Two Liturgical Traditions.* Notre Dame, Ind.: University of Notre Dame Press, 1999.

Bradshaw, Paul F., and Maxwell E. Johnson. *The Origins of Feasts, Fasts and Seasons in Early Christianity.* Collegeville, Minn.: Liturgical Press, 2011.

Buber, Solomon, ed. *Midrash Psalms.* Vilnius, 1891. Reprint, Jerusalem: Vagshal, 1977 (Hebrew).

Calvin, John. *A Treatise on Relics.* Scotts, Valley, Calif.: CreateSpace Independent Publishing Platform, 2015.

Cantalamessa, Raniero. *Easter in the Early Church: An Anthology of Jewish and Early Christian Texts.* Trans. and ed. by James M. Quigley and Joseph T. Lienhard. Collegeville, Minn.: Liturgical Press, 1993.

David, Rosalie. *Handbook to Life in Ancient Egypt*. Rev. ed. Oxford: Oxford University Press, 1998.

Dever, William G. *What Did the Biblical Writers Know and When Did They Know It?* Grand Rapids, Mich.: Eerdmans, 2001.

Doukhan, Jacques B. *Israel and the Church: Two Voices for the Same God.* Peabody, Mass.: Hendrickson, 2002.

Eby, Aaron, et al. *Meal of Messiah: The Wedding Supper of the Lamb.* Marshfield, Mo.: Vine of David, 2010.

Ecker, Avner. "Dining with Herod." In *Herod the Great: The King's Final Journey.* Ed. by Silvia Rozenberg and David Mevorah, 66–79. Jerusalem: Israel Museum, 2013.

Episcopal Church. *The Book of Common Prayer and Administration of the Sacraments and Other Rites and Ceremonies of the Church: Together with the Psalter or Psalms of David According to the Use of the Episcopal Church.* New York: Church Hymnal Corp., 1979.

Eusebius. *The Ecclesiastical History.* Trans. by Kirsopp Lake. Vol 1. Loeb Classical Library. Cambridge, Mass.: Harvard University Press, 1926.

Eusebius of Caesarea. "On the Paschal Solemnity 4." In Cantalamessa, Raniero. *Easter in the Early Church: An Anthology of Jewish and Early Christian Texts.* Trans. and ed. by James M. Quigley and Joseph T. Lienhard, 67. Collegeville, Minn.: Liturgical Press, 1993.

Eusebius of Caesarea. "On the Paschal Solemnity 5." In Cantalamessa, Raniero. *Easter in the Early Church: An Anthology of Jewish and Early Christian Texts.* Trans. and ed. by James M. Quigley and Joseph T. Lienhard, 67–68. Collegeville, Minn.: Liturgical Press, 1993.

Fischer, John. *Messianic Services for the Festivals and Holy Days.* Palm Harbor, Fla.: Menorah Ministries, 2006.

Fraser, Michael A. "The Feast of Encaenia in the Fourth Century and in the Ancient Liturgical Sources of Jerusalem." PhD diss., University of Durham, 1995.

Freedman, H, and Maurice Simon, eds. *Exodus in Midrash Rabbah.* Trans. by S. M. Lehrman. New York: Soncino, 1983.

Fu, Janling. "Feasting in the Biblical World." In *Behind the Scenes of the Old Testament: Cultural, Social, and Historical Contexts.* Ed. by Jonathan S. Greer, John W. Hilber, and John H. Walton, 464–467. Grand Rapids, Mich.: Baker Academic, 2018.

Gaster, Theodore H. *Festival of the Jewish Year.* New York: Morrow Quill, 1953.

Gilat, Y. D. "On Fasting on the Sabbath." *Tarbiz* 5/1 (1982): 1–15 (Hebrew with English summary).

Glatzer, Nahum N., ed. *The Passover Haggadah with English Translation and Introduction.* New York: Schocken, 1969.

Goldman, Ari L. *Being Jewish: The Spiritual and Cultural Practice of Judaism Today.* New York: Simon & Schuster, 2007.

Goldstein, Bernard R., and Alan Cooper. "The Festivals of Israel and Judah and the Literary History of the Pentateuch." *Journal of the American Oriental Society* 110/1 (1990): 19–31.

Goodman, Philip, and Abraham E. Millgram. *The JPS Holiday Anthologies.* 8 vols. Reprint, Philadelphia: Jewish Publication Society, 2018.

Greenberg, Irving. *The Jewish Way: Living the Holidays.* New York: Summit Books, 1988.

Gregory of Nyssa, "On the Three-Day Interval between Our Lord's Death and Resurrection." In Cantalamessa, Raniero. *Easter in the Early Church: An Anthology of Jewish and Early Christian Texts.* Trans. and ed. by James M. Quigley and Joseph T. Lienhard, 77. Collegeville, Minn.: Liturgical Press, 1993.

Hammer, Reuven. *Entering the High Holy Days: A Complete Guide to the History, Prayers and Themes.* Philadelphia: Jewish Publication Society, 2005.

Hareuveni, Nogah. *Nature in Our Biblical Heritage.* Trans. by Helen Frenkley. Kiryat Ono, Israel: Keot Kedumim, 1980.

Heschel, Abraham Joshua. *The Sabbath.* Boston, Mass.: Shambhala, 2003. Originally published 1951 by Farrar, Straus and Giroux.

Ignatius of Antioch. "Letter to the Magnesians." In *Early Church Fathers.* Ed. by Cyril C. Richardson. Vol. 1 of *The Library of Christian Classics*, 94–97. New York: Touchstone, 1996.

Instone-Brewer, David. *Traditions of the Rabbis from the Era of the New Testament.* Vol. 1 of *Prayer and Agriculture.* Grand Rapids, Mich.: Eerdmans, 2004.

Janicki, Toby. *God-Fearers: Gentiles and the God of Israel.* Marshfield, Mo.: First Fruits of Zion, 2012.

Jerome. "Commentary on the Gospel of Matthew 4, on Matthew 25:6." In Cantalamessa, Raniero. *Easter in the Early Church: An Anthology of Jewish and Early Christian Texts.* Trans. and ed. by James M. Quigley and Joseph T. Lienhard, 99. Collegeville, Minn.: Liturgical Press, 1993.

Jerome. "Commentary on the Gospel of Matthew 4, on Matthew 26:2." In Cantalamessa, Raniero. *Easter in the Early Church: An Anthology of Jewish and Early Christian Texts.* Trans. and ed. by James M. Quigley and Joseph T. Lienhard, 99–100. Collegeville, Minn.: Liturgical Press, 1993.

Josephus. *Against Apion.* Trans. by H. St. J. Thackeray. Loeb Classical Library. Cambridge, Mass.: Harvard University Press, 1926.

Josephus. *The Jewish War.* Trans. by H. St. J. Thackeray. Loeb Classical Library. Cambridge, Mass.: Harvard University Press, 1927–1928.

Kinbar, Carl. "Messianic Jews and Jewish Tradition." In *Introduction to Messianic Judaism: Its Ecclesial Context and Biblical Foundations.* Ed. by David Rudolph and Joel Willitts, 72–81. Grand Rapids, Mich.: Zondervan, 2013.

King, Philip J. "The Marzeah Amos Denounces." *Biblical Archaeology Review* 14/4 (1988): 34–44.

King, Philip J., and Lawrence E. Stager. *Life in Biblical Israel.* Louisville, Ky.: Westminster John Knox, 2001.

Kitov, Eliyahu. *The Book of Our Heritage: The Jewish Year and Its Days of Significance.* 3 vols. Jerusalem: Philipp Feldheim, 1999.

Kloner, Amos, and David Davis. "A Burial Cave of the Late First Temple Period on the Slope of Mount Zion." In *Ancient Jerusalem Revealed.* Ed. by Hillel Geva, 107–110. Repr. and rev. ed. Jerusalem: Israel Exploration Society, 2000.

Kraemer, David. "Leavened or Unleavened: A History." *Forward.* March 30, 2007. https://forward.com/articles/10411/leavened-or-unleavened-a-history.

Lacey, Robert, and Danny Danziger. *The Year 1000: What Life Was Like at the Turn of the First Millennium.* London: Little, Brown and Co., 1999.

Lancaster, D. Thomas. *King of the Jews: Resurrecting the Jewish Jesus.* Littleton, Colo.: First Fruits of Zion, 2006.

Lancaster, D. Thomas. *Restoration: Returning the Torah of God to the Disciples of Jesus.* Marshfield, Mo.: Frist Fruits of Zion, 2009.

Lancaster, Steven P., and James M. Monson. "Isaiah's Exalted Servant in the Great Isaiah Scroll." Special Supplement to *Messiah Journal* 107 (2011): 1–65.

Langer, Ruth. "Revisiting Early Rabbinic Liturgy: The Recent Contributions of Ezra Fleischer." *Prooftexts* 19/2 (1999): 179–194.

Lauterbach, Jacob Z. "The Origin and Development of Two Sabbath Ceremonies." *Hebrew Union College Annual* 15 (1940): 367–424.

Leaver, Robin A. "Passiontide Music." In *Passover and Easter: The Symbolic Structuring of Sacred Seasons.* Vol. 6 of *Two Liturgical Traditions.* Ed. by Paul F. Bradshaw and Lawrence A. Hoffman, 146–180. Notre Dame, Ind.: University of Notre Dame, 1999.

Levine, Lee I. *The Ancient Synagogue: The First Thousand Years.* New Haven, Conn.: Yale University Press, 2005.

Levine, Lee I. "The Nature and Origin of the Palestinian Synagogue Reconsidered." *Journal of Biblical Literature* 115/3 (1996): 425–448.

Lewis, C. S. *Surprised by Joy: The Shape of My Early Life.* New York: Harcourt, Brace and Co., 1955.

Leyerle, Blake. "Meal Customs in the Greco-Roman World." In *Passover and Easter: Origin and History to Modern Times.* Ed. by Paul F. Bradshaw and Lawrence A. Hoffman, 29–61. Notre Dame, Ind.: University of Notre Dame Press, 1999.

Lichtheim, Miriam. *The Old and Middle Kingdoms.* Vol. 1 of *Ancient Egyptian Literature.* Berkeley: University of California Press, 1973.

Marcus, Joel. "Passover and the Last Supper Revisited." *New Testament Studies* 59/3 (2013): 303–24.

Marshak, Adam Kolman. *The Many Faces of Herod the Great.* Grand Rapids, Mich.: Eerdmans, 2015.

Matthews, Victor H., and Don C. Benjamin. *Social World of Ancient Israel 1250–587 BCE.* Peabody, Mass.: Hendrickson, 1993.

McDowell, A. G. *Village Life in Ancient Egypt: Laundry Lists and Love Songs.* Oxford: Oxford University Press, 1999.

McKee, J. K. *Moedim: The Appointed Times for Messianic Believers.* McKinney, Tex.: Messianic Apologetics, 2013.

Melito of Sardis. "On the Pascha." In Raniero Cantalamessa, *Easter in the Early Church: An Anthology of Jewish and Early Christian Texts.* Trans. and ed. by James M. Quigley. and Joseph T. Lienhard, 41–46. Collegeville, Minn.: Liturgical Press, 1993.

Meyers, Eric M. and Mark A. Chancey, eds. "Early Judaism and the Rise of the Synagogue." In *Alexander to Constantine: Archaeology and the Land of the Bible.* Vol. 3 of The Anchor Yale Bible Reference Library, 203–238. New Haven, Conn.: Yale University Press, 2012.

Michael, Boaz. *Tent of David: Healing the Vision of the Messianic Gentile.* Marshfield, Mo.: First Fruits of Zion, 2013.

Miller, Robert D., II. "Modeling the Farm Community." In *Life and Culture in the Ancient Near East.* Ed. by Richard E. Averbeck, Mark W. Chavalas, and David B. Weisberg, 289–309. Bethesda, Md.: CDL, 2003.

Millgram, Abraham E. *Jewish Worship.* Philadelphia: The Jewish Publication Society of America, 1971.

Monson, James M. *The Land Between: A Regional Study Guide to the Land of the Bible.* Jerusalem: James M. Monson, 1983.

Monson, James M., and Steven P. Lancaster. *Regions on the Run: Introductory Map Studies in the Land of the Bible.* Rockford, Ill.: Biblical Backgrounds, 2019.

Morgenstern, Julian. "The Calendars of Ancient Israel." *Hebrew Union College Annual* 19 (1934): 15–28.

Murphy-O'Connor, Jerome. *The Holy Land: An Oxford Archaeological Guide from Earliest Times to 1700.* 5th ed. Oxford: Oxford University Press, 2008.

Olitzky, Kerry M., and Daniel Judson. *Jewish Holidays: A Brief Introduction for Christians.* Woodstock, VT: Jewish Lights, 2007.

Oppenheim, A. Leo. *Ancient Mesopotamia: Portrait of a Dead Civilization.* Rev. ed. Chicago: University of Chicago Press, 1977.

Oswalt, John N. *The Bible among the Myths.* Grand Rapids, Mich.: Zondervan, 2009.

Parker, Richard A. *The Calendars of Ancient Egypt. Studies in Ancient Oriental Civilization* 26. Chicago: University of Chicago Press, 1950.

Pogrebin, Abigail. *My Jewish Year: 18 Holidays, One Wandering Jew.* Bedford, NY: Fig Tree Books, 2017.

Pohl, Christine D. *Making Room: Recovering Hospitality as a Christian Tradition.* Grand Rapids, Mich.: Eerdmans, 1999.

Prager, Dennis. *Exodus: God, Slavery, and Freedom.* Washington, D.C.: Regnery Faith, 2018.

Rainey, A. F. "The Order of Sacrifices in Old Testament Ritual Texts." *Biblical* 51 (1970): 485–498.

Reif, Stefan C. "Prayer in Early Judaism." In *Prayer from Tobit to Qumran.* Ed. by Renate Egger-Wenzel and Jeremy Corley. 439–464. Berlin: de Gruyter, 2004.

Richardson, Cyril C., ed. *Early Christian Fathers.* Vol. 1 of *The Library of Christian Classics.* New York: Touchstone, 1996.

Robertson, A. T. *Word Pictures in the New Testament.* 6 vols. Nashville, Tenn.: Broadman, 1930–1933.

Robinson, George. *Essential Judaism: A Complete Guide to Beliefs, Customs and Rituals.* Rev. ed. New York: Atria, 2016.

Rose Publishing. *Christ in the Passover.* Peabody, Mass.: Rose Publishing, 2008.

Rosen, Ceil, and Moshe Rosen. *Christ in the Passover*. New ed. Chicago: Moody Press, 2006.

Rudolph, David. "Messianic Judaism in Antiquity and in the Modern Era." In *Introduction to Messianic Judaism: Its Ecclesial Context and Biblical Foundations.* Ed. by David Rudolph and Joel Willitts, 21–36. Grand Rapids, Mich.: Zondervan, 2013.

Sailhamer, John. *The Pentateuch as Narrative: A Biblical-Theological Commentary.* Grand Rapids, Mich.: Zondervan, 1992.

Samuel, Delwen. "Bread." In *The Oxford Encyclopedia of Ancient Egypt*, Vol. 1. Ed. by Donald B. Redford, 196–198. Oxford: Oxford University Press, 2001.

Sauer, Carl Ortwin. "Forward to Historical Geography." In *Land and Life: A Selection from the Writings of Carl Ortwin Sauer.* Ed. by John Leighly, 351–379. Berkeley: University of California Press, 1963.

Schaff, Philip. *History of the Christian Church.* Vol. 2 of *Ante-Nicene Christianity*. New York: Charles Schribner's Sons, 1930.

Schaff, Philip, and Henry Wace. *Nicene and Post-Nice Fathers.* Second Series. Vol. 14 of *The Seven Ecumenical Councils.* New York: Charles Schribner's Sons, 1900.

Scherman, Nossom, with Meir Zlotowitz, trans. and eds. *The Complete ArtScroll Siddur.* Brooklyn, N.Y.: Mesorah, 1997.

Schild, E. "On Exodus iii.14—'I Am That I Am." *Vetus Testamentum* 4 (1954): 296–302.

Schnabel, Eckhard J. *Jesus in Jerusalem: The Last Days.* Grand Rapids, Mich.: Eerdmans, 2018.

Senn, Frank C. "Should Christians Celebrate the Passover?" In *Passover and Easter: The Symbolic Structuring of Sacred Seasons.* Vol. 6 of *Two Liturgical Traditions*. Ed. by Paul F. Bradshaw and Lawrence A. Hoffman, 183–205. Notre Dame, Ind.: University of Notre Dame Press, 1999.

Shafer-Elliott, Cynthia. "Food Preparation in Iron Age Israel." In *Behind the Scenes of the Old Testament: Cultural, Social, and Historical Contexts.* Ed. by Jonathan S. Greer, John W. Hilber, and John H. Walton, 456–463. Grand Rapids, Mich.: Baker Academic, 2018.

Shir HaShirim Rabbah in Midrash Rabbah. Trans. by Maurice Simon. Ed. by H. Freedman and Maurice Simon. New York: Soncino, 1983.

Soden, Wolfram von. *The Ancient Orient: An Introduction to the Study of the Ancient Near East.* Trans. by Donald G. Schley. Grand Rapids, Mich.: Eerdmans, 1994.

Sperber, Daniel. "Social Legislation in Jerusalem during the Latter Part of the Second Temple." *Journal for the Study of Judaism* 6/1 (1975): 86–95.

Stern, Menachem, ed. *Greek and Latin Authors on Jews and Judaism*. 3 vols. Jerusalem: Israel Academy of Sciences and Humanities, 1974–1984.

Stevens, Kenneth. *Jerusalem Revisited: The Liturgical Meaning of Holy Week.* Washington, D.C.: Pastoral Press, 1988.

Strashny, Alex. "Modern Searches for Aviv Barley in the Context of the Hebrew Calendar: A First Description of the Israeli Barley Observational Date." *The Jewish Bible Quarterly* 45/3 (2017): 179–187.

Strassfeld, Michael. *The Jewish Holidays: A Guide and Commentary*. New York: Harper & Row, 1985.

Tabory, Joseph, and David Stern. *The JPS Commentary on the Haggadah: Historical Introduction, Translation, and Commentary.* Philadelphia: Jewish Publication Society, 2008.

Talley, Thomas J. *The Origins of the Liturgical Year.* 2nd ed. Collegeville, Minn.: Liturgical Press, 1986.

Talmon, Shemaryahu. "Reckoning the Sabbath in the First and Early Second Temple Period—From the Evening or the Morning?" In *Sabbath: Idea, History, Reality*, 9–32. Beer Sheva: Ben Gurion University of the Negev Press, 2004.

Thayer, Joseph H. *Thayer's Greek-English Lexicon of the New Testament*. Peabody, Mass.: Hendrickson, 2017.

Thiele, Edwin R. *The Mysterious Numbers of the Hebrew Kings*. Rev. ed. Grand Rapids, Mich.: Academie Books Zondervan, 1983.

Union of Messianic Jewish Congregations. "Defining Messianic Judaism." July 20, 2005. https://www.umjc.org/defining-messianic-judaism.

Vaux, Roland de. *Ancient Israel*. New York: McGraw Hill, 1961.

Vine of David Haggadah: Messianic Jewish Passover Seder. Marshfield, Mo.: Vine of David, 2011.

Visser, Margaret. *The Rituals of Dinner*. New York: Penguin, 1991.

Wasef, Husney. *The Israelite Journey through the Wilderness in the Sinai Peninsula*. Mount Gerizim, Nablus: Centre of the Good Samaritan, 2012.

Waskow, Arthur O. *Seasons of Our Joy: A Modern Guide to the Jewish Holidays*. Philadelphia: Jewish Publication Society, 2012.

Watson, Wilfred G. E. "Daily Life in Ancient Ugarit (Syria)." In *Life and Culture in the Ancient Near East*. Ed. by Richard E. Averbeck, Mark W. Chavalas, and David B. Weisberg, 121–152. Bethesda, Md.: CDL, 2003.

Wenham, Gordon. J. The Book of Leviticus. *New International Commentary on the Old Testament*. Grand Rapids, Mich.: Eerdmans, 1979.

Wilkinson, John. *Egeria's Travels*. Rev. ed. Jerusalem: Ariel, 1981.

Wright, Christopher J. H. *Walking in the Ways of the Lord: The Ethical Authority of the Old Testament*. Downer's Grove, Ill.: InterVarsity, 1995.

Wright, Paul H. "Famines in the Land." In *Lexham Geographic Commentary on Acts through Revelation*. Ed. by Barry J. Beitzel, 279–289. Bellingham, Wash.: Lexham, 2019.

Wright, Paul H. "Geography of the Nations in Jerusalem for Pentecost." In *Lexham Geographic Commentary on Acts through Revelation*. Ed. by Barry J. Beitzel, 105–114. Bellingham, Wash.: Lexham, 2019.

Wright, Paul H. *Heart of the Holy Land: 40 Reflections on Scripture and Place*. Peabody, Mass.: Rose Publishing, 2020.

Wright, Paul H. *Holman Illustrated Guide to Biblical Geography: Reading the Land*. Nashville, Tenn.: B&H, 2020.

Zimmerman, Martha. *Celebrating Biblical Feasts: In Your Home or Church*. Bloomington, Minn.: Bethany House, 2004.

Zion, Noam, and Barbara Spectre, eds. *A Different Light: The Big Book of Hanukkah*. Jerusalem: Devora, 2000.

Index

A

B

C

G

H

Q

R

S

T